Wardell has a sharp eye and a keen ear for Japanese customs, language, and the aspirations of the New Generation. His book is highly readable. Even old Japan hands will enjoy *Rising Sons and Daughters* and benefit from it.

> *Vernon R. Alden*
> President, Japan Society of Boston

Only a young person could enter so intimately into the life of a family and of a school, and only a most unusual young person could describe the people around him with such sensitivity. *Rising Sons and Daughters* also helps us to see, hear, taste, and feel daily life in Japan.

> *Kenneth E. Carpenter*
> Harvard University Libraries

A brightly wide-eyed view of the new Japanese young and a scrupulous accounting of how one young American found that clashing cultures really don't.

> *Donald Richie*
> *Geisha, Gangster, Neighbor, Nun*

RISING SONS

Foreword by Haru Matsukata Reischauer

AND DAUGHTERS

Life Among Japan's New Young

WITHDRAWN

STEVEN WARDELL

Plympton Press International
Cambridge · Massachusetts

RISING SONS AND DAUGHTERS

© 1995 by Steven Wardell

Mr. Tomita is a composite of two people. The rest of the book is as true as the author's memory, aided by his diary entries, could make it. The author apologizes in advance for any errors or omissions in what he believes to be an accurate account of the Japanese young people he was privileged to get to know.

The affiliations of the writers of comments about the book are provided for identification purposes only.

Library of Congress Cataloging-in-Publication Data

Wardell, Steven, 1971–
   Rising sons and daughters : life among Japan's new young / Steven Wardell.
   1. Teenagers–Japan–Social conditions.
   2. Teenagers–Japan–Social life and customs. 3. Japan–Social conditions–1945- 4. Japan–Social life and customs–1945- 5. Wardell, Steven 1971-. 6. Students, Foreign–Japan–Biography. I. Title.
   HQ799.J3W37 1995
   305.23'5'0952–dc20
   ISBN 0-9639230-8-0 (alk. paper)   94–181
   ISBN 0-9639230-9-9 (alk. paper : pbk.)

Manufactured in the United States of America
First Edition 1995
10 9 8 7 6 5 4 3 2 1

Cover design by Barbara Gunia
The acid-free paper in this book meets the guidelines for permanence and durability of the Committee on Production Guidelines for Book Longevity of the Council on Library Resources.

Plympton Press International
Cambridge, Massachusetts

Dedicated with affection
to the Ando family, Ojisan and his family,
Tomita-*sensei*, and
all other residents of
De a i no mura,
the International House of Friendship

RISING SONS AND DAUGHTERS

Foreword by Haru Matsukata Reischauer

Acknowledgements

Introduction

Foreword

by Haru Matsukata Reischauer

author of *Samurai and Silk:*
A Japanese and American Heritage

Rising Sons and Daughters is a fascinating and informative account of an American teenager's encounter with Japan. Despite his Western background and language barrier, he was almost immediately accepted as a member of a family of parents and teenagers. This is a heart-warming narrative of how friendship and understanding between peoples of different cultures can be built through personal interaction, and how both sides can find more in common than not.

As this book so well illustrates, by attaining a better appreciation of each other's values and aspirations, the stereotypical misconceptions, prejudices of race, and differences in culture that have been obstacles in Japanese-American relationships disappear. This is especially true of the younger generation of both countries, who have fewer fixed ideas about each other to overcome. Steve discovered much in common with his peers and formed binding relationships. Interestingly, he found a wider gap in understanding exists between his peers and their parents' generation.

Steve's experience in Japan was made possible by the Youth for Understanding Program, a two-way exchange for young Americans and Japanese. His book is living testimony to the importance of the growing number of such exchanges in the improvement of understanding between our two countries.

These exchange programs started almost fifty years ago, after the War, when efforts were being made to develop relations between the peoples of our two countries. In 1955 I was inspired to write an article for an American publication about the experiences of two young American exchange farmers who lived and worked with Japanese farm families. The International Farm Youth Exchange Program that sponsored them also invited young Japanese farmers to America. The grassroots goodwill they and other participants of such programs have generated over the years has played an inestimable role in the development of friendly bi-lateral relations.

For three generations, my family has been involved in a cross-cultural exchange between our two countries. My grandfather went to New York in 1876 and is credited with starting direct trade between America and Japan. He is also acknowledged to have helped establish close ties between Japanese and Americans. From him I inherited my lifelong interest, and as both observer and participant, I have seen great progress.

Now I put my hopes and trust in the generation of Steve and his peers, who are well equipped to strengthen the ties between Japan and America so together we can contribute to the peace and prosperity of the world.

H.M.R.
LaJolla, California, 1994

Acknowledgements

I am grateful to many people, both in Japan and in the U.S., for their help and encouragement in transforming my observations into a book: my charming host-sister and the author of her own chapter-length commentary on the book, Shika Ando; my Harvard friends Ann Anninger and Roger Stoddard of Houghton Library, Bill Crout, John Fox, Jordan and Judith Dann, Fumiko Cranston, and Wadih Canaan; Philip G. Spitzer of the Philip G. Spitzer Literary Agency; Tom Chapman of Emphasis! (Hong Kong); Rick Kennedy of *Tokyo Journal*; Keiko Enatsu (Tokyo), David Duncan (Boston), and the other fine people at Youth for Understanding; Takashi Seo of Pfizer (Japan); Seymour Shubin; Yoshiaki Takita of Uenogaoka High School; Alan Chalk; Jon Fulkerson; Joe Armstrong; Chris Harvey; Harold Pratt; Asa Phillips; Professor Samuel Hayes; Charles Downer; John and Judith Dowling; and Madoka Tsuda and Mitsuru Tanaka, my editors at *The Japan Times*.

Introduction

A perfectly paternal government; a perfectly filial people; a community entirely self-supporting; peace within and without; no want; no ill will between classes. This is what I find in Japan in the year 1858, after 100 years' exclusion of foreign trade and foreigners. Twenty years hence, what will be the contrast?

            —Letters of Lord Elgin

If you read the many recent books about Japan, there seem to be two Japans. One is good, promising, helpful, friendly, and rather like the one Lord Elgin describes over a century ago; the other is quite the opposite.

Two such disparate views are presented, for example, by Ezra Vogel's seminal *Japan as Number 1* (1979) and Jon Woronoff's reply, *Japan as Anything but Number One* (1990).

Woronoff goes on to divide Japan experts into two opposing camps—Japanapologists and Japan-bashers. (Professor Vogel manages to appear on both lists.)

While I enjoy listening to these debates, I am also glad, frankly, that I hadn't encountered them before I visited Japan. At age 17 I'd had a couple of hours' worth of Japanese history lessons, limited to the arrival of Commodore Perry's "Black Ships" and Japan's role in World War II— events when Japan impacted "World History" as it was taught.

Now, as I read further, I find that wildly differing opinions about Japan began to appear soon after Perry's arrival. Early visitors generalized sweepingly. One declares that "there is a strange, determined, treacherous streak in the character. . . Their impassive expressions make it impossible for Westerners to guess what is in their minds" (Evelyn Adam, 1910). Another pronounces, "The typical Japanese is loyal, filial, respectful, obedient, faithful, kind, gentle, courteous, unselfish, generous." (E.W. Clement, 1903).

The debate continues today in the columns of our newspapers and magazines.

"Japan's bubble has finally burst"; "Japan will emerge stronger still."

"Japan is winning out and will dominate us economically"; "We'll become a better trading partner when we shape up and learn the lessons Japan is teaching us."

"The Japanese have enviable team spirit"; "They are isolationist and insular."

"They learn English poorly, just for exams, and can't speak it"; "Every Japanese learns our language, whereas our business envoys in Japan aren't even sure which lavatory door to enter."

"Japan's schools create an outstanding product that has helped their economy soar"; "Japan's schools create hard-working robots lacking in creativity."

"Japan is a clean, well-run society"; "Japan is polluted and corrupt."

"Exclusionary Japan focuses on its own uniqueness"; "Imitative Japan is eager for 'internationalization'."

Whether Japan is a friend or foe or just an enigma—I had no real preconceptions. I mention this to not to display either ignorance or humility, but only to point out that I hadn't become a partisan in the seemingly endless debate over Japan. I don't consider myself to be one now. I simply came and saw, and—as my homestay-sister Shika mentions—I took lots of notes.

I offer a candid view of Japan's New Young as they revealed themselves to me. I believe they did this fairly uninhibitedly because we shared a close bond: our age. "Culture," surprisingly, turned out to be a second strong link between us. *Rising Sons and Daughters* is, then, a view of Japanese *chiineija* (teenagers) through the eyes of an "adopted" *chiineija*. It is a *shasei*, a drawing-from-life.

I would have liked to stay longer because I enjoyed getting to know the New Young. But I also became aware that, inevitably, the longer I was there the less I perceived; my first impressions not only remained fairly accurate ones, but also were my best.

One thing I noticed time and again is that there seemed to be less of a culture gap between "them" and me than between "them" and their elders. (The notable exception to this attempt at generalization was my "father," Mr. Ando. Despite his forty-ish age, he seems to have been in the vanguard of Japan's "new generation" and has never lost his risk-taking, iconoclastic, innovative, and thoroughly modern spirit.)

In *The Material Child: Coming of Age in Japan and America* (1993), Merry White writes that before she began her comparative study of 100 teens in Japan and 100 teens in the U.S., she had 'bought the notion that the American brand of teen did not exist in Japan.' During her interviews and analyses of diaries and essays she is struck time and again by the similarities between "us" and "them" as young people. I, too, found that we are evolving into similar kinds of people, tested and shaped by our common internationalized cultures, and growing steadily toward each other.

In his 1990 study, *Japan's 'International Youth': The Emergence of a New Class of Schoolchildren*, Oxford professor

Roger Goodman finds that Japan's relatively recent "Returnee Children Problem" (*Kikokushijo Mondai*) has already altered to the point where these once-stigmatized children—some 10,000 a year who, because of their parents' work abroad, have been brought up overseas—are now widely welcomed, admired, and even groomed for future leadership positions. Previously they had been regarded as 'heterogeneous, independent, and argumentative' and ostracized as 'pitiful'—a plight documented by Merry White in her 1980 study *Strangers in Their Own Land*.

Former Prime Minister Nakasone's educational reform council, Goodman points out, has called for schools to promote individuality, internationalism, and creativity, and singled out the Returnee Children as exemplars.

Goodman finds the new status of the Returnee Children to be one more example of "Japanized westernism." This 'new class of schoolchildren' is now recognized as a ready source of "Japanese internationalists" —individuals who, while not losing their unique identity as Japanese, nonetheless recognize their own membership in a larger group of boundary-free people.

The Andos, whom you will read about in this book, are home-grown Japanese internationalists.

The future will clearly bring further rapid change for Japan as the New Young—Westernized and internationalized—assume their positions of responsibility. The greatest transformation will be one of mindset, as the New Young question the operating assumptions of their society. Why do we have to apologize for our past? Why do we need to be so tightly bound by our traditions? Why do we play such a small role in the UN and in other global decision-making? Why have we given in so often to America, and what should our relationship with America be now?

In *The Japanese Market Culture* (1989), George Fields

recognizes three major, lifestyle-transforming "openings" of Japan to the West: the arrivals of Perry in 1853, MacArthur in 1945, and the Olympic Games in 1964. He speculates that the present time may, in fact, be the beginning of the *real kaikoku* – "opening of the country" – a result of the large-scale internationalization that Japan has been enthusiastically undergoing.

The young people in this book are the product of *kaikoku*. They readily accepted me and showed great enthusiasm for the "West" that I instantly represented for them, indirectly demonstrating that someone can be different without being wrong.

I learned from Japan a second "lesson" that I'd recommend to my peers in America, caught up as we often are in bitterly divisive struggles among ourselves. The Japanese have revolutionized themselves and their country without the need for revolution. Around me in Japan I saw people growing, learning, adapting. They were adopting what they considered worthwhile from others, while retaining the best features of their own past.

According to Professor Edward G. Seidensticker, the central paradox of Japan – a paradox that can actually envelop the conflicting theories of Japanapologists and Japan-bashers – is this: "The relationship between tradition and change in Japan has always been complicated by the fact that change itself is a tradition."

For the Japanese, change is a constant, a given. Now we hear that Japan's next goal is to transform itself into a "Lifestyle Superpower." Headlines about Japan regularly trumpet the word "reform." Women emerge on the national scene as political leaders and scholars. The school week and work week are shortened. Consumer demand for Harleys and surfboards explodes, and our pop stars are bigger hits over there than here.

Contradictions – such as we find between the two

camps of Japan experts – can be irritating, but paradoxes are, by their very definition, acceptable. The Japanese live comfortably with paradox.

Ancient and modern, sacred and profane, imitation and innovation, young and old – these and many other apparent opposites don't clash in Japan as they regularly do in the U.S.; they coexist comfortably, at times symbiotically.

How do these changes and seemingly-strange juxtapositions shake out for the individual Japanese person? I wondered, and I learned.

Mr. Ando and Japan are paradoxes in themselves. Mr. Ando states his personal philosophy in terms of a paradox: "I want to be a cowboy who also plants rice." No mixed metaphor – this is simply the Japanese-adopted Chinese notion of yin and yang, or complementary oppositions.

In her groundbreaking study of Japan's culture, *The Chrysanthemum and the Sword*, anthropologist Ruth Benedict compares the rigid constraints she found in Japanese pre-World-War-II society to the tiny, invisible wire racks that Japanese flower-enthusiasts insert in chrysanthemum flowers to improve their beauty for display.

Benedict concludes her 1946 study with the conviction that the seemingly tradition-bound Japanese can indeed make a rapid transition from rigid militarist state to peace-loving democracy. Accurately foretelling the future, she speculates, ". . . The Japanese in Japan can, in a new era, set up a way of life which does not demand the old requirements of individual restraint. Chrysanthemums can be beautiful without wire racks." The Japanese are clearly capable of rapid but also carefully considered, targeted change.

Based on my own experiences, I wager that the person to come closest to predicting where Japan is going is the late Professor and Ambassador Edwin O. Reischauer who, at the end of his book, *The Japanese Today: Change and Continuity* (1988), writes, "The contradictory pulls between uniqueness and internationalism that so grip the Japanese today will be resolved in favor of internationalism." He adds a further note of optimism: "And with the economic power and technical skills of the Japanese clearly lending themselves to that trend, Japan and the rest of the world will come appreciably closer to a viable world order."

*   *   *   *   *

These are my observations today, having read dozens of books about Japan as part of, and outside of, my college courses. In contrast, *Rising Sons and Daughters* was written before I'd done any reading to speak of, and belongs to a moment in time that the visitor to Japan experiences only once.

*   *   *   *   *

Close your eyes and picture a map of the world. Where is the U.S., and where is Japan?

When I first entered my classroom in Japan, I was startled to see Japan located in the exact center of the world map hanging on the wall in front of me. Perplexed, I stared at the map: it didn't look at all familiar.

As I reoriented my mind, it occurred to me that, on the maps I knew, Japan is always on the far right and the U.S. on the far left—as far away as possible, separated by the vastness of Eurasia.

'Western' maps have established and reinforced in our language the artificial distinctions of "oriental" and "occidental," "Eastern" and "Western" —descriptors that are meaningless for a round planet.

To the American schoolchild, Japan and the U.S. exist at opposite edges of the world, beyond which one presumably tumbles into a void—much as Europeans once worried about falling off the edge of the world if they sailed toward the horizon.

We thus fail to see that Japan is actually our neighbor. Professor Reischauer sagely suggests we start thinking of Japan as "Far West," rather than Far East.

In contrast, Japanese children are immediately aware of their proximity to America. The U.S. is just an ocean away—to the East, as a matter of fact—and the "East"/"West" dichotomy has much less significance. Shika, as you'll read, considers herself 'Western,' rather than Eastern.

In his 1983 study of *The Japanese Mind*, Robert Christopher bemoans America's sorry lack of knowledge about Japan. "There are. . . a considerable number of Japanese who know pretty clearly what makes America tick, and Japanese institutions, public and private, have made shrewd use of that knowledge in their dealings with the United States. . . If the United States is to begin holding its own vis-a-vis Japan. . . a great many more of us must come to understand what makes Japan tick. . . Such understanding. . . must become part of the mental furniture of as many as possible of the nonscholarly Americans who, on a day-to-day basis, conduct our business with Japan."

There are many books that can help us get to know Japan by analyzing the Japanese adult mind. But with change so pronounced and so rapid, we also need to look to the future, to Japan's New Young, if we are ever really to catch on, and catch up.

My hope is that this book will help redraw our mental map, and thereby make my Japanese peers—Japan's leaders of tomorrow — less exotic to us, ideally as familiar to us as we are to them.

Meet Shika, Mr. Sumo, the World's Best "Wink" Fan, and the others. Listen to Japan's New Young, and you will hear what I heard — an invitation to work, but also to enjoy life, together.

RISING SONS AND DAUGHTERS

I Am Ando

"You are Steven." It was a statement, not a question. Flying from Tokyo to Oita to meet my host family, I was surprised to hear my name. Looking up, I found an unusual-looking—though clearly Japanese—man dominating the aisle in front of me, smiling.

A chubby, round face with a thick, pointy beard protruded incongruously above a generic gray business suit. His full, black head of hair was mussed.

No other Japanese had looked me in the eye as he did. His open stare unnerved me. When I returned a hesitant "Yes," he replied with satisfaction, "Good. I am Ando."

I was relieved to know that this bear of a man was my host father. As I stood up, my hand extended and a rehearsed smile on my face, I forgot that my seat belt was buckled. It jerked me painfully, clumsily down.

Mr. Ando asked the *bijinesuman* (businessman) in the seat next to me—who'd carefully avoided looking at me the whole pre-departure time—if he'd mind exchanging seats. My silk-suited neighbor readily acquiesced, disappearing into the farthest corner of the plane. My host father was discreet in his manner and careful with his bags as he shuffled to get comfortable. He exuded a relaxed self-assuredness and warmth.

He'd expected me to be on this plane, though there hadn't been time to let me know of the coincidence. I was pleased to meet my new dad suddenly like this because now the nervous first encounter that we exchangers had been trained for was over. He treated me as if I were simply coming home instead of arriving for the first time.

In a kind of English that would take some getting used to, Mr. Ando kept up a lively conversation for much of the hour-and-a-half flight. He'd taught himself. He liked to cut off the ends of his sentences with hearty laughs or boyish chuckles. His own brand of word order and conjugation made some of his talk indecipherable, but he had a large vocabulary and seemed hungry to speak English.

"I been to America and driven on highway, all alone!" he exclaimed, as though waving an imaginary trophy. "In the Plains States, too, many miles." He said he owed the people of America a great debt for all the hospitality they showed him.

"What is it, Japan?" he asked, pausing. My puzzled look prompted him to add, "Your idea of Japan is what?"

I told him about last night in Tokyo, the surprising, debilitating heat, and how lushly green I found the landscape. I said that we exchangers had staggered off the plane jetlagged, to be escorted to a restaurant and a big steak dinner provided by the Tokyo representatives of the Youth for Understanding exchange program. Then we stayed up late worrying and wondering about what was ahead.

"All this left me dead tired," I said, sliding farther into my seat and rolling back my head to mimic what I meant.

He cocked his head at the expression, "Yes, *dead* tired." He laughed and repeated it again, absorbing the new phrase immediately. You could tell he liked it.

The little I knew about the big family I'd be joining for the next two months had arrived in a letter from the family's older daughter a few days before I left Connecticut.

Hello! How are you?

I'm Shizuka Ando. Will be your Japanese sis. We've just got information from the exchange program and are anxious to have this summer with you. Well, I'll introduce a little about us. Hope it will help you.

−Oita −

We live in Oita. It is very hot and so humid in summer.

−My Family −

- Father−owner of barber shops, a hotel man. Very busy. Can speak English. Has been to U.S. twice.
- Mother−housewife. Likes patchwork (country sewing).
- Me (Shizuka) 18 years old. Senior. Been to the U.S. one year. Play basketball, but now study hard to go to college.
- Sister (Minori) 16 years old. Goes to art high school (major in sculpture). Plays basketball.
- Brother (Manabu) 14 years old. 9th grade. Plays basketball. Has to study for the entrance exam for high school next spring. Likes watching baseball very much.
- Brother (Yamato) 10 years old. 5th grade. Plays basketball.

−School−

You'll go to my school (Uenogaoka public high). It has about 1,400 students and many interesting clubs.

We and people at school are looking forward to seeing you very much.

Let's have a good time!

See you soon.
Sincerely,
Shizuka Ando

We deplaned into the intense, humid heat of Japan's southern island. Mrs. Ando, a slender, almond-faced woman in Western-style white blouse and blue skirt, carried a large sign I couldn't miss: "Hello, Steven."

Standing beside her at the bottom of the escalator was a small, slim man in black slacks, white sports shirt, and a backwards baseball cap mostly covering his slightly wavy hair. He was, I would learn, the family's honorary "uncle." As I descended the escalator, he began snapping pictures of me with the large camera slung around his neck.

Meeting Mr. Ando had been impromptu and wonderfully casual. Now as I rode down toward the two strangers, a "predicament-skit" that we exchangers had performed at our week-long orientation session in Seattle came rushing into my mind. Whom do I approach first? What do I do, shake hands or bow? Or both? What if we bonk heads—the ultimate nightmare! Introductions and first impressions are so important, we were told again and again.

The uncle tried to get everything on film as we shook hands. Mr. Ando, who asked me to call him Otōsan (father), introduced us, with appropriate translations for the mother and uncle, who each knew a few English words.

I was a head taller than any of them—indeed, than anyone in the terminal—and that launched Okāsan (mother) and Ojisan (uncle) into a game of comparing me to objects around us to see if I was taller. Otōsan translated for me. How did I fit in the plane? Could I make it out the door of the airport lounge? Were they going to lose me among the palm trees? Where would they put me if I didn't fit into the car? I'd have to make do on the roof.

It was all good fun, and Ojisan laughed most of all. He had a built-in grin—appearing to be pleased even when he was totally serious—and his budding ears accentuated this.

Outside the airport I had to pose again for photos, as Ojisan caught every event—the first time I posed with the group, the first time I went outside, the first time on the street. When we arrived at a large, new Toyota sedan, Okāsan immediately sat in the back, and the two men discussed who would drive. Otōsan would, so Ojisan sat next to him.

The roads around the airport were littered with signs featuring politicians' faces. Japanese election posters contain one or two words, and the rest is simply a big, colorful face. American election signs usually include an eye-catching logo, a name, and the all-important "sign-bite" about some issue. Here the face *is* the sign.

I pointed and said "election." Otōsan nodded, pleased I was catching on, then translated my observation for the others. They nodded too, and Okāsan reached up and patted me on the head.

Otōsan explained, "Japanese vote face, vote person." Additional comments and gestures helped me gather his meaning. The Japanese put great stock in a person's integrity and countenance, even if that means believing in a face on a sign. People care more about what kind of a person they elect than about his or her position on the issues.

Oita ("Oh-ee-tah") City is the largest city in Oita prefecture, or province, with a population close to 400,000, Otōsan explained. A river flows through the city into a bay, but both waterways are polluted by the industries on them.

The mountainous terrain of the island of Kyushu leaves few easy places for roads, I noticed; the tortuous road from the airport traced a ragged coast.

Halfway home we stopped at a pottery shop selling old pots, medieval shards, and faded, dingy scrolls. Everything was the color of bone. Squeezed between the highway and a cliff, the shop resembled a decrepit gas station, piled high with what could have been junk if it were not so unmistakably old. The air was so musty I could almost cup it in my hands and feel its age.

After considerable browsing, Okāsan bought a large

flowerpot painted white with blue cranes. She held it up for me to see, nodding happily, while Otōsan paid. The old shopkeeper wrote out a bill of sale on a scrap of fading calligraphy paper and stamped his chop in a sticky red ink.

We stopped for lunch at a traditional restaurant that Mr. Ando liked to patronize. The chef was an ex-sumo wrestler, and looked it. As such, he was a respected, significant person.

In back of the bar was a traditional, tatami (woven reed)-walled dining room, but we chose one of the common tables crowded against the wall in the front. Sitting down on the low chair, with all eyes in the restaurant upon me, I found to my dismay that my shins were too long to fit under the two-foot-high table, so I had to press my knees to the side and out into the walkway.

My gangly legs threw everything out of joint, disturbing the *wa* (spiritual harmony) of this crammed place. Everyone in our group chuckled over the awkward situation. When I looked around, I met smiles and a general wagging of heads among the regulars, who had momentarily stopped watching baseball on the overhead TV.

We helped ourselves from a central bowl of salad. The family, especially Ojisan, was surprised that I could manage chopsticks. These were *waribashi*—the disposable, soft-wood chopsticks that come in one piece with a lengthwise slit halfway down the center.

"If you to eat well, then break the *waribashi* with spirit." Otōsan held out his own *waribashi* and snapped the pair apart with gusto. The two pieces splintered irregularly. "Arrgh!" he growled. "Bad break."

Ojisan admired my chopstick use, and Otōsan translated for me the uncle's offer to show me how to make my own chopsticks from bamboo, the traditional material.

The main course was tempura—a large serving-bowl of

sea food and vegetables heavily breaded and fried. The three adults studied my reaction to each piece. They'd ordered all types: lettuce, shrimp, sweet potato, soft fish, special roots, and other treats.

When I'd finished, Okāsan asked, "Ichiban?" and Otō-san translated, "What you like number one?" I felt this question was being given undue emphasis—they were all intently listening, and so, it seemed, was the rest of the restaurant. This was one of the first opinions I'd been asked for, and I thought they might somehow gauge me by my answer.

I pointed to a spicy octagonal root. It was full of holes that not even the slushy, grease-coagulated breadcrumb mixture could plug. I'd enjoyed it, but couldn't fathom what it was. Okāsan clapped her hands and shouted. Otō-san explained that it was *her* favorite, too. "When you eat lotus root," he said, "the happiness pours through the holes and into you."

Noodles were popular among the regulars. One of them slurped his noodles with jarring loudness. Ojisan pointed to the slurpers, and Otōsan translated, "He say that the loud suck is to show the food is good and you feel good."

Slurping is also the only way you can get lots of hot noodles, plus a little cooling air, into your mouth in a short time. "Take the noodle fast, right away," Otōsan told me. "If you wait, noodle takes up the water." He shrugged, "Bad."

Our noodles were served steaming hot, which my family didn't mind, but I scalded my mouth. On closer observation, I found that my new family's resistance to heat wasn't genetic, but was an acquired skill: they blow on the food forcefully as they bring it up to their mouths, then inhale equally forcefully as they put it in their mouths, cooling it twice. Clearly I had much to learn as well as some prominent shins to deal with.

We wound our way through Oita's crowded, commercial streets of white and brown buildings, all neon and asphalt, with exterior surfaces that resembled bathroom tiles. Entering a more residential area of cinderblock and wood homes, the car ground up a steep hill that seemed mostly cemetery.

As I climbed out of the car and headed toward the Andos' large white-stucco house, some young children who were bug-hunting along the street gazed at me with stares of astonishment, their tiny nets on bamboo rods hanging limply at their sides for the duration.

I thought I heard giggling coming from inside the house as we approached, but couldn't be sure because the TV was on. I took a deep breath, straightened a little, and approached.

The Andos' house was new and built in a plain, contemporary-style, its front mostly screened doors and open windows. Otōsan led the way as I lugged my suitcase to the door, while Okāsan carried her own precious pottery bundle. Ojisan toted a bag of mine in one hand and his camera in the other, remaining behind to immortalize the moment with a photo.

As Otōsan strode in the front door, he slipped off his shoes in steps so fluid that I never realized he'd done anything. In a fluid motion of my own, I tripped over the half-step that separates the foyer from the rest of the house and fell flat on my face. In doing so, I hurled my luggage out in front of me so that it nearly landed on top of Minori, the younger daughter, who was standing there open-armed to meet me.

"Oh! Oh!" Okāsan exclaimed, her hands to her mouth. She thought I'd broken every bone in my body.

Meanwhile Shizuka, the older daughter, apologized to my prone form. "It's my fault, it's my fault," she moaned in good, unaccented English, a look of deep concern on her face. "I should have told you the step—about the step—in my letter! I'm so sorry."

"No, don't be, please, I'm fine," I said, uprighting myself and testing my limbs. What an introduction!

I got my first good look at Shizuka. She was about 5'3", with thick black hair tied up in a ponytail and a round face that radiated an easy smile.

Minori, like her mother, had a hand to her mouth, but she couldn't hide her amusement. Her face, almond-shaped like Okāsan's, was framed in a stylish bob of short wavy hair parted in the center and swept to either side.

The Ando home was, I quickly surmised, one of the nicest single-family homes in the city. It was set on a green hill on the outskirts of Oita called Sakuragaoka, "cherry blossom hill." Most of the hill had escaped developers until now.

The back of the house overlooked the city. In front there was a basketball hoop in the cement courtyard. Posted conspicuously on the wall inside the front door was a realistic portrait of me that Minori had sketched with colored pencils from a photograph I'd sent.

I settled my belongings in the bedroom I was to share with Manabu, the elder son. Then, after brief introductions and snacks, Shizuka, Minori, and I encircled the TV for the Saturday teen-mania shows that my arrival had interrupted. Minori especially loved these shows and was as excited watching them as the wildly screaming studio audience. It was early afternoon, and the sisters still wore the sailor-style school uniforms from their Saturday-morning classes.

This room, the living room, was dominated by a large table, less than a foot high, and a large, Western-style, leather sofa surrounding the table on two sides. The whole room was arranged like an amphitheater around the large TV set in the corner.

Ten-year-old Yamato, the younger son, spoke no English but was immediately friendly when he arrived half an hour later from school and basketball practice. He was short for his age. His glossy black hair was brushed tight to his head, and his ready smile reflected a calm, happy disposition. After shaking hands, he plopped down next to me with a large history comic book. Absorbed in the comic and ignoring the TV, he began pointing out for me his favorite drawings. The book seemed to be about Chinese warlords beheading each other.

While I was examining the comic with Yamato, fourteen-year-old Manabu walked in and, although his sisters urged him to come meet me, he darted off to his room. I caught a glimpse of a bright white shirt and white socks as he hurriedly closed his door. As I was to be his roommate, this seemed a less-than-auspicious start.

I asked Shizuka why Manabu had disappeared in this way. She said he needed to change out of his school uniform. But he didn't re-appear.

Yamato took me to Manabu's room to see more comic books. He could tell I was curious about them, and would probably be more responsive than his other siblings were. I was a fresh candidate to introduce to the wonders of Japanese *manga* (comics).

Manabu's room was startlingly bare: nothing on the walls or floor. The desk in the corner was covered with folders and other standard school gear. There was a bunk bed, one level of which would be mine. Nothing hinted at his personality except a small bookcase in one corner crowded with *manga* and a framed All Nippon Airways ticket from a trip he'd taken to Tokyo Disneyland.

This colorful corner was all comics, the treasured possessions of the boys of the house. Yamato pointed out that the comics, some thicker than telephone books, were numbered in sequence—44, 45, 46—as they followed some superhero through endless weeks of adventures.

Without words he guided me through the chapters of another history comic as if I were his pupil. His concerned face and expressive gestures kept me interested. Clearly he expected me to get as much out of the comics as he did.

When my new little friend left, I decided to unpack my introductory presents for the family. While I dug in my bags, I became aware of someone watching me silently from the upper bunk—Manabu had been up there all along! This made me feel awkward. We both knew of the other's presence, yet were too uncomfortable or shy to say hello.

The fact that this was our first impression of each other didn't make it any easier on me. He continued to watch, and I pretended not to notice and fumbled more with my bags, debating whether to turn around and say hello. I was nervous, so just standing up and saying "hi" wouldn't have been as easy as it sounds.

At that moment, Yamato returned and, grasping the situation, introduced us by grabbing my arm and gesturing expansively toward Manabu. As our eyes briefly met, Manabu broke into a big grin. From his prone position on the upper bunk he extended his hand. (Handshakes are the first thing the Japanese learn about Westerners, thanks to TV and movies.) "Sankyu for your letter," he said with great clarity, a phrase I later learned he'd been practicing just for this moment.

"Look! Here," Manabu now wanted to show me all the school supplies in his desk, and did so. Unlike tiny Yamato, Manabu was tall for his age. He had Otōsan's suntanned complexion, but a thin build more like Okāsan's. His neat, stylish haircut—like the hair styles of the others—attested to the fact that haircuts were the original family business.

To communicate with the two brothers, I began to do some simple card tricks with the deck I'd brought. They requested instead a game of poker, which they didn't know how to play. They did, however, know how to say "pokaa," a word they volleyed like enthusiastic tennis players. "Pokaa." "Pokaa." "Pokaa."

They didn't really like "pokaa" after I showed them the game; they just liked the idea of playing an authentic game of it with a Westerner. It must be agony to see so many cowboy movies where poker is featured, and never know what it is.

"Go Fish" was more to their liking, but the game broke up when I began to do coin tricks. All the Ando children watched with glee.

The five of us next returned to the teen-cult TV show the girls had been watching since before I arrived. These spontaneous, audience-driven, let's-do-anything-for-laughs shows drag on for hours.

Okāsan served snacks of cheese and seaweed on crackers. Shizuka translated for her mother, "Okāsan says she doesn't like to watch TV. But she likes to be with the family, so she keeps herself busy between the kitchen and TV, preparing snacks for us."

The four children were howling with laughter at the TV, and I joined in at some of the sight gags. Normally I don't like slapstick, and I was surprised that the family found it so hilarious. Okāsan never smiled once, as she sat in front of the TV sewing. Shizuka noticed the question on my face. "Okāsan thinks the program is dumb. She doesn't like today's television."

When the show was ending I decided to deliver my presents. After receiving Shizuka's letter, I'd thought carefully about what to get each child.

Quietly I carried the presents into the living room and left them hidden from sight. I turned off the TV as soon as the commercials came on in order to obtain their undivided attention for what I thought was the most important thing I'd attempted so far—to distribute my gifts and become really sociable with the family.

When the TV snapped off, Manabu's hand shot out desperately for the remote control that I held a few inches from his grasp. "No, no, no. Please. Important, please!" he insisted. Wondering what I should do, I looked at Shizuka, but she shrugged. Manabu eventually retrieved the remote from me and lent me one eye while I distributed presents, but kept the other eye on the TV. It was just what I'd hoped wouldn't happen.

Minori liked her "Ridgefield High School" bookbag but couldn't use it, I soon learned, because a standard bookbag is part of her school uniform. Graciously, though, she hung the bag over her bed. Yamato loved his "U.S.A." stickers, even though they were the simplest of my presents. He took off his shirt and stuck flags, stars, and bald eagles on his shoulders and chest like tattoos.

Shizuka already owned a dictionary that she'd bought in America, a big *Webster's*. Mine was just a simple high-school dictionary. "But I think I will use yours," she said. "The *Webster's*, it is trouble . . . It is complicated. Too complicated. Thank you for such a useful present."

Manabu scrutinized his Aerobie, an aerodynamically designed frisbee ring that once set the world distance-record for a thrown object. It was one of the few toys I could find in Connecticut that was made in America. "I try, now. Sankyu for your letter," he nodded politely and, to my surprise, tore himself away from the TV. He stepped outside, tossed the Aerobie, and nearly lost it over the side of the hill.

"Manabu, you'll have to find a large open space to throw it," I said.

Shizuka sighed, "It's so crowded in this city. There aren't any open areas around here." Manabu had already lost interest in the Aerobie and was back at the TV.

The phone rang, and Shizuka answered. She soon handed me the phone. I gestured "Me?" The caller, Mr. Hiroshi Tomita, spoke good, carefully chosen English. He was an English teacher at Uenogaoka ("High Hill") High School.

"Do you wish to go to school?" he asked. I answered a cheerful yes. Actually, I didn't have a choice. I knew the family had made arrangements for me to attend school for the next three weeks, before the summer vacation started. (I had no idea, though, of how I'd spend the other five weeks of my visit.) But it was nice of Mr. Tomita to ask.

"The students are eagerly expecting you," he said pleasantly. "Would you kindly make a speech to our teachers on Monday, to introduce yourself and tell them about America?"

After I agreed to speak and our brief conversation ended, Shizuka explained, "To speak to all the teachers is a great honor, Steve."

Mr. Tomita soon arrived at the Andos' door, having walked the ten uphill blocks from school in the blistering heat. He wore a short-sleeved business shirt and slacks.

"I received a folder all about you from the exchange program, Steven," he said. "I'll be following your progress."

Sitting on the sofa with Shizuka and me, he spoke with what sounded like rehearsed remarks and witticisms. Little by little he seemed to shed this skin of nervousness and became cordial and jolly—though Shizuka, his former student, maintained her formal politeness.

I guessed that he might be nervous not only about

meeting me but also about being in this house. He had not undergone the formality of meeting Otōsan, the man of the house, who was out on business. Without this introduction he couldn't be fully at ease, I sensed, even though he was a respected teacher and invited guest.

He told me a little about what to expect at school and handed me a roster:

SCHEDULE OF LESSONS

	Mon	Tues	Wed	Thur	Fri	Sat
1	English Readers	English Readers	Analitics	Geogr.	Japanese Classics	Geogr.
2	Algebra& Geometry	Physical Ed	English Grammar	Physical Ed	English Readers	Japanese Classics
3	Health Education	Analitics	Algebra& Geometry	English Readers	Algebra& Geometry	Biology
4	Japanese	World History	Required Club	Home Room	Arts (Electv)	World History
5	World History	Japanese Classics	Biology	Analitics	Physical Ed	
6	Physical Ed	English Grammar	Geogr.	Japanese	Biology	

I noticed with surprise that all the students in the eleventh grade took the same courses, which included two English courses—English Readers and English Grammar—as well as Japanese and Japanese Classics.

Mr. Tomita stayed a long time to explain a little about the school day, while Okāsan repeatedly served him coffee and seaweed biscuits. The coffee was set out in an exquisite set of half-size cups. Okāsan didn't sit with us but socialized politely with Mr. Tomita each time she stopped by with refills. He took a long time to drink his coffee, stirring in his sugar at length, adding a dab of cream and stirring again, then holding the cup in front of his mouth for several minutes, with gestures reminiscent of tea ceremonies I'd seen in films.

Mr. Tomita left after several farewells. Shizuka seemed excited by what it meant for her to have me attend her school. She drew maps of how to get to my homeroom from the school office and how to get to her homeroom from mine.

"Now come see where you'll be staying," she said as she led me on a tour of the house. We went outdoors to reach the basement, which contained a big family-room, with a ping-pong table, portable rostrum, wine storage rack, and fireplace. "Otōsan expects to have large groups here and to give lots of speeches," explained Shizuka. "He'd like to be a community leader. Maybe a leader of our neighborhood organization."

The main floor contained the big bedroom I was to share with Manabu, three other bedrooms, a small storeroom where my luggage would stay, a kitchen, a tatami room, a toilet room, a separate shower-bath room, and the living-room—where Shika said they always ate their meals rather than in the house's formal, Western-style dining area. In the shower room I noticed Yves St. Laurent towels and a small clothes washer, but no dryer; the clothes hung outside. During my visit, Yamato—who ordinarily slept on the bottom bunk in Manabu's room—would sleep with his parents at the other end of the first floor.

The bedrooms of Shizuka and Minori were opposite mine. Minori's was tiny. Her small school desk and one of the household's ubiquitous electric fans took up most of it. She slept on a thin futon laid on a bed-like wooden platform.

In Shizuka's room a frame on the wall held an embroidered cloth that said "Kansas," a souvenir of her year-long exchange visit.

This spacious floor also contained Otōsan's big home office plus another office for Ojisan.

In a room to itself, the Andos had installed one of the most advanced toilets in the world. It looked like an oversized Western toilet except for the electronic console at your right hand to control its heated seat, variable-speed water jets, and air-dryer. I knew I'd need flight training to use it.

The most handsome room in the house was also the simplest. It was the small, bare room with smooth tatami mats on the floor (the other rooms had highly polished wood floors). There was a single work of calligraphy on one wall, paper *shōji* (sliding doors) to the rest of the house, and glass *shōji* to a tiny porch. "Although Otōsan asked Ojisan, who's an architect, to design a modern house for him," Shizuka said, "he also wanted it to have a traditional retreat."

On the top, or second, floor were the bedrooms of some of the employees of Otōsan's barber shops—three young men and three young women. Each of the two groups shared a large room, Shizuka told me. We didn't go up there.

The house was so new that it was still being finished. The gardens hadn't been started, and building materials lay scattered around the property.

Shizuka explained that her father owned four barber shops, one of them inherited from his father, and he was a partner-manager for two hotels in Yufuin, a nearby spa town. He also owned a five-storey office building in the center of the city, which held one of his barber shops and several other tenant businesses.

Before moving to Sakuragaoka a year ago, the family had lived in a large apartment, and before that in a smaller one. It was clear that in recent years the Andos had done extremely well.

I unpacked my things and set up my bed with the help of Okāsan, who was buzzing around energetically. Not much was happening; we sat around the TV, and Yamato led me silently through more comics.

The someone we were waiting for walked in around 7 p.m. Otōsan was home for dinner, and we could start. He was in a jolly mood as he changed from his business suit into dungaree shorts and an LAPD t-shirt that showed off his bulk and roundness. He looked far more comfortable in these clothes. Entered the TV room, he knelt down at the table, and said, so everyone in the house could hear, "I am hungry" −in English. All members of the family dropped what they were doing and trotted in to dinner, promptly served by Okāsan, who'd been working on it all afternoon.

Otōsan's conversation revealed an insatiable curiosity about my trip and life at home. How big was my family, what did we each do, what was I studying, and again, what did I think of Japan? Shizuka translated my information for Okāsan, who acknowledged it with big, appreciative nods.

Although the table was large, it was crowded because each place had many dishes: a bowl for the miso soup appetizer (chopped chives and tofu in a bean-paste-based soup), a bowl for the ever-present rice, another for soy sauce, one for wokked vegetables, and one for beef strips, plus a ceramic block to rest chopsticks on, and a glass of wheat tea−not to mention the serving dishes in the center.

At the end of the meal Okāsan and Minori delivered to my place a big cake with the words "Welcome Steven" written on top with icing. I don't know what kind of cake it was; it tasted eggy. I appreciated the gesture, but with midnight approaching, my eyes were filming over. Everything in my peripheral vision took on a prism-like quality.

After I ate some cake, I bid everyone goodnight and swiftly hit the sack.

The lower bunk was a bare, wooden shelf on which rested a firm, thumb-thick futon. The pillow was Western-style, I was relieved to see; some Japanese use wooden pillows, I'd been told in Seattle.

The welcome peace and darkness of the room was disrupted by the overpoweringly loud ticking of a wind-up clock. When I couldn't bear it any longer, I deposited the clock outside the door and climbed back into bed. In that sleepless state, I took the opportunity to review what I'd learned from Shizuka about names.

Otōsan means father. "*O*" is a prefix for "great" or "honorable." "*San*" also means "honorable"; it's the standard syllable attached to last names, like "Mr.", and it confers respect, as in Ando-san. It doesn't seem redundant to the Japanese to add two respectful epithets. That leaves the middle: "*tō*" means "male," "father," or "husband." Otōsan means Great-Father-Honorable. Q.E.D.

Mr. Ando's first name, Shizuo, like Shizuka, means "quiet one." No one ever called him by his first name, though; outside the family they called him Ando-san, and inside they liked nicknames. That his name meant "quiet man" was amusing because he was the loudest, most extrovert, most outgoing Japanese I'd met.

"Mother" is *kā*, so *Okāsan* means Great-Mother-Honorable. "*Kā*" loosely means "female," but you have to be careful to draw out the nasal "*ā*," because a short "*ka*" means "mosquito."

Shizuka shortens neatly to Shika, "deer." Her girlfriends call her Shika-chan, which adds "beloved," in the sense of good friend.

Minori's name can't be shortened. I thought I heard Manabu calling her "Nori-chan," so I used it, to explosive giggles. Nori-chan means "beloved seaweed."

Manabu means "learning" and shortens to Mākun. Another family might say Manabu-san, "honorable Manabu," because he's the oldest boy, but this family likes informality.

The first kanji character of "Yamato," when isolated, is pronounced "dai." *"Dai"* means "big," and the family has no end of fun calling this tiny child "Dai" in front of guests. His pet names are Daidai (Big big) and Dai-kun (beloved Big).

I decided to use nicknames too.

Mākun strode into the bedroom an hour later, flicked on the bright ceiling light, changed out of his clothes behind the closet door, retrieved the noisy clock, switched the ceiling light to a "night-light" setting that still bothered my eyes, and spent the night peeking down at me from the top bunk.

Rise, Stand Straight, and Bow!

Week 1: July
Sunday

I woke early, even though I'd been up late last night. Maybe it was my apprehension in this strange new place, or the sheer differentness of my sleep that popped my eyes open with the sunrise and propelled me out of bed with little of my usual lethargy. I'm generally not a morning person.

Out the bedroom window I saw an old woman in a Western-style housedress strolling down the Andos' curved driveway toward the house. She called out, "O Haay Ohhhhhhhh" (Hello). After greeting Okāsan, she walked into my room, where I was still in bed in my underwear to say a warm hello. She was Obāsan, the grandmother, and she wanted me to visit her house as soon as I was ready.

A little later, after I'd dressed, Shika took me to her grandmother's Japanese-style house a few doors up the hill. Living so close, Obāsan often dropped in unannounced, Shika explained.

The grandparents' house was surrounded on three sides by mountain wilderness and bamboo groves. The inside contained a handsome, traditional-style pair of rooms with a tea ceremony area and more than a dozen Noh masks displayed on the walls. Some masks appeared to be hundreds of years old; others were so vibrant they seemed alive. The grandfather, a retired barber, made them all.

The grandparents gestured and bowed graciously as they ushered me around the house to see their mask collection. I hit my head on the low ceiling once or twice. They jokingly conveyed their conclusion – Shika translating – that I was just too tall.

High-spirited Obāsan laughed and made pleasant comments that Shika restated for me. Dressed in traditional clothes, the dignified-looking grandfather watched me intently, so I was on my best behavior, trying to act as though I wasn't wearing a bright pink t-shirt and aqua shorts.

In the basement they led me to a showcase of the best of the Noh masks. There were women's faces in severe fright, terrifying faces of demons in agony, and men's faces stern and fretful in ivory or black. The elderly couple beamed at me as I inspected the masks and conveyed admiration with my own set of facial expressions.

One bright-red gargoyle caught my eye because, surreal and distorted, it looked exactly like what I imagined a gargoyle to be. I pointed it out to Shika, who grimaced: "Sometimes I have bad dreams about that face."

We knelt around the grandfather, who picked up an ancient scroll and began to chant in a deep, staccato monotone. Shika tried to follow the text with her eyes, while we both knelt silently for the impressive performance. Later she told me the text was written in ancient Japanese, and she couldn't read it. I had no idea what had occasioned his performance, but from his dignified bearing and close attention to my reaction, I assumed he wanted to provide me with a sampling of still another ancient skill—part of my introduction to Japan.

"It's a wonderful house," I remarked to Shika on the way home.

"Yes, I think it is the nicest house in the whole city," she replied.

The grandparents are so formal and traditional, I mused later, like the Japanese I'd read about in books, whereas Otōsan is ebullient and bold. "How could these gentle, traditional people have such an unusual son?" I wondered.

Late that afternoon, Okāsan took me to the home of a boy my age to borrow a pair of pants for my school uniform. (The shirt was no problem because any short-sleeved, white polyester shirt would do.)

She drove me in her tiny, red Suzuki, which was very dinged-up and left lots of smoke. She had to park it on the driveway because the family's parking slots just off the street accommodated only their van and new sedan. Backing the Suzuki up the steep driveway strained its little engine tremendously. The car whined and made several attempts, rocketing backward and slipping forward, before it finally lurched onto the street. The car was presumably a survivor of their earlier, not-so-affluent lifestyle.

As we drove through narrow streets walled in with gray cinder blocks, we passed groups of students. The boys all wore the same white shirts and black polyester slacks. The girls wore sailor blouses and skirts, but the colors varied from light blue, like Uenogaoka's, to gray—depending on the school.

As if one uniform weren't enough, a dress uniform—plainer and more formal—is worn for special occasions, Shika said. Hers was a dark blue dress. The boys' formal uniform at Uenogaoka was a black Mao suit with its oriental collar and button-up front. I wouldn't be a student here long enough to need one.

The boy we visited was renowned for being the tallest student at the school, but the cuffs of his pants still had to be let down all the way for me. Okāsan did the job while we waited, with sewing materials provided by the boy's mother. The two women sat at a knee-high table, snacking on fruit biscuits and squid.

Meanwhile, the boy gave me a tour of his spotless, medium-sized house, small by Western standards. There was almost on the tatami floors—no chairs, or cabinets, just a couple of tables and little else. Any clutter was piled into unobtrusive closets shielded from view by *shōji*. There were no interior walls, just *shōji* separating the rooms. Theoretically you could remove all the screens to convert the whole house into one big room.

In the boy's room was a dresser filled with clothes, its top nearly overflowing with his heavy-metal tape collection. He selected a tape by Bon Jovi and played it loudly so we could hear it throughout the rest of our tour. This also meant that it was playing in the mothers' ears. They talked right through the obnoxious noise.

There was nothing else in his room, not even a bed. As if reading my thoughts, he slid back a screen to point to his futon neatly folded behind it. As we walked around the house, I banged my head several times on doorframes or hanging lights. Eagerly, as if he'd been waiting too long for the appropriate moment, he asked if he could measure my height. Tape measured, I came out at six feet. He appeared impressed and told his mom the result. She then discussed it with Okāsan as though I were the Colossus of Rhodes.

Back at home, we kids watched TV until early evening. Shika was about to take her exams for college. The Japanese have a name for this time, *juken jigoku* or exam hell. I expected she'd do well in English; Mr. Tomita had told me she's known as one of the best English-speakers in the Oita schools.

She was undecided, though, about which university she'd choose, and what choice she'd have would depend very much on her entrance-exams. She said she wouldn't study just English at university; she'd specialize in something that would provide her with a profession.

"In the U.S.," I commented, "we tend to separate the world into two halves—East and West. Japan, though obviously in the East, is considered special because of its industrialization and close relationship with the West."

Out of curiosity I asked her whether she considered herself Eastern or Western. Without hesitation she replied, "Western."

Shika said Mākun would soon take big exams to get into high school. He wanted to go to Shika's school, Uenogaoka—academically the best in Oita.

"Our family was not planning to invite another foreign-exchange student this summer because Mākun and I need to study especially hard for these exams," Shika explained. "But one day in the spring my father just said, 'We will.' So we did, and I'm glad.

"My father's very international-minded," she continued, "and he wants to have foreign visitors at our home forever. Our exchange student before you was a Hindu girl from the U.S., who couldn't eat many Japanese foods. That's why we're always asking you, 'Can you eat tofu? Can you eat rice? Cabbage? Miso soup? Chicken? Squid?'"

At dinner we watched TV while we ate, the way my American family does. We knelt around the low table on leather cushions borrowed from the sofa. Afterward we pushed our plates into the center, shifted the cushions and ourselves up to the sofa, and continued to watch.

Dai liked to sleep on the floor in his parents' room, so I was glad not to feel I'd evicted him from his bunk. He and his mother were still very close. When boys go off to junior high they become "men" and aren't supposed to kiss their mothers in public or show much emotion. But Dai was still of an age where his mother could smother him with affection.

Okāsan liked to have him with her whenever possible and gave him cute little presents, like chopsticks with Panda heads on the ends. She always had fresh t-shirts and shorts for him, or for special occasions perhaps a new pastel polo shirt and khaki slacks with a good crease. He had only recently moved out of his parents' room and in with Mākun.

I fell asleep on my bunk practicing some phrases I learned from Shika:

Watashitachi Top Gun miru.
   We watch "Top Gun."
Anata wa kādo ga umai.
   You are good at cards.
Korewa ōki-na ōchi des.
   This is a big house.
Motto yukkuri hanashite kudasai.
   Speak more slowly please.
Wakarimasuka
   Understand?
Wakarimasen
   Not understand.
Watashi wa Steve desu.
   I am Steve.
Watashi no heya wa doko desuka.
   Where is my room?
Dōzo yoroshiku.
   Pleased to meet you.

Week 1: July
Monday

We rode bikes to school through the maze of angular, convoluted, walled roads. It was all downhill, which made for a wild ride if you were late. Shika said that because she lived so near, the school expected her to walk instead of cycle. I mentioned that I'd seen a lot of students walking and wondered why they had to walk when they all had bikes.

"It's just what the school says," she shrugged. She rode her bike anyway. Minori's art school was farther still, yet she too was required to walk. So I used her bike.

Bikes were parked two-deep under a small roof, in a line that stretched the length of the school. From a distance the hodgepodge of handlebars and spokes looked like an impenetrable barbed-wire fence.

Two classroom buildings, an administration building, two gymnasiums, outdoor pool, and other facilities like playing fields and tracks, all occupied a deceptively small plot, surrounded closely by the city. Within the grounds, however, the school took on an uncrowded, simple air. Courtyards allowed air circulation to counteract the relentless sun. The buildings were made of worn, gray-brown concrete, not particularly attractive but shiny clean inside and out. The two classroom buildings were each four storeys high, one classroom wide, simple, and box-like.

After parking our bikes, Shika delivered me to the teachers' office and attached me to Mr. Tomita, who seated me in a corner while the other staff members trickled in, chatting quietly.

After they'd assembled and at Mr. Tomita's prompting, I gave a short speech—my name, where I was from, where and how long I was staying. Last night Shika had helped me write the opening sentences in Japanese, and I gave the rest in the simple English that Mr. Tomita had said would be "fine."

In Boy Scouts, when I'm teaching a skill, sometimes the kids—the ones who aren't understanding—look at my belly-button or slightly above and behind me while I talk, but specifically not at me. I always get an empty feeling in my stomach when they do. I got that feeling now from these teachers. Still, they were polite and applauded when I sat down.

After the teachers' busy meeting, Mr. Tomita introduced me to an English Grammar teacher, Miss Hamazaki, a young woman who taught the homeroom class I'd be joining. The first thing she said, after delicately shaking my hand, was a cryptic, almost pleading, "Please help me."

As the meeting broke up, Mr. Tomita led me to an all-school assembly where I'd join my classmates.

A bottleneck of students had formed at the entrance to the gymnasium-auditorium, where they had to remove and carry their shoes inside. Each homeroom class was separated into boys and girls, and these shoeless groups were hustled into the gym by a burly, gruff-looking teacher who tugged and shoved them into their allotted spaces.

After removing his shoes and motioning to me to do likewise, Tomita-*sensei* (Teacher Tomita) led me past the bottleneck. Lost without Shika to explain things and intimidated by the way the students were being packed in, I felt out of place and uncomfortable. Ripple-waves of students gasped and pointed at me. Tension built up, twisting my gut, while I desperately scanned the room for Shika, or the boy whose pants I was wearing, or anyone I might know.

Mr. Tomita found the boys from my homeroom and, having said a few words to them, was gone.

I was met by shy smiles from my future classmates, but they avoided any eye contact and moved slightly back from me. Suddenly a short, bull-like boy with a close crew-cut and a big, impressively confident smile greeted me by yelling as loudly as he could into my chest, "I can't speak English!" Then he ran a victory lap around the other boys, who were driven to titters. Returning to my chest, he announced several times, "Mai neim isu Jani" (My name is Johnny), as if he'd taken a dare to do this. Relieved to know someone, I introduced myself in Japanese, as I'd been taught. After exchanging smiles, we sat down side-by-side on the floor—my first problem solved.

When I thought the gym couldn't hold any more bodies, a teacher shuffled us along the floor and into neat columns, then packed the columns tightly against each other to make way for still more students—far more than a U.S. fire code would permit. Nevertheless, with the exception of Johnny, the students nearest me continued their slow dispersion, allowing me a noticeable and uncomfortably large circle of personal space.

Teachers filled the assembly time with announcements that, of course, totally eluded me. Although the speakers were enthusiastic, the students grew more and more lethargic and apparently uninterested—understandable considering the intense heat and crowding.

The assembly over, I returned with my new class to our homeroom. Every classroom was the same: seven columns of desks, seven students to a column. At Ridgefield High we had only about 20 students in the same-sized room.

I was further disoriented by a map of the world hanging on the wall in front of me: Japan was at its center. My mind spun as I groped to regain my bearings.

My classmates had recently begun their junior year, and in the U.S. I'd just finished that year. But the junior class was the right place for me; in Shika's senior class the novelty of my presence could jeopardize the crucial college-exam preparations.

Shika had also explained that each class contained students of every ability level, who learn to work together. I'd had the impression that Japanese schools were sweatshops of intense competition, but the students I got to know were sociable and helpful to me and, very noticeably, to each other.

Every time a teacher entered the room, the class leader—who sat in the front row, squarely in front of the teacher's rostrum—stood to announce:

KIRITSU! (Rise)
KIOTSUKE! (Stand straight)
REI! (Bow)

With these commands, we stood in unison, bowed, sat down, and began our first class.

English Readers

Teacher Tomita asked me to give my introductory speech again, and this time he had a map of the U.S. ready for me to use. I detected more than a little disappointment that I was from someplace called Connecticut, and not New York City.

Next he had me read from their text, *Sunshine*, following my words closely as I read aloud, and checking them against the phonetic-alphabet legends on each page. He said that my correct pronunciation was helpful for the students, but added, "We won't be spending very much time on pronunciation because the students' exams will be on written, not spoken, English."

He quizzed random students on the meaning of words from the text like "fantastic" and "dialogue." A boy who didn't know the meaning of the word "dragon" was sternly directed by a gesture from Mr. Tomita to consult the dictionary in the front of the room. In total silence and under the teacher's unswerving gaze, the self-conscious student had to locate the word and give a satisfactory answer before the class could continue. This process took some time.

"Gold-haired," I overheard a clique in the back of the room calling me.

Algebra & Geometry

A tremendous amount of time was spent going over math operations in detail and correcting homework, every step. I found the pace laborious, yet the students were attentive. The teacher wrote out on the blackboard the many steps of long problems, and the students meticulously copied them into their notebooks. They wrote neatly, precisely, on graph paper, working in many colored inks—the red reserved for correcting.

Health Education

The class was studying how cuts heal, how to treat common accidents, and what emergency services were available.

A girl in a short ponytail was called upon to read from the text. She spoke softly, not wanting to attract anyone's attention, although she was centerstage. Her classmates did her the courtesy of burying their faces in their books, which also served to avoid attracting the teacher's attention when it came time to call on someone else.

A girl in the front row didn't move all period: her head was hunched down low and her notebook was clasped tightly to her chest. She seemed paralyzed with fear of being called on or standing out.

One of the things that struck me was how uniform all the students were—and not just because they wore uniforms. Certainly the Japanese are known for a homogeneity of looks and body size. Beyond this, the boys had the same haircuts, and the girls' hairdos varied only slightly.

Everyone had the same attentive posture, and their expressions were all the same—as close to expressionless as possible.

Everyone kept a pencil box with similar writing implements in the upper left corner of the desk. Erasers were separate from the pencils, and nobody used wooden pencils, only mechanical ones.

Identical school bags—black leather satchels—hung on clips on the right side of each desk. And students usually removed their watches and placed them in the same spot, the upper right corner. In their shirt pockets the students carried photo-IDs, which included a small booklet reminding them of the words to the school cheer, song, and rules.

Schoolgirls and women acted delicately and spoke in high-pitched voices. The girls seldom mixed with the boys, and there seemed to be that same wall-of-difference between the sexes that's common in the West among younger children and that evaporates, for the most part, by our high-school years. Japanese girls who were friends often held hands in pairs or groups. Boys did too.

The students remained in the same classroom all day except for gym, required clubs, and other subjects that needed special facilities, such as art.

My desk was too small. I devised a theory that school seats in Japan are designed so that a student can't lean far forward or backward; they also have a narrow base so you can't slump effectively. My chair was much too confining for my height and leg size, and I couldn't lean back or put my feet forward for relief.

Eventually I found a way to overcome this constriction. I stuck both legs out through the front of the desk and rested my feet on the back of the chair ahead of me. In devising this *modus vivendi*, I attracted the intense interest of my staring classmates, their lessons forgotten for a happy moment.

My legs now stopped complaining, but my shoulders and small-of-back were worn out from a cramped morning, so I planted my elbows firmly on the desk and rested my forehead in my clasped hands.

My neck still hurt from trying to sleep on the plane to Tokyo. My shoulders and back ached, too, from the heat and new postures. In resting, I looked as though I were praying. The students pointed me out to each other, murmuring worriedly. I appreciated their concern, but then my aches again took charge of my ability to concentrate.

During the break after health class, Johnny leaped at me, rubbing his hands with excitement. "Stibu!" he bellowed so loudly that my chest resonated. He wasn't shy like the others—or maybe he was and was overcompensating.

"Now to show . . . toilet!" he shouted, overjoyed. With a group of merry sidekicks, he escorted me to the school bathroom. Inside, at the mirrors, boys were meticulously combing their hair, which didn't need combing because it immediately returned to its buzzed state.

He swung open a stall and pointed, docent-like, at the ceramic bowl set into the floor. "Japanisu toireto!" (Japanese toilet), he announced, erupting in a ridiculous staccato laugh that was echoed by his friends, who looked expectantly at me. I acknowledged this information with a smile, then eagerly led the troop back to class, having decided to re-explore the bathroom later.

Lunch

Classes lasted 50 minutes, but were really closer to an hour because teachers continued lecturing into the ten-minute breaks. Lunch was only 40 minutes.

I was surprised when the school authorities piped hard-rock music into our classroom over the loudspeaker during lunch. They also played some love songs and Top

10 hits—all Western music. It seemed out of character for this strict school, or maybe for any school.

Balconies spanned the length of the school, allowing students to socialize outside their classrooms during lunch and breaks. A girl waved at me from the balcony in another building. When I waved back, she and all her friends were at first startled, then laughed and hid their faces behind the fans they were cooling themselves with.

Some of the boys gathered in a tight group on our balcony to eat and laugh. This balcony group was the class's coolest clique, and they loved to converse about heavy-metal music. To my delight, they figured that, being American, I was a punker too, so they readily admitted "Gold-haired" to their circle. After High Fives all round, they offered me roots or interesting parts of fish from their lunchboxes as a gesture of friendship, but also to watch my reaction—sometimes quizzical but always gratifyingly enthusiastic—to these foods.

In particular, the boys wanted me to sample their umeboshi, a popular lunch that's uniquely Japanese and considered patriotic, even nationalistic. There it was, a round, red pickled plum in the middle of a field of white rice, like the flag. The bite-sized plum was incredibly sour and salty and made my mouth hurt. Umeboshi comes in different strengths and, among these boys, you earned respect if you could eat the sourest.

The boys taught me to eat the umeboshi whole, then spit out the stone. The bitter taste is supposed to last for the whole bed of plain rice, which is actually the meal and which is pleasantly sweet by comparison. Sometimes the umeboshi taste lingers all day.

The students' *obentō*s (lunch boxes) typically contained leftovers from last night's dinner, plus rice and some new side-dishes, like pickles. Everyone wanted to trade lunches with me. When I told Okāsan this later, she was tickled.

When the students found I could do coin tricks, I became even more "cool" and the center of attention. They'd ask earnestly to see each trick again, then invite their friends, who also had to see the trick a second time. They never tired of the same tricks, which I appreciated, given the limited number in my repertoire.

Japanese

Outfitted in a trim robin's-egg-blue jacket-dress, her lips accented with dark-red lipstick, stylish young Miss Watanabe spent 30 minutes of the period filling a medium-sized blackboard with kanji. It takes a long time to write these Chinese-based characters correctly and aesthetically. Kanji also take a long time to learn, and constant exposure to retain.

So far, none of the teachers had asked for hands to be raised. They'd called on students, but their classes weren't oriented toward free-response or discussion, or even questions from the students. Teachers didn't always seem to prepare for class, I noticed, and often ended up doing something boring like rote memorization or repetition at the end of the period to fill time.

World History

I wrote a note, the first of many, to the boy sitting next to me, who'd been pointed out at lunch as probably the best student in the class:

> Me: DO YOU STUDY HARD?
> Boy: NO
> Me: ME, TOO!

Soft-spoken and reticent, he wore thick-rimmed glasses and his posture was poor. When the national sports proficiency scores were passed out today, I was surprised to learn he'd gotten very high scores, and the boys at lunch had also indicated that this nerdy kid was the school expert in kendo. I nicknamed him Kendo Kid to myself; publicly I called him Ken.

Kendo Kid had a Mickey Mouse watch; Mickey's eyes blinked as each second ticked by. I asked to see it, and he shrugged indifferently as he handed it to me, then studied my face closely as I inspected it. He took a new interest in his watch when I gave it back.

Japanese students study both European/American and Asian/Japanese history. They calibrate Asian history by their own Emperor-date system (and sometimes by the Chinese emperor-date system), and Western history by the B.C./A.D. system. The two dating systems never meet! Plus there's the schizophrenia of modern-day officials using both, say, "1989" and "1" (the first year of Akihito's reign) to describe a particular year. These multiple dating systems are dizzying to contemplate, let alone to learn history by.

Physical Education

I was confused. Some boys left with their kendo gear, but most headed for the pool. Other kids stayed behind as if waiting for me to make up my mind. Finally, one pantomimed a few strokes and said "Swimming?" I saw no alternative, so I nodded and threw myself into the group. The kids whooped and frolicked, carrying me forward in their middle, like a hunting party returning with its trophy.

I was swept off to the changing room, a balcony above the gym with canvas tarps strung around to shield it from the view of the girls playing volleyball below. Copying the other boys, I rinsed myself in an ice-cold shower before diving into the less frigid outdoor pool.

We played "tag" in the water to warm up. Next, we clambered out for a lengthy dissertation by the head coach—the same man who'd packed us together earlier at the all-school assembly. Then he led us through calisthenics before we did time-trials back in the pool.

Johnny clowned throughout the class. The swim coach was also the judo coach, and because Johnny was the best judo student in the school, he could get away with his antics. When the coach was about to start the first race, Johnny leaped off the starting block, hugged his shoulders as if shivering, and bellowed, "I can't swim!"

Back on the block, he jumped in before the starting gun, swam corkscrew for a while, then backstroked toward the far wall. On the way back, he faked drowning twice. Approaching the end of his two-lengths, he stood up in a pose of absolute exhaustion. Putting his feet down disqualified him from the time-trial, completing his farce. The cheers and laughs of his audience egged him on.

I swam seriously, and the on-lookers hushed up to watch. A member of my high-school varsity swim team, I swam a strong breaststroke. When I finished, Johnny shrieked "BEST!" I don't think I was the best, but I couldn't understand the other students' times. From that point on, Johnny proclaimed that whatever I did was "BEST!" As I climbed out, the group applauded and shook my hand. I felt a little sheepish at the lavish praise, but also realized I was among friends.

Top members of the swim team were distinctive. They swam every day, and the heavy chlorine bleached their hair reddish over time. This was no badge of distinction, however; these students were laughed at. They were called "Red-head Hideo" (or whatever the student's name was); they felt different and uncomfortable.

After school today I saw students mopping floors, sweeping, and leaning far out windows in order to wipe the outside of the glass. Two girls worked from either side of a window to make sure they shined the outside completely, each holding the end of the same long towel and pulling it back and forth like a pair of lumberjacks sawing a trunk. Students delegated to sweep and wash could merely go through the motions because the floors were already clean, thanks to the special slippers the students wore inside the school.

In America students mess up the school, and janitors clean it. In Japan the students have to clean the school during a daily 15-minute clean-up period, so they don't dirty it. Cleaning is neither a reward nor a punishment; it's simply each student's responsibility.

The classroom walls were dingy and cracked, not having been painted recently. Some windows, broken a long time ago, were painstakingly taped up. But the room was clean. This time of day therefore became a social event, with everyone participating and chatting cheerfully.

The students were not so meticulous at their end-of-day cleaning as I'd thought they might be. Dust—what little there was of it—was swept under the unused chairs and desks in the far corner. Some students, the ones not socializing, looked bored by the routine and were going through the motions ineffectually, but not resentfully.

Students, especially the girls, liked to wave to each other in the halls, saying "Haro" (Hello) during the day and "Baibai" (Bye bye) after school. They did this to me, too. I liked to see this, and to smile and receive a sincere smile in return.

Within my hearing, a group of girls decided "Stibu pretty boy."

"Do you have girlfriend?" I was asked a dozen times a day by both boys and girls. Also, "Do you think Japanese girls are pretty?" When I asked Johnny if he had a girlfriend, he looked wild-eyed, hauled me into a corner, hunched over low, and put a finger over his mouth, "Shhhh. Secret."

Not long after Shika and I got home, a girl from my class whom I nicknamed Diana called to see if I'd arrived safely. She was a friend of Minori.

"Sure, he's OK," Shika informed her, handing me the phone.

"Hi. It's nice of you to call," I said, wondering what she'd say next.

"I'm sorry," said Diana. "I don't speak English very well." She sounded nervous, and I think others were listening at her end of the line—I could hear giggling. She repeated the fact that she didn't speak English, then we both fell silent.

"Thanks again for calling," I concluded, unsure what else to say. I returned the receiver to Shika and pondered why Diana had called to check on me, and why she wanted to talk to me if she didn't have anything to say. Shika didn't know either.

Despite important exams less than a week away, Shika and Mākun didn't seem to be spending a lot of time studying. I'd had to do much more preparation for the final exams I'd just finished in Ridgefield.

We watched a TV show consisting of popular Japanese rockers filmed in the U.S. Tonight's stop was Utah, where the rockers danced to a dubbed song in front of the American flag, the Statehouse, mountains, and some American by-standers. The video segments had subtitles—for example, "Utah State capitol building" —in English. Another group was filmed at the base of the Statue of Liberty, where they encircled some curious American teenagers and serenaded them.

"Japanese," Shika told me, "like New York City and the Statue of Liberty and rock videos filmed there." The Japanese, I learned, also like California, except for L.A., which is getting a bad press as a combat zone full of gang wars and drug-trafficking.

The Japanese women I saw in music videos didn't dance well. They stood in one place, moved their arms around feebly, and smiled. The very popular female duo Wink, which had just sprung into the limelight, was distinctive because the two girls didn't even smile or show any expression as they delicately waved their arms and hips.

As we watched, I realized I was witnessing a TV-centered cultural revolution, complete with teen idols and pop cults, and reminiscent of the fads and variety shows of the U.S. in the 1960s.

I helped Shika with her English homework before dinner. She'd taken a difficult college-entrance English exam upon arriving home from Kansas and had failed it. "Many English teachers in Japan fail this same test," she said. "Because I took it immediately after returning from America, I thought I might be able to pass it, but it was still too advanced." So I began working with her on pronunciation rules, word choice, difficult grammar, and sentence construction. A sample exam question was "Gold is heavier than lead. How do you pronounce 'lead'? 'Leed' or 'led'?"

The test also asked you to make a sentence out of a jumble of words; only one sequence was deemed "correct," although several combinations sounded right to me. I found Shika was much faster than I. She jotted down the possible ways that three or four of the words could fit together into phrases. Then she compared these building blocks to each of the sentences given in the multiple-choice answers. Very scientific.

Actually, I got a few questions wrong that she got right. She used a more direct method that didn't allow for the variations that my aural approach did. Interestingly, the subject of her reading-comprehension test was the correlation between Japan's high test scores and high teen suicide rate.

Toward the end of the evening Shika eagerly asked, "Steven, want to look at Yamagata pictures tomorrow? He is a modern painter I like."

"How can you take the time to go to an art exhibit just two days before your exams?" I questioned her.

She closed her eyes wistfully, then broke into a grin, "I don't know, but the exhibit won't be around after the exams. Therefore we must go! And the museum will be as much fun as the exhibit, because it's an old castle surrounded by a moat."

I could tell she didn't want to return to her books and relished the breaths of air she took outside her room. When she was in her room, I could not have yanked her out because she was a serious student. Once out, though, she savored this conversation stolen from her studies, a look of edgy satisfaction on her face.

Week 1: July
Tuesday

At school I took the stairs two at a time because they were small, like the ones I remembered in my elementary school. Everyone stared at me when I did this, murmuring "Ohhhh." Again I was conscious of my too-long legs.

English Readers

Tomita-*sensei* asked my assistance with an exercise. "The wind blows through the trees," I read aloud from the textbook, and the class chanted it back to me in hushed tones. They began their response together, but *very* softly. No one wanted to stand out. Then the choral reading disintegrated, as some read fast, some slow, and others got stuck. It ended pathetically in chaos.

For homework they were assigned chapters from a book about American culture and history—about the Chinese New Year in San Francisco, the sinking of the "Titanic," and the taming of the Wild West. They went over the reading in class to learn pronunciation and correct emphasis, which was particularly difficult because the Japanese language emphasizes all syllables equally. They took turns reading and "discussing" each chapter, but the teacher dominated the proceedings like a judge at a trial, all dialogue coming directly to and from him. Some intelligent remarks were generated in this class, but seldom a conversation and never a debate.

"Does anyone know what today is?" Mr. Tomita had an impossibly big smile on his face. No one knew. He asked me directly. I could've kicked myself. It was the Fourth of July, and I'd forgotten. Finally I blurted, "American Independence Day." Then I remembered the American flag I happened to have in my backpack and waved it to cheers and roars of laughter. Johnny and I hung up the flag in the front of the room to a standing ovation. Mr. Tomita asked me to write a little speech about the Fourth of July to present to their English Grammar class later that day.

Someone began humming the tune to "Reveille," apparently believing it to be the American anthem, and I felt obliged to explain: "In America, that song is played to wake people up."

I pursued the instruction by singing the complementary "Taps." "That's what is played when you go to sleep."

This commentary caused a stir among the students, who exchanged wondering glances. A quiet boy I'd nicknamed Bobby, an aspiring civil servant, came forward hesitantly with a question, "Do all Americans sing these songs each day?" I replied that I meant just soldiers and perhaps Boy Scouts on a campout.

I began to sing the appropriate song for the day, "The Star Spangled Banner." The students were happy to hum along; they knew the melody but not the words. Humm-umm-umm hum hum hum . . .

When I got back to my seat, Bobby leaned over to ask in a soft voice, "Do you always carry American flag?"

"Only to school," I reassured him. His eyes bugged out, so I quickly corrected myself, "Only to *this* school." He went back to his notebooks with a quizzical expression on his face, only partly satisfied. So many of my exchanges with Bobby ended this way.

Physical Education

This time I chose kendo and followed Kendo Kid to the sports lockers outside the classroom, where the students kept their sports equipment and gym uniforms. The lockers were small, so the boys had to leave their kendo swords propped up in the hall. Their bags said "KENDO," in English.

When I asked Kendo Kid how good he was, he responded, "No, very bad." He was the kendo-class leader and a blue *gi*, which is roughly equivalent to a black belt in karate.

The healthy-looking, 60-ish instructor advised me to watch during my first class so I'd understand what was involved. The kids raced about foolishly and played with their swords like samurai, whirling and leaping, before settling down to an orderly teaching session.

Analitics

I spent third-period studying the Japanese-language workbook given to me by Youth for Understanding during our orientation session, while the class hammered away at calculus.

I'd noticed that if a teacher was a little slack about discipline, there could be quite a bit of fooling around in class. This might consist of whispering to neighbors, making faces at other students, or getting the whole class involved in a note-passing gig. Sometimes a few daring students actually conversed, like the heavy-metal-rocker clique that had formed in the back of the room.

The attitude of the students changed with the different teachers, though. Like students anywhere, they'd figured out how much they could get away with in each class. Their attitude also varied with the different moods of a teacher.

The students didn't seem to respect younger teachers as much as older ones. This was evident as soon as a young teacher entered the room. These teachers usually smiled a lot—a sure sign of weakness—and I could hear the class let out its breath and relax. But if a young teacher was strict or suddenly became strict, he or she could not ever be as intimidating as an older teacher—like this analitics teacher, who could sink a whole class with a glare.

A teacher might also drop to a lower-level of respect by not punishing students as often or as severely as other teachers did, or by engaging in Western forms of teaching, like calling on individual students or letting students raise their hands or talk to each other.

In response to a teacher's joke, laughter erupted in bursts—enthusiastic, but a canned sort of laughter. I often heard such an explosion from a class down the hall or across the school. Miss Watanabe, the pretty Japanese teacher, enjoyed making jokes; through the open windows I heard several of these explosions from her classes in other parts of the building.

Johnny liked to look out the window at the birds during class. Small swallows, chirping furiously, congregated in the garden-courtyard between the school's two largest buildings.

Johnny approached me after analitics class was dismissed.

"It is dunch," shouted Johnny.

"You mean runch," I replied with a grin.

"Yes!" he agreed with his boisterous laugh. I thought I'd had the last laugh, but wasn't sure.

The heavy-metal clique caught onto one of my tricks: I found them practicing the coin-palm trick. One of them did it correctly, whooping with surprise and delight; he did it again and was equally delighted.

Japanese Classics

A sudden abdominal sensation sent me scuttling out of class and into one of the bathrooms down the hall. Scouts are taught to "Be Prepared," but I wasn't. There wasn't any toilet paper. The Japanese know to carry their own.

I leaped out of the first stall and checked the others. No toilet paper, not even a spool for it. Beyond caring, I dashed into the last stall, found it already occupied (no locks), doubled back, and squatted again.

I made a tough choice and took from my pocket the only assignment I'd yet been asked to do—my speech in simple English called "The Fourth of July Is Fun," to be presented next period. I'd written it on the pulpy newsprint used here for assignments, and having made use of newspaper as toilet paper in Scouts often enough, I made short work of it. "Spontaneous" is about the kindest comment that could be made about my Independence Day speech next period to my assembled classmates.

English Grammar

Class began with the passing out of papers. From separate corners of the room I heard two students whisper, in English, "I can't speak Japanese." (Lots of laughs.)

The speech Mr. Tomita asked me to write for this class had been short and simple. Now, without it, my remarks were even more so. I talked about what the Fourth of July represents and how I usually spend it—attending a small-town parade, picnicking, and watching the big Boston or New York fireworks on TV.

During the rest of the class, Miss Hamazaki meticulously dissected the grammar of sample sentences in many colors of chalk, while the students copied everything into their notebooks in matching colors. The class focused on rules of English suitable for memorization. The course was difficult, and the students worked hard. They used "The Queen's English," perfect but wordy, upper-class English – American spelling, though.

Hamazaki-*sensei* told her students they were now finished with the year's English grammar lessons, so they could take the rest of the period off. She mingled with the students to chat and instruct a little. The students were in a jovial mood, mostly chatting in groups, while a few worked on assignments.

I was surprised that only one foreign language was taught at this high school: English. They did teach Chinese Classics, but mostly in Japanese translation. They also taught Japanese Classics, which were written long ago in obscure kanji. Shika told me that classical Japanese is highly stylized and hard to understand, perhaps like Old English would be for me.

All Japanese children must study English for three years, starting in the seventh grade; those who go on to high school add three more years of it. My classmates were just completing their fifth year of the language.

Most of the English Grammar class was taught in Japanese. The students spoke English only the few times they were called upon. Shika had to remind me, "This is because they are learning not so much to speak it well, but to pass a college-entrance exam."

After school, Shika and I were to "look at pictures." Rather than bike to the museum, which was in the center of town, Shika said we should take the bus, so I'd learn how to ride it myself if I ever needed to. The crowd at the bus stop included many students. Some lived so far away, she said, that they took three or four buses each way.

On a bus map Shika pointed out the kanji titles of the routes and where they went. The map was useless to me because I didn't know anything about the city, but I hoped to memorize the kanji so I could be independently mobile.

Transportation in the city was chaotic. The buses were too large for the narrow roads. They drove over the center line, and at the same time crowded the cyclists on the edge. The drivers did seem to be accurate at avoiding obstacles, but they drove hair-raisingly fast.

Standing on the bus—Shika wouldn't sit while any adults remained standing—proved a difficult feat. The bus swerved for cyclists and braked violently at bus stops as if they'd been forgotten until the last moment.

Oita was full of noises, from the background babble of packed pedestrians to the random punctuation of traffic snarls. From a restaurant emanated the hollow wail of a Buddhist monk's prayer. . . on audiotape. An election van broadcast a lively message from the crown of amplifiers on its roof. From the stores, picking up and fading as we passed, emanated soothing Muzak and raucous announcements of sales and bargains.

A backing-up bus added a piercing beep-beep. With every pedestrian WALK signal, a little song played—a signal for the blind. Whenever the bus pulled up to a stop, a taped female voice politely announced the destination, rules, and cost of the trip to the newcomers boarding the bus.

The city even smelled busy. Too many people were breathing its hot, humid air, and the crowded buildings blocked the breezy respiration of nature. Fumes and gases assailed my nose.

We alighted at the city's castle, a massive fort that's now a museum, to enter "The Fantastic World of Yamagata," a collection of wonderfully detailed, bright, happy landscapes. Yamagata studied art in America and fell in love with the place; many of his patrons are Americans. His full-of-life-and-color paintings were favorites, I learned, of Arnold Schwarzenegger and Ronald Reagan. In a video-tape played over and over in the exhibit hall, Schwarzenegger described himself as an "art freak," adoring Japanese art, and most of all, Yamagata's.

Yamagata paints a dream world of rainbow-colored scenes, mainly of urban and rural America. I liked his work because it provided a great escape from the heat, noise, and crowding outside, but I was still curious why Shika had brought me here so shortly before her exams.

She walked around in a daze, not wanting the exhibit to end, not wanting to let go of it, staring deeply at each canvas as her feet carried her forward. When we left the museum, she snapped back to reality with a moan. "I'm not getting my work done, and I've got so much more to do."

After watching Shika at the art show, I knew why she'd gone there. At home, she'd have to study again, intensively. She was not a slacker. Her studies would draw her back to them. She wanted—needed—this time to herself, a time to dream.

Reality engulfed us again as the bus returned us to the high school and we rode our bikes home.

Ojisan, who often smoked, had left his pack of "Hope" cigarettes on a table. I asked Shika if Otōsan smoked, and she said, "He doesn't smoke often, only when he drinks. I guess that makes it all right, eh?"

She wanted to speak English with me now, perhaps in preparation for her exam, and so before dinner we sat in the living room and talked. Her voice changed when she switched from English to Japanese. Her Japanese voice was high, sometimes shrill, and surprisingly loud. By contrast, her voice was low and very controlled in English; she was good at speaking it, but it came out pale compared to Japanese. Shika translated for me a comment contributed by Okāsan, "Whenever Shika speaks in English, she sounds tired."

The campaigning for Japan's elections was tumultuous, and I asked Shika a question about it. "I can't tell you much because I guess I'm just not interested in politics," she shrugged. She was also surprisingly naive about world events when I asked for news about some of the international issues I'd been following prior to my trip.

Instead, Shika switched subjects. "In the auditorium for the all-school assembly on Monday, you were a head taller than everyone else, and your blondish hair stood out. Did you know that everyone was staring at you and whispering '*gaijin*,' foreigner?"

"Gosh, I hope I haven't caused you any embarrassment or problems," I responded, uncertain what her point was. She said I didn't, but I think I may have.

Shika's not like the other Japanese girls I've met, though. She may have acquired her different perspective from her year in America, or from the bold, new ideas of her iconoclastic father. Teasingly, I hazarded a comment, "Maybe I'm also bringing lots of attention to you and you like that."

"Well, maybe I do a little," she confessed.

Otōsan entered and announced with appropriate gravity, "Shika has to make a big decision tonight. She thinks about the university. And maybe you can talk to her. I already give her what I know."

"Yes," Shika explained. "I must decide if I'll apply for a special exam-free acceptance to Meiji University in Tokyo—my #2 choice—or take my chances with the na-

tional exams and try for Jochi, which is another name for
Sophia University, also in Tokyo and my #1 choice."

At Otōsan's request I described some American colleges and how I would choose among them—both Otōsan
and Shika listening intently—but concluded with the obvious: "I guess I can't really be much help to you with your
choice."

Shika responded, "I know. This is such an important
time for me because, in Japan, your choice of college con-
trols your destiny." Outwardly, during the rest of the evening, she seemed collected and detached, taking her mo-
mentous decision in stride.

As usual, we had miso soup with dinner. I loved most
Japanese foods, but I didn't like tofu. It's made from bean
curd, and it's healthful, but it has a sickly-sweet taste, so I
avoided it in the miso soup.

"Slurrrp!"

"Schrumpffff!"

What was that racket, I wondered, looking up from
my meal. It was Otōsan, Mākun, and Dai, all slurping
their soup contentedly. Once or twice I winced, and the
family could see I was unnerved by the slurping. Translated by Shika, Okāsan gently reminded me, "You slurp to
show your enjoyment." She brought her bowl up to her
mouth and demonstrated by sipping with minimal noise.

"Sh-h-luuunnmff!" Mākun made his slurps louder.

A busy lady, Okāsan worked long hours before and
after meals, preparing and cleaning up. Today she made a
vegetable sushi, starting from scratch with rice, seaweed,
and vegetables, and also cooked side-orders of beans and
small servings of spiced fish.

We were served large meals, but if I was ever extra
hungry, they said, I could eat more rice. If you put a root
or pickle in your mouth and add lots of rice, it tastes as

though you're eating many pickles, as I'd learned at lunch with the umeboshi. The same goes for beef. The Japanese are practical in eating matters, drawing out the taste of expensive foods so as to make more with less.

I missed a glass of water or milk with meals. Traditionally, the Japanese seldom serve anything to drink with meals; small cups of tea are an exception. Nor did they seem to me to drink much between meals. However, that's changing with a diet that now includes more Western foods.

The Andos kept milk in their refrigerator, something I drank with every meal in the U.S., but they used it sparingly—in coffee, for instance. Where my parents bought half-gallons, Okāsan stocked cartons about one-fifth that size. Yesterday I poured myself a large glass of milk when I should have had juice or cold tea, and Okāsan gasped. Land-intensive milk is a delicacy to the Japanese, the way labor-intensive sushi is a delicacy to Americans.

I also missed napkins.

Okāsan had set the low living-room table earlier in the day and now served us while we ate. She somehow managed to eat with us, too. We cleared off our own places afterward. Next she served dinner in the dining room to the barber-employees from upstairs, who sat on chairs at a Western-style dining room table. Finally, she washed and put away the dishes from the two sittings and packed up the food.

She was always cleaning, shopping, preparing food, helping her children, entertaining guests, or, if all else was done, working on her sewing and quilting.

After dinner, while Shika returned to her studies and the rest of the family watched "Poseidon Adventure II," I spent some time gazing alone from the tatami-matted Japanese room at the fabulous view of the city.

Downtown Oita was composed of nondescript

cement-and-glass office buildings and honeycombed apartment buildings. Visible on the skyline was a three-level, mesh-covered, golf-driving range. The city's many neon signs were beginning to flash and twinkle. But you could also see the ocean in the distance and the tranquil hills on the far side of the bay.

Small Rebellions

Week 1: July
Wednesday

Every morning, Mākun's alarm clock went off loudly at 6:30. He jumped up to shut it off, then returned to bed for another half hour—just as I did at home. But a sudden touch of anxiety cleared my head this morning. I was to give a talk to the English Grammar class.

At school the pallid, study-worn students fanned themselves and mopped their brows in the hot, still air of their homeroom. Next, in Analitics, the students laboriously inscribed formulas on the board that I understood, a satisfying change from my near-total incomprehension in other classes.

English Grammar

Mr. Tomita introduced me, his beaming eyes following me as I stood and walked to the front of the room. The students regarded me politely, masking their curiosity. I remember thinking: In America, some of the students would be whispering wisecracks behind their hands.

I spoke to them about my impressions of Japan, and the differences between Japanese and American schools. "In America we do not wear slippers, we do not bow to our teachers, and we usually do not have a uniform. We do not clean our school, except as punishment. I think schools in Japan are friendlier than those in America. I have many friends in America, but I think I now have even more in Oita. I am touched by your friendliness, but in America I think we are not as shy as you are . . ."

I told them that when I was young I learned how to make origami, and I'd also taken karate lessons for many years. I concluded, "I am glad that, of all the countries in the world, America and Japan have become friends. And I am glad that, of all the people in the world, we are friends."

At Tomita-*sensei*'s request, the students asked questions: "How old are you?" "How many TV stations are there in America?" "Do you have own car?" "What do you like Japan?"

Next, Mr. Tomita directed students to stand up to perform a self-introduction in English. They clearly regarded this as torture.

"I am 17-year-old. I have one brother. He is bigger than I am."

"Hello, Steven, my name is Haruko Matsui. I like the Beatles and Madonna. My hobby is American movies. My English is a . . . My English is very bad. I am a bad student too."

Each student's response was subjected to roars from classmates. I could hardly hear—the speaker's whispers were drowned out by the laughs. The students were still shy toward me, and now they were being stared at and corrected by their teacher as well. They whimpered out their name and age and whether they had any brothers and sisters. I asked each one a question like, "Do you have any hobbies?" "What's your birthday?" "What street do you live on?" The students muttered inaudible answers.

Because I still felt odd in my three-inches-too-short pants, I decided to ask the students how they felt about school uniforms. "Do you like having a uniform?" I asked a girl, who stood to reply and simply nodded her affirmative answer.

"What do you think?" I asked a boy, who stood and managed a "Yes" before sitting down again.

"Do you like your uniform?" I persisted, nodding to another boy. This boy—who'd never spoken to me because he was so shy—replied clearly in English: "No, I don't like it." He remained standing and looked proud.

If he'd sat down promptly, the class might never have caught on because no one was really listening. Now they seemed worried and concerned about me—or him—and astonished that this small rebellion had occurred. I lingered in the relative silence to see if anything more would come of my daring question and his bold response, but nothing did. Mr. Tomita called on the next student to introduce herself.

I used this opportunity, during their introductions, to ask the students if I might give them American nicknames, like Johnny's. I asked a boy with an impossible name that began with "Ha—," "Can I call you Harry?"

"How about 3-D for you?" I said to a boy whom I'd seen sporting a pair of white cardboard glasses with one red lens and one blue lens, obviously a leftover from a 3-D movie.

To a bold, heavy-set boy who'd described himself to me jokingly as "Japanese wrestler," I said, "Can I call you Mister Sumo?" This last question nearly ended the introduction session: the students burst out laughing, and the noise went on for nearly five minutes. In an un-Japanese manner, Mister Sumo beamed and shifted his girth a bit. He said "Yes, yes" again and again.

Third period

I went to see Mr. Tomita in the teacher's lounge, and he dropped everything to talk with me.

"So, you don't like uniforms." Rather than appearing

defensive, he exuded a confidence that suggested, "We all know uniforms are the best way, and we are comfortable enough in this knowledge to humor a bit of, hmmm, dissent."

He provided me with some background. "As you may know, Steven, there is a 'Society of Shame' in Japan, meaning that the group is more important than the individual, and people are highly conscious of what society thinks of them. Shame is considered the worst fate, so people become very careful, modest, and sometimes averse to standing out.

"So the Japanese like uniforms," he concluded, in his polished English. "Students and others become more conscious of themselves and their actions, and they behave and work together better because now they each represent more than just themselves."

I'd already noticed that in Japan almost everyone seemed to have a uniform. Industrial workers wore their company's uniform. The universal office uniform was the *sarariman*'s dark suit or the Office Lady's neat white blouse and navy or gray shirt. Every third car was driven by someone in a uniform with a name tag.

I asked Mr. Tomita what "required club" I should visit after lunch, and he produced a long list of "sports clubs" and "cultural clubs" for me to choose from. Then, handing me his English Readers textbook, he asked that I go over the next lesson and write some true/false questions for the class.

Lunch

I heard a guffaw behind me, then a boy in the back shouted, "Tom Cruise!" Some boys in a rear corner were trying, in a zany way, to out-do each other in resembling Tom Cruise. They kept flicking their collars up, patting down the backs of their hair, licking their fingers to smoothe their eyebrows, shaking their shoulders, and announcing themselves "Tom Cruise!"

American movie stars are idolized here. When I asked a group of girls "Do you know Tom Cruise?" they screamed in unison, threw up their arms, and covered their faces. They listed off as many of his films as I could.

One of the girls motioned me over to a corner. "Secret," she confided in hushed tones, "Here is my boyfriend." She held a photo of a member of a Japanese rock group that had been laminated to the hard plastic board that students place behind the paper in a writing pad. "I carry this picture everywhere," she added, pleased and relieved to share her confession with someone she knew would be interested and who would—mostly through ignorance of the language—keep her confidence.

Required Club

From Tomita-*sensei*'s list I chose Origami Club, and he said he'd take me there. We met some girls from my class in a finely tended floral walkway between buildings (it occurred to me that such a place couldn't exist in an American school, at least not for long). Mr. Tomita left me with them since they were going to Origami too.

Diana asked me several questions. "Do you know 'Genki TV'?"

"No, I don't."

"Oh, it is my favorite *terebi* (TV) show. I hope you to see it."

"Do you know Will Wheaton?" she asked, continuing the "Do you know" game I was always encountering.

When I nodded to indicate I understood, she yelped with surprise and covered her face with her hands.

"Do you know American movie star who played English boy in 'Empire of the Sun'?" She drew his picture, cut from a magazine, from her purse. "I love him," she added, suddenly bashful.

Another girl changed the subject, "Did you like Yamagata exhibit?"

I said "yes" adding, "I even saw Schwarzenegger on
the video there." The girls became surprisingly talkative
and wanted to know what he'd said. For a moment I lost
all my foreign novelty value except as Arnold's advance
man.

At Origami Club the students—about equal numbers
of boys and girls—giggled and stared when I arrived. I
noticed that no one was folding paper. It was so close to
exams that the teacher had let them use club time for
studying.

When a period is set aside for study in America, the
students usually do everything *but* study, and it was the
same here today. They talked loudly in small groups and
read glossy magazines with English-language titles like
*Popeye: Magazine for Nice Boys, Fine Boys, Up to Boy: Private
Room Bible,* and *McSister.*

The teacher tried to show me how to fold a goldfish.
This task took nearly the whole period, and he had to
check his progress in a book more than once. Meanwhile
each conversation cluster now made origami—cranes, samurai, boats, cups, and a dragon—and presented them to
me with great delight.

Biology

The biology teacher was very young, but he had a
confident air, and the class did not get out of hand. "Are
you understanding everything?" he asked me jokingly.

I nodded and grinned, but thought to myself, "Not a
thing." I had picked up only the words "RNA" and "DNA"
from his monologue.

"What are you writing?" he wanted to know. He
beamed when I explained I was keeping a diary. Many
students have walked up and appreciatively flipped

through my notebooks. They hand them back with two hands and a reverent "Ohhhh."

There was another *gaijin* at our high school, a Canadian. Yesterday I saw him driving out of the school fast. When I asked Shika about him, she said she'd heard of him but didn't exactly know what he was doing here. He was a bit of a mystery to everyone I've talked to. All I could find out was that he was from the English-Speaking Society.

Today I met him. I was entering the teacher's lounge, and he was coming out. "I'm an English teacher," he told me, when I stopped to introduce myself. "Here's my business card." Glancing at it, I noticed that he offered "English Conversational Classes."

"I want to learn some Japanese while I'm here," I began, by way of opening a conversation.

He broke me off with a shrill laugh. "Don't even try. I've been here six months and can't understand a thing."

I could sympathize. A "returnee" from the previous year's exchange explained to me during our Seattle orientation session that the Japanese have perhaps the most complex writing system on earth.

One of their four alphabets is kanji, which are the famous ideograms borrowed from the Chinese a few thousand years ago and the main staple of the Japanese writing system. Chinese and Japanese characters, while identical once upon a time, have changed in application over time and are now incompatible.

It takes hours of study to be familiar with even a few of the characters. About one thousand are taught to the end of junior high school, when compulsory education ends. Newspapers and television use the 2,000 most suitable for mass communication, and college entrance exams also assume about 2,000. A college student should know closer to

3,000 to tackle sophisticated texts, and there may be 8,000 kanji in all. Actually, the total number isn't known, as there are many variations, plus old ones not in use, and the total also depends on one's definition of what a kanji is.

If you do manage to memorize a quantity of them, you must practice them constantly. Even the Japanese lose their familiarity with kanji after a prolonged absence.

A second alphabet is hiragana, which is flowery and stylized and difficult to write. With these 77 characters, making up sounds like "ka," "no," and "yu," the Japanese can spell their words phonetically. Hiragana are used to fill in the holes left by the Chinese kanji as imported into Japan.

There's a third alphabet paralleling hiragana called katakana, more angular and straight than hiragana. Katakana are used to spell the many adopted foreign words: *beisuboru* written in five katakana characters represents "baseball"; other examples are *aisukurīmu* for "ice cream," *hatto dogu* for "hot dog," *kukī* for "cookie," and *futoboru* for "football."

Japanese borrows its many foreign words mostly from English, though some are from Portuguese and German. The popular *gairaigo* (imported words) dictionaries have to be updated often. To understand themselves, the Japanese are constantly playing catch-up with their runaway language.

Finally, the Japanese have adopted Roman characters as their fourth alphabet: rōmaji is used to spell out *Japanese* words phonetically. It's taught in all the schools and seen everywhere, on signs, magazine covers, and corporate names. For example, "Sony" and "Mitsubishi" appear in rōmaji around the world, as well as here in Japan.

Rōmaji is considered useful for product names and advertising because most people know and accept it, and the Roman characters expose the product to a vastly wider audience – including the rest of Asia. Also, rōmaji is thought chic and cosmopolitan, especially by the young.

Perhaps most amazing is that all four written forms are mixed indiscriminately. A sentence may begin with the stylized hiragana, add a rōmaji name or date to give an international flair, switch to katakana for a foreign word, present the bulk of the sentence in kanji, and end with more hiragana. It might even include a straightforward English word: "Elvis Presley" or "microchip."

English Grammar

I gave my introductory speech again, this time to Teacher Tomita's sixth-period class, a different homeroom group for me. It was a disaster.

After waiting patiently for someone to ask me a question, Mr. Tomita broke the tension I felt by asking, "Please show some of your tricks to the class." Someone produced a deck of cards, but they were a different size from American cards. I dropped some of them and felt clumsy and phoney. The class tried to ignore my ineptitude.

Hands sweating and shaking from that debacle, I self-consciously led the day's reading – my real purpose for visiting the class. Mr. Tomita asked the class some questions from it. He also used the true/false questions I'd written. "So who was the U.S. President who built the Panama Canal, Tadao?"

The student bolted out of his seat to stand for a while and think. After giving his successful answer, "Theodore Roosevelt," Tadao paused for Mr. Tomita to say "Hai" (Yes) before sinking into his chair.

"Steven, would you now please criticize each student's reading?" asked Mr. Tomita. I felt awkward. They all had the same petty pronunciation problems, and when I mentioned one of these (for example, "th" pronounced "ss," as in "bath"), Mr. Tomita took charge again. "Now class, you heard Steven. We are going to drill on that problem. Repeat after me. Bath. Bath . . ."

The poor student I had corrected, standing throughout the drill, bowed his head and seemed crushed. After "bath" had been repeated for the fifth and final time, I reassured him that he was good in everything but had messed up just a little on that one point. He smiled wanly as he gratefully regained his seat.

As I was leaving Mr. Tomita's class, a group of girls was waiting for me in the corridor. Some appeared on the verge of tittering. One finally spoke up, "You–come?" She fluttered her hand. I found they'd come to escort me back to our homeroom so I wouldn't miss today's cleaning session.

At home that afternoon Mākun tapped my shoulder, "Please to go to town and video." On the way, we dismounted in an urban residential area where Mākun pointed, "This is long ago house." It was where the Andos once lived–a simple, Western-looking building containing three small apartments on a street densely packed with dull-looking concrete apartment buildings.

Crammed in between a Fuji film shop and a corner grocery, the Mom-and-Pop video shop had too little space to be called a store, really. We were met at the door by its owner, a courteous, smiling old woman, who carried a tray of glasses of iced tea for her patrons. Mākun was a horror aficionado, but since I wasn't, we settled on "Red Heat" with Arnold Schwarzenegger.

Japanese video stores hold much variety and, perhaps, a window onto their popular culture's mix of East and West. I saw Chinese kungfu films and ninja movies. Most of the non-cartoon videos came from America with their soundtrack still in English; they were subtitled in Japanese rather than dubbed, probably to preserve the authentic tones of Western speech. Old American TV shows like "Street Hawk" and "Air Wolf" were also favorite videos.

Perhaps half the films packed into the small shop were animations, which were hugely popular. In addition to the usual adventure and romance cartoons, they even offered cartoon series on relatively serious topics, such as sports or history. A particular style of drawing pervaded: the characters were instantly recognizable as Western, yet they were drawn in Japan—tall people with blond or black hair and large, round eyes. Sometimes these characters were Westerner heroes or villains, and sometimes not.

We stopped at a flower shop because I wanted to get Okāsan a gift. In Seattle, one of the YFU returnees had told us his host family really appreciated flowers. The parents of a friend of Mākun owned the shop, but it was closed. I said, "Tomorrow. Shhhh. Secret."

He grinned conspiratorially, "OK."

Farther down the street we passed a *hana* (flower) shop that was open, so I bought a single flower for 200 yen (about $1.75). The store owner pulled a red rose out of a glass refrigerator and went through an elaborate four-minute procedure of pruning, de-thorning, watering, tissue-wrapping, plastic-wrapping, foil-wrapping, and taping it.

Mākun and I agreed to race home, and soon to my surprise—I have almost no experience with bikes—I was winning . As we neared the house, he suddenly called out, "Wait! I have to talk to you." I braked, and he zipped past me, chortling. I buried my chagrin.

At home, Okāsan was delighted with my gift, displaying the package to Shika and Minori before she carefully removed the layers of wrappings and put the rose in a vase. She was beaming.

In return she gave me a special pair of chopsticks with "*otemoto*" written in calligraphy on the wrapper. This is the fancy name for chopsticks, ordinarily called *ohashi*. Her mother had made the *otemoto*'s paper sleeve, and the tiny origami doll pasted to it. A toothpick (the Japanese are proud to have invented the toothpick) cleverly attached the doll's head to its origami body and was removable for use. Inside were the nicest disposable chopsticks I'd ever seen, made of the finest pine. Yet they were meant to be used only once. They were so lovely, and so lovingly handcrafted, that I knew immediately I'd never use them.

People here become embarrassed at any show of emotion. Girls frequently put their hands over their faces to cover their surprise, but this response just makes them look more surprised.

Minori had been watching fad-TV ever since she got home from school. These programs were like the old "Gong Show" and "The Tonight Show," but had no real parallel in America. Though there was no-one around to observe her, she still put her hands over her face when she laughed, like the teenage-girl studio audience.

Dai, who went to elementary school in the center of the city, was a silent but lively child. He developed the habit of hopping onto my lap or tickling my leg in a way that was unbearably funny. He let his fingers crawl over my knee like a spider, while he gazed absentmindedly at the ceiling or TV. He looked so detached and innocent that, even if you weren't ticklish, you couldn't help laughing.

When I wrote in my diary, he'd flip through its pages as though he were reading it. Then he'd give me a present, like a Mickey Mouse wallet he got at Tokyo Disneyland or a pretty bow he'd saved from one of his gifts.

Today after school Dai brought me a rubber ball with some elastic string attached to it. I think it was half of an old paddle-ball set that broke. He showed me how to play

with it: swing it over your head, around and around. Pro-
tectively he pantomimed a warning not to swing it below
head level, or it would hit me with dire results.

Dinner tonight was an elaborate, traditional meal: a
big, covered wooden box holding lots of cold, raw fish,
tangy vegetables, and seaweed.

A young family with an infant son stopped by the
house after dinner. They looked so wholesome and neat
that I could picture them in an American yuppie hand-
book. Their child stared at me, unblinking and unmoving,
during their entire stay.

Okāsan immediately took charge of the infant, croon-
ing over him. She murmured, "Okāsan six beibi (babies),
one, two, three, four, five, six." For Number Five, she
pointed to me; the sixth was the infant she was cuddling.

Week 1: July
Thursday

Our start to the day was always the same. We ate jam
on the good bread Okāsan made, fresh from her bread-
maker oven. While we ate, she filled our *obentōs*. These
finely-made, lacquered-wood boxes were then wrapped in
a handkerchief and stuffed in our schoolbags.

At 8:12, before classes began, the students were fanning themselves more vigorously than ever. Most were
finishing their homework while the homeroom teacher
made announcements. In front of me two students were
slouched over their books, asleep.

The first few days of school, I followed along in all the
classes with interest—absorbing the structure of what was
happening, if not the content. While I couldn't understand
much of what was being said, I got the general idea in,
say, geography class. In some classes, like math, I was
familiar with the work; in others, like Japanese Classics,

I'd pay attention to the teacher for the first few minutes, then start eyeing the students who were passing notes to each other around me, or write in my diary, or do exercises in my copy of *Japanese in 10 Minutes a Day*.

Much of that time my behavior during class was interpreted as attentiveness by my fellow students, who normally looked glazed while "participating" in class.

Geography

The class learned about the climates of tropical rainforest Africa, southern India, Southeast Asia, and Micronesia. In a lecture about plantations, the teacher asked me in English to say something about American plantations.

"We grow tobacco and cotton in the South," I answered.

"Bananas?" he asked.

I told him no, the climate wasn't right. He was pleased to have this information from the source, before returning to the Japanese text. In turn, I was gratified to have justified, a little, my distracting presence in his class.

Physical Education

The judo teacher, Mr. Kuriyama, was the same one who did the swimming time-trials and packed us into the gym on the first day. He lent me a spare judo uniform, which didn't fit in a dozen ways—especially in the pantlegs, which came halfway up my shins.

Today he taught us the shoulder throw, front sweep, roll, and fall. I knew roll and fall from karate and could do them almost as expertly as Johnny. Towards the end of class, when we were showing the teacher what we'd learned, I demonstrated my techniques on Johnny about 20 times. Each time Mr. Kuriyama patiently corrected me, a determined frown on his face. I felt hopeless at the sport.

Later that day, after third-period English Readers class, Mr. Tomita approached me: "Good news. Mr. Kuriyama, who is a judo master of some fame in Japan, came to me after the class to say that you show promise. He wants to teach you individually on the days when the other students will be busy with exams. This will be Friday, Saturday, Monday, and Tuesday, directly after exams, at noon for an hour. This is clearly an honor."

I hesitated before saying thank you, not knowing how this kind and surprising offer would work out. Mr. Kuriyama didn't speak English. He was stern, and I'd have to work hard to please him. Also, I hadn't spoken with the Andos about the family's plans for me.

When I told Johnny, his mouth dropped open. "He is to . . . Kuriyama-sensei will teach you alone? Oh . . . You are lucky man. Lucky man!"

Lunch

On my way back to the classroom, I nearly collided with a girl as I quickly turned a corner.

"Aaahhh eeeeee!" she screamed, jumping aside just in time.

"Sumimasen" (Excuse me), I nodded, continuing on my way. But she and her friend—who'd rushed to her aid—remained at the corner and started giggling. All the way up the stairs I heard them chortling about her close encounter.

I wore uncomfortable plastic slippers inside the school; they either fell off or came up short on my heel. Diana noticed earlier today that I carried my outdoor shoes around with me all day in my backpack. She told me she knew where my shoe locker was and would take me there immediately. I didn't know that I had a shoe locker, so I asked her if she'd please show it to me sometime but not just then.

There weren't any female leaders in the class, certainly no official ones. Petite Diana came the closest, if only because of a certain bold impishness about her appearance and demeanor. Perhaps it was her black braid of hair, worn as long as permissible and whipped through the air as she tilted and turned her head in animated conversation with her girlfriends. My impression of Diana's status was reinforced by the fact that she was one of the few girls who ever initiated a conversation with me.

Now, near the end of lunch I noticed a group of nine girls forming behind me and knew I was in for another "Do you like what movies?" session, where a group of girls interrogated me about movie stars. While they were apparently mustering the courage to come forward to pepper me with questions, I spotted Diana among the group and sought to divert the course of events. "Diana, can you show me my shoe locker right now?"

So off we went, all ten of us, along the hall, down two flights of stairs, and outside to a vast metal cabinet containing many lockers. Belying the name, none of the lockers was locked. Diana began opening them to find an empty one. The ones she tried were full, so I opened some too. The eight other girls watched. I placed my street shoes in empty #36, and hurried back to the classroom, nine people in tow.

Heading upstairs, by mistake I got off after one flight instead of two, and began walking swiftly to where I thought my classroom was. (This was easily done because the Japanese start with 0 for the ground floor; so my room "on the second floor" was actually on what I'd call the third.)

All nine girls followed me nearly to the end of the hall before I realized my error. They'd been either too polite or too shy to tap me on the shoulder and say, "Wrong way." No one had broken away from the group either; no one had said, "Forget this!" and taken off back to class.

Later that day I found locker #36 had been neatly labelled "Steven Wardell."

Home Room

Fourth-period was devoted to something I couldn't understand. While the class fooled around lightheartedly, a student spent a long time writing kanji on the board. Another student stood at the rostrum, doing nothing, while Mrs. Suzuki, the "Home Room" teacher, sat in the back, nodding her encouragement.

I watched Mister Sumo make an origami hat out of his handkerchief. Then, with pronounced self-control holding back a frenzy of merriment, he placed it on the head of the unfortunate girl seated in front of him. While he laughed and pointed, she sat immobile and tried to disappear or die.

It may have been Current Events that they were speaking about. Whatever it was, the class began splitting up into little groups like the lunch groups, and the only thing that suggested to me what their topic might be was one discernable word, "apartheid."

Kendo Kid, the only student I could speak much English to, deferentially slipped me a note: "What do you think Negrophobe?"

I corrected his grammar and made several false starts at trying to answer. Finally I wrote back to him, "Unfortunate consequence of slavery that we Americans are trying to overcome." He spent some time looking up the words in his dictionary, let out a satisfied "Aaaah," nodded many times, and returned a comment: "You will be President."

Analitics

The math teacher is one of those old-school disciplinarians, and his students know to buckle down. Even so, throughout today's test I could see Kendo Kid to my left, head hunched down over the paper, mouthing the words to a song some of the boys had been raucously singing during lunch—"I'm Popeye the Sailor Man."

Japanese

I continued my exchange of notes with Kendo Kid. Having heard he might be the best student in the class, I wrote, "Who is the best student in the class?" After a long pause, he returned my note with "Detail" written on it and a big arrow pointing to my word "best."

I tried to "detail" what "best" meant: "# 1 student, highest achiever."

He kept evading, "I don't know. No one. Class is best," refusing even to admit there was a "best" in the class.

During clean-up Diana insistently wanted to know if I knew Japanese calligraphy. She looked so disappointed when I said no, that I volunteered that I knew several forms of English and American calligraphy and showed her an elaborate version of my signature. She and the rest of the girls in the class promptly lined up to have me sign the inside covers of their notebooks.

When Teacher Tomita arrived, to end clean-up and hand back papers, he read aloud from a certificate with fancy calligraphy and an official-looking seal. He said "America" a couple of times, so I thought it might have something to do with me or perhaps with Kendo Kid, who'd been to America. Maybe "Most Helpful to the *Gaijin*" award for Kendo Kid, who'd helped me understand what was going on in classes through our regular exchange of notes.

It turned out that Kendo Kid, who hadn't wanted to name the best student in the class, had won some distinction and therefore would study English for a year in Washington, D.C.

Johnny tore out of the room during clean-up and reappeared only after it was over. He hadn't participated in any of the clean-ups so far, managing his disappearances to coincide with our manual labor. Kendo Kid explained that Johnny was the school president and had other duties to perform at that time.

Johnny was unlike his classmates. He alone, on my first day, had the nerve to address me. He was loud and sometimes mischievous. Actually, I'd say Johnny was rather American in his style.

When I talked to Johnny and others, I generally pointed to them when I said "you," hoping to help avoid confusion this way. However, they typically indicated themselves, "I," in their conversations, by pressing down hard on the tips of their noses. Sometimes they held their fingers on their nosetips for what seemed like half the conversation. Johnny pressed down so hard that I thought any second the cartilage would snap.

Squid-on-a-Stick

That evening, as Mākun and I were leaving the house, Okāsan rushed over to us, "No, no, no, no!" She reached out to hand Mākun a 1,000-yen bill (close to $9) and said, "My son."

Turning to me, she presented the same amount. "My son," she repeated, with a gentle smile.

I felt a little quiver go through my arms as I accepted both the spending money and membership in the family. "Thank you, Okāsan."

"No, no," she said, shaking her head. "You," she nodded at me. "You." She was thanking me.

Mākun had finished his exams today, so he and I were off to one of the town's annual festivals. Minori would take her last exam tomorrow, when Shika's exams began. I was happy to think that the girls would be able to study better with us out of the house.

A friend of Mākun's joined us, and we made our first stop at an immaculate snack-bar on the top floor of a Macy's-like store. Mākun could hardly control his excitement. Not only was he showing off his *gaijin* to his friend, but he had been planning a "hot-dog-with-an-American" trip ever since he knew the family would have an exchange student.

So we ate "corn dogs" (a cornmeal-coated hot dog) on a stick, while Mākun pointed out the window to a brightly lit section of the dusky city that had been cordoned off for the festival. The streets looked like rivers, with currents of people being swept along their vendor-lined banks.

Red and green paper lanterns were hung everywhere, and the many stores tried to attract attention with bright lights, colorful window displays, and pop music.

Street vendors hawked machetes, squid, goldfish, color-dyed chicks, lottery tickets, a special festival soda, shish-kebab of fish parts, fans, gags for kids and adults, and other toys that wouldn't last the night. Many of the women and girls in the crowd wore ceremonial regalia – bright, flowery kimonos, mitten-like socks, wooden sandals, and stark white make-up.

Dutifully we began our visit to the festival – once a religious celebration and now more like a carnival – at the shrine in its center. We stood in line to toss money into a big, white sheet stretched on wooden stakes. Mākun handed me a 10-yen coin to throw, then showed me how to tug on one of the loops of a rope hung from the rafters, for good luck. The rope was connected to a big tinny bell decorated with colorful tassels.

When we reached the front of the line, we clapped our hands and clasped them to pray for whatever we wished. Since college applications were looming, my wish was for something my heart had been set on for as long as I could remember – to go to Harvard.

An open spring welled out of a large rock in the center of the semi-circular shrine. The stream had been tamed with bamboo gutters to flow into a pool, where we ceremoniously washed our hands with a simple bamboo ladle.

At an outdoor theater next to the shrine, a Noh production was in progress. Fabulously dressed actors in masks danced majestically to a drum's changing tempos – slow, quick, slow. The characters moved all over the stage, sometimes attacking each other, sometimes freezing in the middle of their actions as the symbolic spotlight switched to a different set of performers. Sometimes they'd all stop, and someone would sing in a lonely, droning way, alternating his music with a solo by a reed-flute or the monotonous bashing of cymbals and drums.

At the booth of a toothless old man, Mākun and his friend each chose a live squid and motioned invitingly to me to do the same. Fresh squid is very popular, especially at festivals. I pointed to mine in a tank clouded by the jet-black ink that squids spray as a last defense. The vendor deftly reached in bare-handed to grab my choice and cut it open in front of me.

He sliced the back of the squid's neck, killing the squid but leaving its tentacles dancing. He was careful to leave the head on the body, because—as both Mākun and the vendor indicated to me—the head's considered the best part.

He slid the squid onto an intensely hot grill for a few seconds, coated it with a special thick, sweet soy sauce, flipped it, added more soy, then in one motion skewered it and handed it to me, hot and dripping, tentacles waving in the wind. Squid-on-a-stick.

It was awfully chewy but tasty. I found the suckers too tough and had to spit them out, like watermelon seeds. Mākun and his friend relished the suckers. I started on the main body but couldn't finish it because it was too tough. I carried the remains around with me for some time because I couldn't find a garbage can. There weren't any, but neither was there any litter. Finally, we discovered a single courtesy can outside a closed restaurant, piled to twice its height with neatly stacked garbage.

The boys gravitated toward a huge glass bowl with hundreds of tiny fish. For 300 yen (about $2.60) Mākun's friend was given a net made of tissue paper to ladle a fish into a smaller, empty bowl. If he succeeded, he'd win the fish, and could keep catching more until the paper broke. The boy dipped the net after a fish, as if trying to stab it. The paper broke before his net was halfway into the water.

Fortunately, I'd spotted someone playing the game with the proper technique. I described it to Mākun: wait for a fish to swim close to the surface, then gingerly skim it off. Mākun caught two fish. He was so pleased and grateful that he gave me the fish right away. The fun for him was in the catching. They were two tiny, oddly shaped and colored "gold fish." The whole pool of them was probably not worth 300 yen, so the concessionaire had the last laugh.

I turned around, fish in hand, to find myself staring at an evening news team—blinding light, video camera, and reporter. They filmed me but didn't ask any questions, then drifted away to film others.

I told Mākun that because I wanted the fish to be gifts—one for Shika and one for Minori—we should ask the vendor for a second plastic bag.

"No, no," Mākun frowned.

I thought perhaps he hadn't understood, so I repeated. "Another bag," I said, tapping the one I was holding. "One—Shika. One—Minori."

"No! No!" He seemed agitated and began walking away.

"Mākun!" I called, perplexed.

Returning reluctantly, he whipped out a pocket dictionary, and searched for a word. Finding it, he gave me a determined look and said, "Unreasonable."

Even in service-conscious Japan, he was reluctant to ask for such a minor extra service. He was adamant, so I let the matter drop. But I'd learned something more of Mākun, if not of Japan itself.

His friend, meanwhile, had noticed some shelves of toys in the next booth and led us toward them. It was a simple cork-gun game where light corks were loaded into a pop gun and shot at prizes. The toys were cheap and mostly heavy, so the odds were gravely stacked against anyone's actually toppling a toy to win it. Four corks cost 300 yen.

I watched the boys ahead of us take careful aim from their position in front of the counter. Invariably they failed because the cork lost all momentum by the time it reached the target.

Younger kids extended their whole arms so as to get the barrel closer to the target. Gripped one-handed and held out in this way, the barrel wobbled. Yet these kids did win a few prizes because they shot at the tiny, light-weight plastic cars or gumballs. Their eyes weren't bigger than their corks.

Mākun and his friend each wasted 600 yen on this game, trying to discover a winning strategy. They brought the rifle up to their eyes in order to shoot accurately, but the corks bounced harmlessly off the targets.

When Mākun hopefully asked me to try his last cork, I held the gun at arm's length the way the little kids did. If I stretched my long arm out and held the rifle tight and steady, I could even touch the toys. I shot off the toy car that Mākun had been aiming at. The boys and I chuckled delightedly, but the concessionaire let out a disapproving cry. As would often happen to me in Japan, I felt two distinct emotions at once: in this case, glee but also guilt.

As Mākun, his friend, and I were leaving the festival at 8:30, Mākun heard some fireworks go off in a nearby abandoned lot. His face lit up like a bulb. Nothing would do but we must go back and buy some. We stopped at several stalls to gaze at their displays. The colorful pictures on the wrappers showed kids having fun, their faces full of delight as bangers went off in their fingers. Mākun bought a box of varied kinds, and his friend bought some too before leaving us for his own home.

We brought the festival back to Shika and Minori. "Here you go!" I handed them each a candy apple, a festival treat, and gave Mākun the bag of goldfish to present to the girls.

"We're worn out. Thanks very much!" The gifts gave the girls a needed pickup.

Mākun and Shika then pleaded with Otōsan, who was in the basement conducting an important meeting—community leaders, I think—to be allowed to light the firecrackers. He agreed and returned to his meeting.

Every sparkler, every rocket, every pop and bang was greeted with screams of delight. Our evening's fun ended suddenly when a ring-shaped cracker that Mākun lit rolled, alight, all the way down the curved stairs to the open door of Otōsan's basement conference room. BANG!

That night I watched TV, as usual. A news report covered today's earthquake damage in the Tokyo area. Yesterday there'd been "unnoticeable tremors," and the news had said there'd be no more today. There were more, though—serious, noticeable ones. There were two-to-three-inch-wide rips in roads, major cracks in walls, and fallen trees. I hadn't felt any tremors, and none were reported in Oita.

Many programs on TV were bilingual: the TV could broadcast in both languages simultaneously. There was usually an English track to the evening news from Tokyo, and I'd seen American sports events dubbed in Japanese, with the English soundtrack retained. I chose the English soundtrack simply by pressing a button.

The Andos had a cute, medium-sized spaniel in the dog house on the patio. Teri ate rice, cabbage, and any leftovers. He was young and frisky, but though he was well cared for and got some attention, he was seldom played with. He sometimes let out mournful cries, especially when the kids were watching TV close by and could have been playing with him.

If I tied my shoe just out of his leash range, he'd go wild, leaping at me to get my attention, and if I wandered within range, he'd sniff and lick me and roll over, waiting eagerly to have his tummy scratched. I often played with him as I did tonight, because I enjoyed him and missed my two pet rabbits.

The family had a story to tell about Teri. He'd been with them only a couple of months when they moved into their new house. The dog didn't know anything about the Sakuragaoka house and soon went missing. Mākun found him standing outside their office building downtown. The dog was celebrated among the Andos and their friends for this feat.

Partly through Teri, I figured out the Japanese characteristic mix-up of "l" and "r." This was one of those things I'd set out to do while here. The truth is that they say neither "l" nor "r." They say a soft "d" for both, which to us sounds like an "l" when we expect to hear an "r"—and like an "r" when we expect to hear an "l." Teri's name always came out "Tedi."

Week 1: July
Friday
During breakfast, at 6:45 a.m., Okāsan suggested I go back to sleep because my wooziness was obvious. I didn't have to get up today until we left for a trip to scenic Mt. Aso. This was an exam day at school so I didn't have to go.

Before I went back to sleep I had a conversation prompted by Otōsan about Mākun. "This is my first breakfast, donchyu?" Otōsan initiated our discussion, using his favorite sentence-ending, "don't you know?" This was indeed his first breakfast with the family since I'd arrived; he was normally too busy or already at work.

He didn't always have to leave home to work because he had an office in the house. "My jobs, I have many jobs, I go downtown and to Yufuin all the time, donchyu? And I have to meet, for the social, with my partners all over the prefecture."

Becoming more serious, he continued, "I want Mākun to be with you, same room, share time, so he can learn Western thinking and English speaking. Very important. I admire the Western idea, donchyu, of individual and initiative. I think the person who can have that in Japan, that person is special person.

"I think maybe you help him not so shy, too," he added.

Mākun was certainly less shy than his friends from what I'd observed, but even so, Otōsan hoped I could work some "Western magic," as he called it, on him.

"He is resistance," Otōsan pronounced, referring to his own efforts to transform Mākun.

Listening from the kitchen, Okāsan expanded graphically on what Otōsan had said, "Say Mākun right, Mākun left. Say Mākun left, Mākun right." Reflecting on some of my own encounters with my parents, I knew just what she meant.

A picture now adorned the wall of Mākun's once bare room, so maybe some of my ideas had already rubbed off. It was a magazine photo of the duo of dainty young girl rock-singers who call themselves Wink.

Toward noon, Otōsan, Ojisan, Okāsan, and I sped off in Otōsan's luxurious Toyota Chaser sedan. The car was so new it still had its plastic coverings to protect the cloth interior. The car's labels, I noticed, were all in English, from its automatic transmission to its tape player. For some time I'd thought this was Ojisan's car. Ojisan drove again today, and he drives fast.

Ojisan, or "Great Uncle Honorable," wasn't related to the family. He was Takumi Iwasaka, Otōsan's best friend. Taller than Otōsan at about five-eight and as thin as Otō-san was chubby, Ojisan had curly hair that was pretty much flattened to his head and a ready smile that showed crooked teeth. He sometimes slept in his office at the An-dos' or in their Japanese room. He designed Otōsan's home and office building in addition to his own home. The two men were inseparable.

"Otōsan, like Ojisan, will probably have only one 'best' friend in his life," Shika once told me. "Each will make great sacrifices for the other, even when the other doesn't know it—like turning down job offers in other cities—because they mean so much to each other."

Another example of the close connection between the personal and the professional in the Andos' lives was the way some of Mr. Ando's employees lived on the upper floor of his home. He had a friendly relationship with them. They ate dinner in his dining room and occasionally wandered down to talk. If they'd ever let him down in business, they'd also let him down personally. They lived and worked as a team.

As we drove we listened to a radio station that played music from 1950s America—"Jailhouse Rock," "That'll Be the Day," "Baby Face." Okāsan loved it, and Otōsan sang fragments of the words.

We dived down country roads so tortuous, steep, and narrow that they put Connecticut's winding roads to shame. Kyushu's not a large island, but the distances are long because the roads are circuitous. For all the twists and turns, the grown-ups were enjoying the ride; like children, they laughed and exclaimed as they swerved around curves and roared up and down hills.

One curve was so tight that Okāsan was jerked almost across the car. "Okāsan need seatbelt," she laughed, promptly buckling up.

"So Stibu, tell me what Mākun said on the bike. Heh, heh, I want to hear again," Otōsan requested. When I finished retelling the incident of the bike race, he raised his eyebrows and asked, "He really did that? What a mischief, donchyu?" You could see Mākun's winning ploy had tickled him. He felt proud of his son.

The trip wasn't all hills and valleys. We saw jet-black cattle grazing on a wide plain. Kyushu is one of the few places in Japan where there are plains and ranges, and land is treated more casually here than in, say, Tokyo. Hokkaido, the colder fishing and dairy land of the north, is one of the only comparable places in Japan.

Little Buddhist shrines decorated the roads and villages. These tiny, similar-looking booths appeared randomly by the side of the roads, in fields, or at street corners. Some marked where people had been killed in road accidents. Some were holy spots revered for centuries. Some were placed in convenient locations for travelers to pause and pray for protection from misfortune.

We stopped for lunch at the El Dorado Ranch in central Kyushu, a hotel-restaurant decked out like a dude ranch, complete with settlers' wagons, Indian wigwams, and stables. Flags from Texas, California, and one of the American Indian nations were flying, in addition to at least two dozen large U.S. flags—they wanted people to get the point. Everything recalled the Wild West except the kanji on the signs and the rice paddies in the distance.

"Howdy, pardner. Name's Mack." I turned to meet a gregarious Texan—Frank McLaughlin—who handled the horses for the Japanese owner and, dressed in cowboy gear, helped make the place look American.

He was eager to chat and tell me his story. "In college I trained to be an English teacher but didn't much like the idea of teaching. See, I grew up on a ranch, so I jumped at the chance to work here. I reckon I'll spend a few years here, maybe start my own business. I've begun by studying the language on my own."

Curious about this ambitious plan, I asked for details.

"Well, I started by memorizing 15 kana characters each night," Mack explained. "So I knew them all in a week. Now I'm studying the common kanji and memorizing phrases." His regimen put my attempts to shame.

The stable was Mack's domain, because no one else in the valley knew how to handle the horses. He saw lots of possibilities for them. He'd just finished planning a horse trek several miles to Mt. Aso, and people often stopped by for rides in the fenced-in paddock. "Horses are prized and grossly overvalued in Japan," he observed, "so I'm looking into bringing a few over from the U.S."

He was also amazed at the demand for Americans. "I can sing in a bar for $500 a night, even though I wouldn't mind singing for free. The big money's certainly one of the attractions that drew me to Japan."

The ranch was designed, according to Mack, from a postcard of a Mexican villa that the owner thought was an American dude ranch. The white stucco buildings did look like Taco Bell, I chuckled to myself.

Mack said he was looking after the place now because he'd arranged for the owner to visit a genuine dude ranch in Colorado, to see what one was really like.

Otōsan, Ojisan, Okāsan, and I served ourselves an American barbecue at picnic tables in the ranch's central dining hall—cooking our own chunks of steak, chicken, tomatoes, and cabbage on a gas grill. Then we ate them with chopsticks!

As we neared Mt. Aso, the one-car-wide road clung to the mountainside. Its median strip was pointless. Small pockets of pavement expanded its width briefly, so that if two cars met, with luck one could zip aside while the other passed.

Looking down from the top of a hill, I viewed a flat valley filled with paddies and surrounded by green mountains. The rice in the paddies grew in straight lines in large puddles of mud. To keep the water in, the fields or terraces were watertight. The water flowed from one paddy to the next through channels. Using his own kind of sign language, Ojisan explained that, to reduce erosion, no two paddies faced the same way.

The sun reflected off the half dozen rice paddies whose rows ran straight out from our perspective into the distance. As we drove, this particular selection of paddies shifted out of the glare, and other paddies shone as we moved into alignment with their rows. It was a pretty sight: a shifting, glinting quilt.

Watching the peasants moving slowly through the paddies in their wide-brimmed sun hats, long robes, and many layers of bulky clothing, I wondered how many thousands of years people had been doing the same work in this spot. Aso was one of the earliest places in Japan to be cultivated.

We entered a small, well-established resort and rice-farming community nestled below Mt. Aso's active volcano, where young children walked to school in yellow hard hats.

By the roadside I saw several randomly placed cement bunkers about the size of a car, with cavities in the side facing away from Mt. Aso—shelters for those caught walking or working outside when an eruption occurred. The population's attitude toward Aso, as with the Tokyo quakes, appeared to be one of acceptance and quiet concern.

Most of the signs were in English. "Camp in Aso." "Parking." "Refreshments." At this popular resort, the majority of its foreign tourists were Americans.

At a souvenir store in a shopping center, Ojisan bought me a packet of postcards with stunning pictures of the valley and mountain. Okāsan wanted to get some ice cream from a freezer there, so she asked Otōsan. With his 1,000 yen bill she purchased sundaes for all of us.

This was not a plastic charge-it society. Otōsan carried big wads of bills in his wallet and took his time counting them out. He held the money up against his palm, as if shaking hands with it.

We rode a gondola to the top of Aso, where the live mouth of the volcano oozed white steam and dirty-yellow sulfur smoke. Concrete bunkers stood like sentinels every 100 feet around the rim. The acid atmosphere was eating away at all the man-made structures on the mountain top, from pavements to shelters.

While they'd all been to Aso before—probably many times—the Andos and Ojisan were having fun, too. For one photo, I lay down at the rim of the volcano and gripped the outer edge, while Ojisan took a low-angle shot so it'd look as though I were dangling over a sheer drop to the center. In another shot, to get me to smile, Okāsan said, "Think Pocari Sweat," and imitated the grin of a mindless-looking girl in the soft drink's commercial.

Okāsan and Otōsan hugged in front of the volcano for a few light-hearted shots—the first time they'd hugged in public or in front of me. Their lives had hitherto been so widely separated by their different roles. I seemed to be an excuse to take them away from their otherwise draining responsibilities.

Back at the bottom, we stopped at another souvenir store to buy pickled roots, a specialty of the region. Okā-san eyed a bowl of samples, and after pausing to decide her course of action, she picked up the bowl. Using its chopsticks, she placed one of the dark-green pickle shavings in her hand, then tested it for taste. She dipped in again and delicately dropped several pickle shavings onto my palm. A smile, a tilt of her head, urged me on.

She paused for my reaction. When I smiled, she smiled back, broadly. "You—like?" she said, with a look of expectancy.

"Very much. Thank you." They *were* good, like firm dill pickles with a sweet aftertaste.

Now Otōsan strode over and picked up the bowl. With the chopsticks he deposited a large quantity of pickle in my hands, then helped himself to a similar portion. He liked what he ate, so he bought a couple of jars.

We all joked about how Okāsan, a small person, had given me a little, and Otōsan, a large person, had given me a hefty serving. To explain this to me and to the puzzled clerk, Okāsan spread her arms as if embracing a tree and said, "Otōsan is big heart."

Okāsan was an excellent complement to Otōsan. He laughed loudly, and was energetic, open, and talkative.

She was extremely polite. Kind, considerate, and responsible, she also "knew her place." Sometimes I thought Otōsan wished she didn't. He certainly allowed his children a lot of latitude and encouraged them in their innovative pursuits. Otōsan made the family successful and outgoing. And Okāsan was the hub around which this family spun, a gracious person with a lively sense of humor and the inner strength to recognize and maintain her own gentle influence over the family.

We stopped for gas. Five attendants ran out to wash the car, gas it up, raise the hood for a long time, and polish the car down to the hub caps. This, I thought, is what you call service.

There wasn't space for pumps in the cramped station, so the hoses dangled from a roof. A carwash at the side of the station looked like an upside down U, designed to roll over your car, so it would take up less space. The gas station crew, perhaps as many as 12, all bowed to the car as we drove away. You're not supposed to bow back, I knew, because it's their job to be courteous to you. Nevertheless I always felt as though I should bow back.

After a plentiful restaurant meal of sushi, we headed back to Oita. Okāsan told me to keep our sushi meal a secret. The children, who'd been at school all day, loved sushi and would be envious if I told them what we'd eaten. They were to make themselves cup-o-noodles for dinner.

Shika and Minori greeted me with friendly cries of "Iina"—loosely, "I wish I were you"—envious that I'd been to Aso. On the kitchen table lay their empty bowls. Shika asked if I'd like some noodles, and I said no thanks.

Shika had put our festival goldfish in a rice bowl full of water in the kitchen. She pointed them out to me in their new location and said, "Fish." I didn't see her point and thought she was offering me some fish to eat. Having just eaten lots of sushi, I said, "No thanks, I'm full." The sushi was a short-lived secret!

Week 1: July
Saturday

Yesterday, in a farmer's front yard, I'd noticed a tree with its branches full of short, fluttering paper ribbons. The ribbons had poems, prayers, and wishes written on them. It was a good-luck tree, part of the national *Tanabata* celebration on the seventh of July. According to a Chinese legend, the Cowherd star can cross the heavens to meet his lover, the Weaver star, once a year on this night.

Early this morning Ojisan made a good-luck tree for me from a branch that resembled a miniature tree. He used play-dough to create flowers at the tips of the small branches and tied on ribbons of paper. This was a spontaneous demonstration of welcome from Ojisan—more than he would have been able to put into English, had he spoken the language—and it made me feel good.

I set off for a long-awaited judo lesson. Everyone had told me a different story about how great and famous a teacher Mr. Kuriyama was and how lucky I was to study with him. Some said he'd competed in the Olympics; others said he was one of the best in the all-Japan tournament.

Mr. Kuriyama stood alone in the *dojo* (practice area) underneath the school's gymnasium when I found him. We got started right away. He liked my falls. Right, left, back. Wordlessly, he taught me throws using a belt tied to the wall. Instead of throwing a person over my shoulder, I grabbed and tugged at the belt. The belt is used so you don't become accustomed to an opponent's weight and rely on it for balance. Making assumptions about another person's inertia is bad form in judo, because the sport is all about using your own weight and that of your opponent to gain an advantage. Working with a belt also saves another person some bad bumps.

He taught me the one-step throw, two-step throw, trip throw, and sweep throw. He brought out his own English-language picture book of basic moves to get across the more complicated ideas. I was so full of aches by the time we got to throws that mine were sloppy. Kuriyama-*sensei* wore a constant scowl and remained ominously silent.

Later we were joined by some black belts, who'd finished their exams. They treated the *dojo* with the utmost respect, removing their shoes, tiptoeing, and bowing at intervals, seemingly to no one. To practice throws and falls, we tossed each other around—effortlessly on their part, painfully on mine.

After my grueling judo lesson in the humid, 98-degree heat, Shika and I biked into town, her day's exams over. We'd come to visit one of the city's largest bookshops—its two floors crowded with books, periodicals, comics, and people. The comics appeared to be the big sellers. There was also a small section of books in English.

The learn-English section was full of depressingly similar titles like "English the Easy Way," "English in a Snap," "Learn Light English," and "Have Fun With English." All were written by Japanese. That's one of the remarkable things about English that makes it so pervasive and established here—the Japanese produce it for their own consumption.

A section was set aside for girls' romances—hundreds of books in each series—Japan's own combination of Nancy Drew and Harlequin romances.

When I brought *Easy Hiragana* to the check-out counter, the lengthy procedure of calculating the bill and writing the receipt was done by hand. Only a week ago I had visions of a monolithically computerized Japan, or an acceleratingly frenzied Japan, but the reality I found was often quaint, even dreary.

I learned half the hiragana tonight, with Okāsan cheerfully testing and encouraging me.

When Dai got home, he immediately took it upon himself, as if I were a helpless little brother, to teach me more hiragana. I liked this, and he was elated to play teacher to me. He tested me a couple of times on how to write his name, then neatly corrected the shapes of my letters.

Week 2: July
Sunday
All this morning, Shika read aloud for her Chinese classics exam. She was supposed to learn a long poem in classical Chinese. There was an explanatory Japanese translation in the margin of her text, and because she was only studying to pass an exam, she simply memorized the translation without bothering to learn the Chinese original. She'd be given only the Chinese version in the exam to refer to, but if she'd memorized the translation, she could answer any questions without ever looking at the Chinese text in front of her!

In the early afternoon, Minori returned from a museum where there was a display on Nazi concentration camps. When I asked her about it, she fanned her face, mime-ing sickness, and disappeared into her room. Intrigued by Minori's report, Mākun said we must go see it, too.

On the way to town, in two separate incidents, people I didn't know waved to me and called "Haro!"

Cycling down a city street, Mākun and I passed a phone booth with a Japanese punk rocker inside. I gave the rocker a passing glance, noting his studded, black-leather belt, the obnoxious painting of a Rolling-Stones tongue on his jacket, and large earring mostly obscured by his long blond hair.

After we wheeled around the next corner, Mākun, a pop-culture enthusiast himself, hopped off his bike and doubled over laughing. It was the blond hair that really got him.

Rock culture here is pervasive and prominent; rockers are commonly referred to by disappointed elders as *shin-*

jinrui, "a new breed of human being." One of the shyest boys in my class—so shy he had to be pushed toward me to say "haro"—turned out to be a punk rocker. I nicknamed him "Heavy Metal." He loved Bon Jovi, Bruce Springsteen, and the European hard-rock group called BOOWY. He posed by donning mirror shades, then whipping them off again.

Whenever I tuned in a radio station, I found little difference between its music and the music of any pop station in America. The hit-parade sounded like the one I knew in the U.S. because it included many American pop songs or translations of them. When big-names like Madonna and Sting release new songs, they're as great a hit in Japan as in America, and rock stars often find the Tokyo stop on a world tour to be their most profitable.

Wherever I went, the question my peers most often asked me—besides "How tall are you?"—was "Do you like Bon Jovi?" I always said yes, even though I'd never heard them, because I, too, like to be cool. Heavy-metal music seemed to be more popular among my peers in Japan than among my American classmates. While there was a clique at my Connecticut high school that loved heavy metal, most of my friends were turned off by its raucousness.

When a song is recorded by a European group, there's often a separate version in their native language—perhaps German—as well as one in English, so as to reach the greatest international market. In contrast, some of the Japanese pop songs are released only in English. Others are first sung in English, then repeated in Japanese. Even the most thoroughly Japanese rock song may have some English words thrown in or used as a refrain, like "love," "tonight," or "dreaming."

We decided to get haircuts en route, but Otōsan's barbershop was too busy. Mākun knew we couldn't take the place of paying customers, so each time a barber chair was vacated, he deferred to someone else.

The back room, where we waited, was an exception to the neatness of the shop. A blanket and cabinet separated it from the main room. The barbers' personal things were flung around the room, including immense comics stacked against a wall, starting with number 30 of a series and ending with number 60. There was also a sink and hot plate. The two barbers had brought their bikes into the shop and parked them here. Japanese bikini-girl posters lined the wall, all labelled with American names like Melissa and Leslie.

Mākun wanted to go bowling now because he saw an ad—"Let's Bowling"—in a newspaper. But I wasn't interested; I was groggy and tired.

We'd been waiting for haircuts about an hour when I remembered with a start that I'd left my backpack with its precious diary and camera outside the barber shop, with my bike, on a busy sidewalk. When I ran out to check, the bag was still there, untouched. I was pleased that the Japanese respect for others' personal space extends as far as their bicycle baskets.

At a Mom-and-Pop stationery store I ambitiously bought some paper ruled vertically for kanji. An old lady ran the store and lived right in the middle of it. The shop was small and a step lower than the rest of the house, but all around it were her living quarters: kitchen, living room, and dining room, each separated from the shop only by ceiling-to-floor strings of beads. We could plainly see and smell her family eating lunch and watching TV.

We didn't visit the exhibit that day, although we did get soaked from riding aimlessly through pouring rain for several hours; I learned later that Mākun hadn't been able to find the museum.

Shika's former private calligraphy teacher still paid frequent visits to check on her progress. She was also a family friend. Today she brought some cake, plus two of her current students to chat with Shika and me. Her calligraphy students were husky boys who also studied judo and resembled football players.

"These fellows don't look like what I thought a calligraphy student would look like," I said.

Shika laughed, and the calligraphy teacher responded, defensively and in excellent English, "The greatest sumo wrestlers study calligraphy. It's the best subject to study for concentration and strength." For nearly an hour she gave me lessons on the proper way to write hiragana, and she told me the history of this alphabet and the stories behind some important kanji.

"How would you represent a hand?" She paused for me to think, then answered, "Instead of drawing all the fingers of a hand, the Chinese and Japanese believe the three creases in your relaxed palm are the important characteristic. So we draw three lines and add a perpendicular line through them to represent a hand.

"Another example," she continued, pen in hand, "is 'sun'—originally a circle with a dot in it. Over the years it's been standardized into a square with a horizontal mark in the middle so as to conform to an imaginary kanji grid. Also, the symbol for tree looks like a tree, but if you emphasize the root, its meaning changes to 'root,' 'book,' or 'source.' These two kanji together, 'sun' and 'root,' mean sun origin, or the land of the rising sun!

"And one more thing, Steven. You need to know that there is one specific way to write kanji, stroke by stroke, and any other way is wrong," she concluded. "Shika studied calligraphy with me for six years. In fact, Japanese have to continue learning their words and language all their lives."

All this time, the 'football-players' watched, listened, and nodded. I had the impression they spoke little English. They stayed a long time to help me with my first kanji, while I worried that the polite Shika was being kept away from her studies again.

Dai and I communicated well, so it was easy for me to forget that he spoke no English. Speaking English with Mākun, however, was often awkward. He might blurt out an English phrase for no reason, like repeating at odd intervals his memorized "Sankyu for your letter."

Otōsan taught himself English and had done an impressive job; I learned today that he was also trying to teach himself something else.

While writing at Mākun's desk I heard a tortured moan. It didn't stop. At first I thought it came from down the street, then it became clear it emanated from this very house, from everywhere and nowhere.

"Shika," I called out. "Are you torturing animals?"

A short search revealed that Otōsan was practicing his saxophone and, sorry, but he wasn't very good. He is a man of diverse talents, but playing the saxophone did not appear to be one of them.

He was considerate enough to practice in his office. Even so, we could hear him all too well. When Okāsan heard him begin, she shut the kitchen door and window, turned on a fan, and started humming loudly while she worked. She noticed me watching her and commented, "Otōsan very good clarinet," while putting her fingers in her ears and scrunching up her face. She meant "saxophone," but her message couldn't have been clearer.

Shika gave me some news: Otōsan and Ojisan were going to Spain for a vacation soon. She once said she'd been "Americanized," and Ojisan had been "Spanishized." Ojisan had been to Spain before, with the manager of El Dorado Ranch, and loved everything about that country.

I remembered seeing a Spanish lesson book on the kitchen counter. I supposed Otōsan was teaching himself Spanish too. Strangely, it was an American high-school Spanish text, which meant he'd be learning Spanish in the most difficult way imaginable–through English. But perhaps this would reinforce his English at the same time.

Today Otōsan alternated meetings with playing the sax. We saw almost nothing of him except at mealtimes or when he'd pop in for an hour.

Okāsan asked if I'd brought any photographs from home. While she was looking at a photo of the Wardell family, she asked how old my mother and father were. When I told her, she looked at me.

"Me," she said, tilting her head and touching her nose. "Tell me."

I cocked my head, unsure what she meant.

"Age." Her smile broadened. "Me–age–you say."

Oh. I tried to think–not to *guess*, but to come up with something diplomatic.

I'd given my mother's and father's ages in Japanese. Now I said politely, "Ni ju hachi" (28). She went wild and hugged me, asking me to say it again.

Shika overheard and commented wryly, "How *could* she be 28, though . . . Ohhh! Brown-noser, brown-noser!" I was laughing too hard to respond. Okāsan was wearing an impossibly big smile.

My favorite Japanese TV program became the one Diana had recommended: a goofy but popular show about current events, fads, and fashion called "Genki TV." "Genki" means "spirited" or "high-energy." There was no parallel for this show in America. It ran Sundays during prime time. Mākun had a plastic bag that described the show:

"Enjoy! GENKI TV. HERE IS A SPECIAL PRODUCT OF TOKYO. IT IS WITTY.IT IS TERRIFIC.IT IS A WAKENING. YES THE GENKI TV!"

The bag itself bore the extraordinary label "100% COTTON SUPER FABRIC"—it was made of plastic.

In one part of this show, a greasy "Joe-Isuzu"-type tried to find the most beautiful woman in Japan. With a camera crew he talked his way, uninvited, into people's homes and accosted women on the street, his purpose being to put women in ridiculous and compromising situations.

If he thought a woman was beautiful, he'd whip out a comb and eagerly slick back his greasy hair; if he thought she wasn't, he'd give her a hug. He ended each encounter by making the woman give him a big kiss on the cheek for the camera, regardless of whether he decided she was beautiful or not. These were ordinary women, not actresses; the spontaneity brought the laughs.

On today's edition, this "Joe Isuzu" was bowled over by the beauty of the woman he'd found, so he went through his hair-slicking routine with extra vigor. The camera operator panned out for a larger view, showing that the anonymous five-person camera crew that followed "Joe" everywhere had gotten out their combs, too, and were working on their hair. Then "Joe" barged into the woman's apartment and went through her underwear drawer. This kind of humor brought howls from the kids.

Another part of the show featured Japanese heavy-metal groups. Their zany antics were genuinely funny.

Around midnight on the day before Shika's last two days of exams, the four children watched "USA Express," a show about what's hot and hip in America. Its hosts were a Japanese and an American, a Mormon who spoke perfect Japanese.

This edition of the program, called "Prom," showed the glitz and incredible expense of high-school senior proms in America. It included the story of a boy who was a no-show: his date sued him for the cost of her dress. The story tickled my host brothers and sisters and made them gasp. They watched cruise ships being rented for proms, and stretch limousines carrying seniors to and fro. Some American teenagers complained that the cost was too much and not worth it, but most said this was their blow-out time and they wanted to make the most of it. The children adored this late night show. Shika gave up her study and sleep time to watch it.

Week 2: July
Monday

Today I got up around 11 because I'd been up past midnight watching TV with the children, who were none-theless in school by 8! I felt drained.

While I was sleeping, the kendo teacher had stopped by to invite me to take kendo! What do I do? I didn't think I could do both kendo and Mr. Kuriyama's judo. I also hoped to study karate, cartooning, and calligraphy. I liked judo more than kendo, but I didn't want to give up any of it.

With the kids taking exams, I wondered what to do with myself at the moment. I thought about sending off a dispatch to *The Ridgefield Press*, the newspaper back home that I wrote a weekly teen column for. Instead, I decided to wander around the neighborhood, to get a better feel for the area.

Sakuragaoka has been built on for centuries, a fasci-nating mix of old and new buildings. You can find a small shrine in a grove next to someone's fancy new house, or a large farmhouse in a state of disrepair with only its small front and back lawns being cultivated, or an old concrete path that changes into an ancient footpath, then abruptly back to sidewalk again. The newer houses—some cheap, others expensive like the Andos'—blend comfortably with this hodgepodge.

I didn't think there was another neighborhood like it for sheer variety. It was built into a steep and unforgiving side of Sakuragaoka. The Andos' house was near the pinnacle, an enviable spot, but it was torture for us kids to climb the hill on bicycles or even on foot.

Later that afternoon Otōsan took me, Okāsan, and two of her friends to an expensive restaurant for lunch. Okāsan tied her wavy shoulder-length pageboy into a bun and added a touch of mascara and lipstick for the occasion— the first time I'd seen her wear make-up.

Driving to the restaurant, I thought how wonderful the Andos were to me. I didn't think Mr. Ando was as well hosted when he visited in America. He drove across a good portion of the continent by himself, even though he wasn't accustomed to using the right-hand side of the road. He visited a lot of people and made many friends, but some of the customs puzzled him.

He told me he'd go to an American friend's house, and the American would say, "Are you hungry?" He'd politely say no, even though he'd have liked some food. The American would say "OK," and go on to the next activity. In Japan, if you said "yes," they'd take you out to dinner, and if you said "no," they'd still take you out to dinner.

He told me that one of his American hosts gave him the keys to the house and was gone the next morning before Mr. Ando woke up—letting him fend for himself. In Japan they'd take care of you, every step of the way. They'd ask, "Where do you want to go? Give us the address and we'll take you there." The American was saying by his actions, 'You have free run of this place.'

The restaurant Otōsan chose for our luncheon overlooked the beautiful castle-museum where Shika and I saw Yamagata's paintings last week. The castle was once a great *daimyo*'s (lord's) fortress, and the city was built around its moat.

"Look, look at fish in pond," Otōsan said, drawing my attention to some colorful carp.

"Otōsan, we'd call that a 'moat'," I said gently, not wanting to appear to correct him, but recalling his interest in enriching his vocabulary.

He beamed, "Moat, moat. These are nice fish in moat, donchyu?"

Pointing to the trees ringing the moat, he said, "In spring season this is beautiful cherry blossom."

"Kore wa sakura des," I replied. "This is a cherry blossom." Everyone at the table applauded. Little did they know, this was the only Japanese I'd known two weeks ago.

"Won't you come stay at my house soon?" one of Okāsan's friends asked.

"I am sure he can," Okāsan remarked, "because I want him stay in Japan as fifth child forever."

Okāsan's other friend was another calligraphy teacher, and she offered to give me lessons. Later, during a lull in the conversation, she started humming a tune. Okāsan enjoyed the little recital, commenting, "She has very voice"—meaning that her friend had a good voice.

"Ho! Look what bad English Okāsan has!" said Otōsan, making a big deal of this, and everyone laughed.

"I had no trouble understanding Okāsan," I said, coming to her rescue. She took it all in good humor. She's a rare person—fine-mannered, quiet, helpful, intelligent.

Indeed, Otōsan later told me, "Okāsan maybe knows *all* the kanji!"—a mark of real schooling and distinction.

Okāsan and the calligraphy teacher asked that I evaluate the English of everyone at the table. I felt up a creek again, so I said, "Okāsan has very English."

"Okāsan very English!" she repeated with delight. But her friends caught on to my joke. Okāsan let out a yipe and ran over to me, grabbing my hands and rapping my knuckles. We didn't stop laughing for a long time.

When we got back from the restaurant, the TV was broadcasting more about the bad quakes in Tokyo. Mt. Aso had a small-scale eruption a couple of days after we'd visited it. Geologically, I missed it by a whisker.

Tomorrow I was to give a talk to the English class at Minori's art and music high school. In preparation, I stopped by Minori's bedroom to ask her what she does at school. She didn't study music, just art, and she showed me some samples of her work—excellent sculptures and drawings. I especially liked her sculpture of a rabbit, and she often created realistic, life-sized heads of people.

She was clearly talented. A charcoal sketch had won her a prize in a show: her still-life included a broken wine bottle amid some cinder blocks, executed with perfect perspective and shading. I said, "It's very good." Usually very quiet, she replied with startling emphasis, "No!"

In America you're expected to acknowledge praise, even glow under it. Here, when praised, you say "No." I shared this observation with Shika, who relayed it to Mā-kun and Okāsan. They laughed at this example of "clash of culture," with all its potential misunderstandings.

Minori's course would make her more liberated than most Japanese women. She intended to be a sculptor and would probably go to an art college. She won't be limited, as most Japanese women are, to a lowly job, such as sales-clerk or bow-er—one of the women who bow to you throughout department stores – followed by marriage and full-time housekeeping.

I asked Okāsan to help me prepare a bath in their traditional bathtub, just for the experience.

It turned out to be an ordeal. I washed before I entered because the small, square tub was only for soaking. After scrubbing down, I tried to step in, but the water was unbearably hot. Okāsan had checked the temperature a quarter of an hour earlier and reported it was "good." I added lots of cold water.

Seated in the tub I felt claustrophobic from the thick, humid air pressing in around me. I threw my head back and breathed upwards to get some cooler air, air I could breathe.

I started to itch. First, I thought it was mosquitoes or gnats from the open window. It wasn't. It was my pores, itching from the inside. I didn't want to move to scratch, because the water would burn me more.

When the itching became too intense, I climbed out and covered the tub with its special insulating pads to retain the heat of the water. The rest of the family would use the same water in the order of descending familial status, and someone would probably complain about its tepidness.

I dried myself, then was surprised to find I was totally wet again. Sweat was spurting – not running – out of my pores. I was sure I wouldn't get over this bath for days.

The Andos took showers. That surprised me, as did the fact that they always wore typical Western clothing. I'd expected them to wear kimonos and take a Japanese-style bath every night.

I also had a lot to learn about shoes.

Footloose

Off and on, shoes are a major fact of daily life in Japan and a potential pitfall for the unwary foreign visitor. Here, the *faux pas* is – literally – a lurking, minute-by-minute possibility. For a *gaijin*, it's easy to put a wrong foot forward.

The Japanese don't like to wear shoes indoors. Many homes have unprotected wooden floors, or floors made of delicate tatami, and they like to keep them perfectly clean. Therefore, every house has a foyer where you remove your shoes.

In their own homes, or at homes of good friends, the Japanese walk around in socks. More formal guests may bring their own slippers, or the host will give them a pair.

You'd think that separate footwear for inside and outside would be enough, but outside the bathroom door, there's always another pair of slippers. Here's how it goes: you change out of your house slippers and into the bathroom slippers in two well-coordinated steps, avoiding putting your feet on the bathroom floor in between.

Bathroom slippers come in garish colors and often have "W" and "C" written on them – for Water Closet – so that they unmistakably belong to that room. A *gaijin* comes to realize this, but only belatedly.

After using the facilities, the careless *gaijin* walks out, by-passing his own slippers, to return to the social function he left. If the party doesn't stop there in astonishment, the guests will be chortling all evening. Eventually some will become anxious because the house slippers that the *gaijin* left behind in front of the bathroom door are signaling that the bathroom is continuously occupied.

Interest in footwear doesn't stop there, though. The toilet room is separate from the bath/shower room. The bath is often used for washing clothes that are large or require special handling. (Washing machines are small to save space.) So there are special rubber slippers—more like galoshes—to save getting the bath/shower area dirty and the hall floor wet.

What's more, there's a tiny porch off one side of the Andos' house. It's made of a special wood, so it has a matching set of special wooden sandals for wearing on it when you want to catch a sunset.

Special sandals or not, the Japanese clean their floors meticulously. The floors never actually get dirty, by Western standards; the effort is spent in polishing off any scuff marks made by the already-clean slippers.

I couldn't catch on to shoe-etiquette; I was always out of step. I continued to wear the bathroom slippers around the house, or I let my socks touch the ceramic-tile foyer inside the front door where shoes are left—a no-no because my socks would then track dirt.

Once I entered the Andos' house by the side door, took off my shoes, then realized that I ought to be going in by the front door. That was the door I always used and I'd forget where my shoes were if I left them anywhere else. To rectify the situation, I carried my shoes across the porch to the front door. That meant I was technically walking outdoors, briefly, in my socks. "Oohhhhhhh," a muffled cry emanated from inside as I passed by the window. I tiptoed the rest of the way sheepishly. Okāsan didn't need to say anything; her expression was enough.

Each member of the Ando family also had a special

pair of flip-flops for the courtyard. Their basement was not connected with the first floor, which was not connected to the second. They walked outside to get to them. So these slippers were for the *sole* purpose of walking down the outside stairs, perhaps to play ping pong in the basement.

One day as I wandered into the bedroom I shared with Mākun, he took one look at my feet and put his hand over his mouth and nose, "Socks dirty!"

I was embarrassed because my socks were old and, while a grayed-out white, not really dirty. So I said, "No, not dirty."

With that he jumped down from his upper bunk and pranced across the room insisting, "Yes, yes, very, very dirty!" He left to get the rest of the family to confirm this.

"Stibu! What are you doing? Oh, Stibu! Ahhhh!" I tried to look innocent, as in trotted Shika, Minori, and Okāsan, who went wild over the socks. "How long have you been wearing those socks, Steve?" Shika translated for her mother. I couldn't bear it.

When Shika and Minori tried to grab my socks for the washer, I leaped into bed and pulled the sheet over my feet. This drove them into a frenzy. Now I'd put "dirty" socks on the snow-white sheets!

The worst of my missteps occurred as Mākun and I were about to go locust-collecting, a favorite pastime for kids. I'd been bitten by insects all afternoon, and, as we left, I thought I'd better take some repellent. I'd already laced up my shoes—an activity that had become a time-consuming bother, rubbing my fingers raw. (The Japanese buy sandals or shoes without laces.) So I crawled back to my room on my knees to get the repellent, my shoed feet waving in the air. Alas, this became a major incident. Mākun's eyes popped open, and again he mustered everyone to see what I was up to.

I was surrounded by the time I reached my suitcase. "What are you doing?" the family members asked. I told them, and they all concernedly searched the bedroom for the repellent and buzzed around me as I knelt helplessly over my case, waiting for them to go away. "Why are you wearing your shoes?" Shika translated Minori's question.

Today I was all alone in the house and went exploring, dutifully putting on flip-flops as I left the house, then changing into the special basement sandals as I entered the outside door to the basement. I walked into a large basement closet; at the far end of it was another closet, opening into a tiny, unfinished earth-floored storeroom built into the side of the hill.

The sloping ceiling was laden with utility pipes, and the walls had racks bolted to them to hold general household items. There was no light fixture, but the bulb from the first closet cast its light upon the packed damp-earth floor of this innermost room of the basement. There—on the earthen floor—was the room's very own pair of slippers.

Week 2: July
Tuesday

I gave my talk at Minori's school, introducing myself with the Japanese sentences that Shika had painstakingly taught me. Afterward, when I asked for questions about America or American schools, five brave students took turns shyly raising their hands. The class exclaimed "Ohhhh" in unison at each of my answers. Minori, meanwhile, had now become centerstage, to a greater extent than I. With everyone asking her about me, she was embarrassed and kept her hands over her face.

The assistant teacher, Mary Alonzo, was a young woman from a small town in Pennsylvania. She translated for me. She gave me her name and phone number, and said she knew of about 20 Americans in Oita, most of them members of a group called FOR, Foreign Oita Residents.

A young Japanese teacher of English shook hands graciously and led me on a tour. A queue developed behind me as the students took renewed interest in the things I stopped to look at. I paused to admire a student's pointillist painting, and the queue halted to admire the painting anew. The students in the rooms we visited smiled, waved "Haro," and beamed every time my teacher-guide said "America."

I went to a movie with Shika and several of her friends—an American adventure film with kanji subtitles. The theater was packed with uniformed students, many of whom waved at me, though I'd never seen them before. I waved back at one of the girls, who then screamed and covered her face, while the group around her broke out in titters.

As Shika and I were walking up the steep hill after the movie, we passed four or five young children in a playground, who sang out a cute little melody when they saw me. It had only one word for lyrics, "*Gaijin, gaijin, gaijin.*" While '*gaijin,*' is sometimes used in the pejorative sense of 'outsider,' or worse, I found the little scene touching. A boy of perhaps five years hopped the fence and touched the hair on my legs. Another followed. Then, on a dare, they all surrounded me to do this. Even though I gave them my most evil look, they trailed me for quite a distance, bursting into the *gaijin* song at intervals.

When we got home Mākun and I played basketball in the yard—he was good at the sport. In fact, all the Ando children were excellent players.

Dai practiced basketball long and hard—Shika said his team shows great promise and might be the best in its league. Minori actually *studied* basketball. She was the captain of her school team and kept a notebook, called 'MENYU,' with each day's schedule. (The Japanese use the English word "menu" to refer to lists.) After practice she wrote up the day's results. The coach checked it, adding his comments in *English*—"good practice" or "nice work."

When I asked Shika if she herself was good at basketball, she promptly responded "Yes," which surprised me. What, I wondered, happened to saying "No" to questions like that? Maybe she stayed too long in America. As if to justify her iconoclastic frankness, she added, "I was on the varsity team in Kansas."

I talked with Shika in the Japanese room about school life. She had time now that her exams were over. There were seven days of school left. "I'll be taking practice college-entrance exams each morning before school, so I'll have to arrive there an hour early," she explained. "The exam is little like the SAT in the U.S., I think. I don't have to study for these practice-exams, so I won't have to work as hard now. I'm glad."

Summer seemed to have caught up with her, at last. She gave a long sigh, "I do not want to go to school tomorrow."

Shika made dinner for the family. Her curry—called *kari*—was not very good. For the first time nobody finished what was on their plates. Mākun made some disparaging comments about the *kari* before shoveling it grimly back and forth in his bowl. A highly spiced version of *kari* is increasingly popular in Japan. Because it's poured over rice, it fits in nicely with the rest of the Japanese diet. There's even a curry-flavor for cup-o-noodles and ice cream.

"I used to make this dish for my host family in America," Shika shrugged, noting the leftovers as we cleared the table.

"Well, I liked it," I said consolingly.

She may have caught the expression on my face because she replied, "They didn't like it either."

During dinner a TV newsbreak appeared called "Sports and News." It seems the Japanese have their priorities straight! It began with a baseball wrap-up and moved on to earthquakes in Tokyo, showing police handing out white air-raid-type helmets for protection from falling glass, roofs, and walls.

That evening, Otōsan called us all into the bar in the office section of the house to meet the kendo teacher. The old man had also been Otōsan's teacher at high school. Otōsan took out a 1960s yearbook that showed a photo of them both. Not surprisingly, the outgoing Otōsan had been president of his class, and later of the school.

With Otōsan as translator, the kendo-*sensei* complimented me on my judo—he'd heard from judo-*sensei* Kuriyama that everyone admired my falls. He'd now made a second trip to the Andos to offer to teach me kendo, and I readily agreed. He presented me with a gift, a fashionable handkerchief for wiping a sweaty brow.

Later that evening, on hearing the story about the little kids singing "*gaijin,*" Otōsan launched into some serious comments about Japanese society. He seemed to worry that I'd been offended by the children's song. His conclusion was "Gaijin! You are not gaijin in my house. Japanese sometimes too closed up. Look at high school—only Japanese students there. Some never know an American. Maybe only know American movies—too bad. New and different is good. Important everyone to be open, to be understanding. That's what we need."

He was rather unlike his usual self. I gathered that he wanted to apologize for the kids and to explain why he wanted exchange students to live with his family. Using his own brand of English, he wanted me know that, since his stay in America, he was convinced that meeting people and visiting places was the best way for everyone to overcome prejudices. He concluded, "Everybody must be friends, donchyu?"

Week 2: July
Wednesday
Exams over, my classmates were bleary this morning. School hadn't even begun for the day, and already it was so hot that most were vigorously fanning themselves with traditional fans while they sauntered around, proclaiming the day to be "Atsui!" —hot!

Johnny liked to confront these students. Typically, he stared them down so they stopped saying "Atsui!" Then he bellowed "Atsui!" down their throats, his ridiculous laugh following as an afterthought.

Johnny was very popular. Unlike the other students, he didn't feel bound to any one clique.

In free moments, the class polarized at opposite corners into boys and girls, and each side further subdivided into stratified layers of popularity. One group talked about girls, another about heavy-metal music, and another about math homework. Because I was no longer a curiosity, the groups didn't encircle me now, but if I invited myself in, I was made welcome.

In the girls' half of the room, the stratification was less noticeable. There was one big group I call the "UNO" club, because they liked to whip out their "UNO" deck for a sociable session of the game. Beyond that, there was a handful of girls doing their homework or each other's hair, plus a few leaning out the doorway to talk with some "hallflowers." "Hallflowers" was what I called the girls who lingered in the halls before school, chatting when they should have been in their classroom.

I saw Johnny blending into each of these groups. He

floated from one to the next, fitting in and taking command, the center of attention.

It was almost incomprehensible to me, but there appeared to be no competitive rat race in this class, no conspiracies. I thought if I were down, I could expect help, not trampling, from my peers here. These teenagers maintained a sheltering social environment for themselves, a by-product of the mutually supportive attitude of their society.

I recalled that last night Otōsan had told me that all the neighborhoods of the city organize into communities—with centers, leaders, and social functions—because the family, while a well-established group, was not alone sufficient to fulfill the strong need for a group identity.

He said that Japanese society is made up of groups within groups that, in turn, overlap with others. The definition of each group blurs as people migrate among them. There's seldom a conflict of interest because the pecking order is well established—for example, school comes before sports, and work before personal life.

This paradox of a unity arising from the layering of separate groups became real for me as the charismatic Johnny made his rounds a second time. "Atsui!" he bellowed, nodding from one member of a group to the next until all were shaking their heads yes. He left them with a final "Atsui!" before heading on to the next clique. The previous group, its leadership having been usurped by Johnny, babbled "Atsui! Atsui!" to itself for a few seconds, heads nodding, before starting a new conversation.

Johnny carried an "I Feel Coke" fan and fanned himself so vigorously that when he stopped, his face turned red. While the fan made him a "cool" dude—figuratively, at least—its slogan meant nothing. Nevertheless in his hands the fan was a symbol of power, as if everyone was gearing up to play football and Johnny was the only kid in the neighborhood who owned a pigskin.

My arms stuck to the table with sweat as I wrote, and I couldn't find a comfortable sitting position. Gazing around somewhat stupefied as we settled down for class, I noted that everyone's face was shining with sweat.

English Grammar

Those students who hadn't yet been called on to stand and formally introduce themselves to me, now had to do so. Most were still shy about speaking to me, which surprised me because this was *my* class; I'd been with them all day now for several days.

Blushing deeply in her light-blue sailor suit uniform, Tomoyo added a whispered "Please come to tea ceremony club" to her self-introduction. According to other students' introductions, the English-Speaking Society invited me to come talk, and the school newspaper wanted to interview me.

Heavy Metal, the rocker who hangs out with the coolest punkers in the class, was asleep when his turn came. He awoke to the jeers of his classmates and took a moment to contemplate how to inform me of his name and interest in heavy-metal music before managing to blurt out these two unadorned facts.

"My hobby is watching movies," said Takeshi. "I love 'Locki'." For the life of me I couldn't figure out what "Locki" was. Noting my puzzlement, he danced around the room, shadow-boxing and taunting some of the big boys with jabs and messing up their hair—to thunderous applause. "Rocky."

"Are you a good boy or a bad boy?" I interrogated Johnny when his turn came. The question was calculated to put him on the spot and get a laugh. It did. It was simple enough English for everyone to grasp immediately, and the shift of attention was as dramatic as if a spotlight had just been focussed on him.

The students jeered, in good humor, while he beamed. He responded with his usual roar, "Jani isu gudo, gudo, gudo, very boy" (Johnny is good, good, good, very boy). Then he bowed, American-style, to more hearty applause.

Lunch

A boy walked past our the classroom door wearing a new-wave t-shirt underneath his uniform. The t-shirt was fluorescent orange with a surf wave design on it—you could see it through his white shirt. "Coooolll!" grunted Heavy Metal, who'd also spied this singular innovation in dress.

Bobby wanted to know about the variety of languages taught in U.S. schools, the sequence of our science courses, and the priorities we give to various subjects. I gave him this information, then took the opportunity to tell him, "Mr. Tomita says you're a very good boy. Very responsible." Bobby giggled. Recalling his interest in joining the civil service after college, I added, "Maybe you'll be prime minister some day."

"No, no, no . . . no. Only people go to Tokyo University become prime minister. They make elite," Bobby concluded with a touch of awed humility.

As lunch period ended, I asked Johnny to take me to a water fountain. I asked by pressing down on my nose and saying, "I am get drink." He understood perfectly, but I gasped at my English.

Required Club

I approached Kendo Kid, "What required club do you go to?"

"English Conversation Club," he told me. I was lacking a club (origami class had turned into a study hall), so I said I'd like to join him.

Waiting for the teacher to arrive, the students in the

club formed little groups to read Japanese magazines about rock groups, chat, and play cards. Multicolored English sentences, meticulously parsed by a previous English class, surrounded us on the blackboard that dominated three sides of the room.

Kendo Kid had written me a cryptic message in math class: "Japan is a rich country, but it is not true. Do you understand it?"

I'd replied "No," correcting his grammar, as he'd asked me to.

Now in English Conversation Club he had time to explain what he meant. "Maybe foreigners think Japan is very rich, but the Japanese do not feel that way because life goes on the way it has for the last 40 years. Attitudes do not change here, I think. Money is re-invested in industry, so new wealth is not felt as much by the people."

I studied his face to see how he felt about this phenomenon, but saw no sign of approval or disapproval—just acceptance.

When the teacher didn't show up after about five minutes, I joked, "Perhaps the teacher is skipping." The class laughed, even though it was unlikely they all understood me completely. One said "skipping," then I heard "skipping," "skipping," repeated from different directions.

Most of the boys changed into their sports uniforms then and there—in spite of the presence of the girls—just because it was so hot. They dropped their slacks, exposing bulky boxer-shorts, then slipped their baggy sports shorts on top. They replaced their white, buttoned shirts with blue and white sports t-shirts. From his tardiness I could tell that the club's teacher used an informal style.

The Japanese "English Conversation Club" teacher finally arrived, a copy of one of Japan's English-language newspapers under his arm. He was surprised to see me, a surprise that modulated quickly into delight.

He beckoned me to come to his desk, where he and I talked about American and Japanese high schools. His English was better than most. When I spoke about exams and colleges in America, he was especially interested, and a group of students gathered to hear. I listed the U.S. national exams and talked about the many colleges near where I live in New England. He got out a map. I told them I wanted to go to Harvard. They'd all heard of it.

The club ended when the teacher left five minutes early and the students reverted to their earlier activities. My American classmates would have been out the door fast.

It was the end of the day, and no teacher was present in our homeroom. I noticed that no one stood up to start the usual cleaning and looked over at Bobby.

"Why—no cleaning?" I asked.

I wasn't sure if he understood me because he just frowned.

"No cleaning?" I repeated.

"I am don't know," he said with a shrug.

I turned to Kendo Kid. "Can we go now?"

He gave my question a moment's thought, then a tentative "Yes."

When I picked up my things to leave, a chorus of voices stopped me.

"No go!" Diana called out above the chatter.

"Not to go," said Kendo Kid in unexplained contradiction of himself. I sat down confused. We were apparently to leave in a group, but no one would or could tell me when.

Finally, after a few slow minutes, the class swept me downstairs with them toward the gymnasium. First we visited our shoe lockers, which are located in the dirt courtyard but on wood platforms slightly raised to keep the slippers clean. We put on our outdoor shoes, packed our homeroom slippers into the locker, and walked 50 yards across the courtyard to the kendo gym. There we joined a long queue outside the door—a bottleneck caused by the need to replace the outdoor shoes with special gym slippers from a pile at the door.

Shoe etiquette again. I noticed that the students were courteous both to others and to their slippers. They wouldn't think of treading on someone's shoes, and they held their own shoes out of harm's way, so they didn't brush anyone with the soles.

Because shoe-changing was taking a long time, our group broke apart, everyone milling about in high spirits.

Some boys were playing with a weighted string that they tossed to each other, drawing attention to themselves. Two other boys were searching for their friends in the multitude. When one of the two started up a conversation with an unsuspecting victim, the other crawled on his hands and knees behind the victim's legs. The first then gave a shove, sending the victim toppling backwards over the accomplice. This caused our whole group to liven up immensely.

New pairs of students picked up the trick. You could no longer trust your friends, girls became targets, and no one could stand in one place for long. You had to keep turning around, or someone might sneak up.

"Stibu!" a voice called. I saw a boy wave to get my attention, then shove an unsuspecting student over backwards. The fallen student uprighted himself, chagrined that I'd been watching. All this was happening, I guessed, because exams were over.

Finally inside, we remained in our class groups—boys separate from girls—and sat on the floor. The heat from hundreds of densely packed bodies intensified the sultry conditions.

The stern yell of Mr. Kuriyama, the burly judo instructor, put an end to all tittering and rowdiness. This was a
meeting to instruct the students on what they needed to
accomplish over the summer.

During the ensuing silence I glanced behind me—a
daring move, because the teachers were looking for someone to flinch so they could issue a reprimand. I saw everyone looking as far away from me as possible. They could
have been whistling for all the innocence they emanated.
No-o-o-o, they hadn't just been staring at me.

I enjoyed the game they were playing and later teased
them with another backwards glance.

Several teachers took turns lecturing, while another
paced up and down the rows to distribute papers and
ensure silence. This patrol-teacher caught someone nap-
ping and yanked up his head by the hair at the back of his
neck.

I had no idea what any of the speakers was saying,
until my Japanese Classics teacher, Miss Watanabe, took
the mike. Bobby dared to slip me a note: "She is persuad-
ing about examination for university."

When everyone stood up for the principal's announcements, I left my notepad and pen behind on the floor.
There didn't seem to be room to stoop and pick them up to
make some jottings, and this wasn't a good moment to try.
Because I was bored, I began to fiddle for the pen with my
toes. It was difficult, but using my other foot to push
against, I clenched the pen between my toes and lifted it to
hip level where I snatched it.

I'd attracted attention from the boys around me and
now felt pressure to get hold of the paper. I didn't want to
fail in front of them, whether I was actually going to write
anything or not. I had not only to retrieve the paper (a
good deal harder than grasping the pen), but also to do
the job with finesse—to show what an American can do. I

couldn't pinch the pad between my toes, so I dragged it up my left leg with my right foot.

My actions went unobserved outside the circle around me (the students were too closely packed for anyone to see very far), but drew barely audible applause from my neighbors and muffled cries of "Bravo!" and "Fantastic!" I heard Johnny add his "Best!" to the accolades. A minute or two after I'd completed my stunt, the principal ended his speech, and we were allowed to sit for the rest of the meeting.

Later on the principal stepped forward to the microphone again to make an announcement, and a few students stood up. More students tentatively followed. I assumed they were being rewarded or honored. They looked, however, as though they'd swallowed a giant Kyushu cockroach, as they shuffled to the back of the room. Several teachers then harvested the aisles, picking more students to go to the back, where they faced the rear wall for the rest of the assembly.

By note, though it was hardly a safe thing to do, I asked Bobby what was going on. He wrote back, "Dress code penalty—girls hair touching shoulders, or not tied up, or ribbons. Boys no undershirts, or wearing clothing not uniform." The boy with the orange surfer undershirt was one of those who got nailed.

I saw a dozen students sleeping. Their heads were tilted forward, and if I craned my neck I could see that their eyelids were closed. Their palms were anchored under their knees in a way that ingeniously kept them upright. There was no noise or applause as the teachers marched up, gave their speeches, and stepped down.

The assembly over, Shika said we ought to swim instead of going home. I biked home, got my suit, came back, and swam. The pool was divided into two sections, boys and girls. Even though it was "free swim," all wore swim uniforms with identical bathing caps and towels.

I challenged a student to a race. The first time I beat him, but he'd hit a lane marker when jumping off the starting block, which slowed him down. We raced twice more, and he won.

There were only a few kids in the boys' half of the pool. Some were racing each other in brief sprints; others played a rowdy game of tag. The numerous girls, on the other hand, were crowded together in their half of the pool, bobbing sociably in groups.

On the way home I walked through the basketball practice, and the teacher, who is also the kendo *sensei,* called me over because he wanted to see me shoot the ball a few times. Practice stopped as everyone gathered around the hoop, staring at me as if I were the victim of a bloody accident. It became a bigger event than I'd have liked. I did a passable lay up and rim shot, leading everyone to think I was a good basketball player. I wasn't, but how could I tell them that without setting them up to think I was just being modest?

Tonight Mākun got a lecture from Otōsan. It lasted over an hour, prompted by a grade Mākun received on a test. Otōsan kept his voice between a growl and a confident sternness. He didn't shout, but he talked on and on.

Shika summed up for me what had been said. "Otōsan told Mākun that he wanted him to be the *best* at something. It didn't much matter what, but Mākun needed to dedicate himself to something, and he knew Mākun had it in him to do just that."

The lecture cast a pall on the whole family, and we didn't indulge in our normal after-dinner jokes and wrangling. It wasn't just as though one member of the family had a problem; it was as though your own arm or neck—

an integral part of you—was in trouble. We weren't the same people tonight.

I never seemed to get to sleep before midnight. Everyone at the Andos' was a night person. At 10:30, when we'd all be asleep at my home in the U.S., the Andos were working, snacking, and maybe watching TV. I was perpetually sleepy as a result.

Otōsan was usually out nights—sometimes in his home office all night, sometimes in his office in town until late, or out at Yufuin at his two hotels. The nights he was home he spent with the kids doing whatever they were doing, usually watching travelogues or dating-games on TV or a *hora* (horror) movie Mākun had rented.

Shika often shut herself in her room after dinner to do homework and came out for a late snack. She liked to do her memory work in front of the TV, staring from book to TV and back while repeating passages softly.

Minori got home as late as 5:30 because her school ended late, and afterward she had basketball practice. She had less homework because she did her art work in the school studio. Each day she rested for a while in her room. She was very quiet. But she had her favorite TV shows and never failed to come out for them.

Mākun started his homework as soon as he got home and took breaks to stretch out the time. A true homework-Parkinsonian, he let his work absorb the whole evening, because that was the time he allotted. He went from studying English to solitaire, to baseball-on-the-radio, to math, to listening to music, to reading magazines in the Japanese room, to writing an essay, to watching TV or bugging Okāsan by sneaking his hands into the dinner.

Dai also arrived home late, usually after Minori, because he, too, had basketball practice. Most of all, he liked to sit with his older siblings as they randomly mingled before returning to their private spaces. Sometimes he pretended to read the newspaper. He especially liked to do this when someone else, like Otōsan, was reading it, so he could mimic what they were doing. Or he read his special comics, where the difficult kanji had explanatory hiragana in the margins, a bit like training wheels. Often he ran out to the park down the street to play with neighborhood kids or to the basement for a game of ping pong with me.

Everyone congregated around 10 or 11. Okāsan—who wouldn't sleep while anyone in the family was awake—prepared orange slices and other snacks, or she lay on the floor next to the living-room couch and rested, or she cleaned the kitchen and did the laundry.

When we finally got to bed, Mākun left his ceiling light on low. His beloved *hora* movies made him afraid of the dark. He also continued his habit of leaning over his bunk to stare down at me. I wore my airline-handout eye mask because of the light, but I could still feel his gaze and flipped off the mask to catch him. It became a game, but it also made me paranoid: every time he shifted in bed, I whipped off the mask to see if I could catch his stare.

What we had in the Andos was a happy family. Everyone knew his or her place. There were no fights that I saw. The kids got along well, and, despite Mākun's disappointing grade, they did well at school and outside activities. I didn't even see any of the small arguments I thought every family had.

This family's operations were complicated by the fact that their oldest child was a daughter—in fact, they had two older daughters. How did the son fit in, I wondered.

Mākun certainly held a position higher than Minori, even though she was 16 and he 14. Yet that didn't seem to apply to Shika. I never learned for sure who was on top because there wasn't a test or forcing of the issue. Shika's eminence in the family and worldliness (thanks to her U.S. exchange visit) placed her above Mākun, I believe—a delicate situation in a society that still reveres and promotes boys. Still, this family was different, I knew, and fairly far along in a transition from an old order—represented by the Ando grandparents—to a new, more American-style menage.

Beyond the matter of birth-order, there was a clear clash of values between Shika and Mākun. I recall Mākun's returning from a record store with a pile of magazines about Wink and a cassette of their latest recording. Shika followed him into his room and talked authoritatively with him for ten minutes. When she returned, I asked what was going on.

"It's Mākun. He is spending all his gift money on that Wink stuff. I just don't . . ." Shika paused.

"Is it that expensive?" I asked.

"Yes, it *is* expensive. Even the magazines are about $10 each. But that's not the point. When Minori bought her stereo, she thought about it long before. It's not the same with Mākun. He sees something and he buys.

"I grew up when our family lived in a small apartment," she continued. "We didn't know Otōsan would do well. Mākun doesn't remember any of that. It's different with him. So when I see him just spend his money without thinking it, without feeling it, I have to tell him that's wrong."

What held everyone together was Okāsan's graciousness, Otōsan's commanding presence, and Shika's benevolent leadership during his frequent absences.

Soccer Through a Purple Haze

Week 2: July
Thursday
Today was Class Match, the sports day and one of the biggest celebrations of the school year. I ate a big rice, bread, and jam breakfast to be ready for it, even though this meant I'd be late.

Shika had left a note on my washed and folded swimsuit and towel.

> Steve:
> Good morning!
> Take your swimming suit & white T shirt and short pants. (Go to school in your uniform though.) You'd better leave here as early as possible because you have to change at school by 8:10, I guess.
> Shika

I read the note, grabbed my things, and arrived at school 15 minutes late. The teachers stationed at the gate clucked at me as I cruised past.

The entire junior class had gathered on the soccer fields for the opening ceremonies. After one of the speeches ended, I was allowed in and had to walk down my classmates' aisle to the end. One after the other, everyone mockingly whispered, "Stibu bado boy" (Steve bad boy) and "Bado!" as I ran the gantlet.

When I reached the end of the line, I responded with a "Stibu gudo, gudo, gudo very boy," borrowing Johnny's memorable description of himself during the introductions.

I was just in time for the school exercise, a predefined set of perfectly sequenced calisthenics that varied systematically with each run-through. As soon as I caught on to one pattern, they'd switch. The exercises finished with a teacher's exhortation, translated earnestly for me by Bobby, "Try hard and participate energetically on our teams."

Before being dismissed, my classmates and I were provided with purple socks and purple headbands with our names embroidered in black. Rival classes got different colors. Shika told me last night that boys could swim or play soccer or basketball.

"What you do, Stibu?" asked Bobby.

Assuming I could pick my sport, I replied, "Swimming."

"Yes, yes," nodded Bobby.

In the melee that followed, I joined up with some students who were rushing to the changing room, then jumped into the pool with them.

After a warm-up splash-fest we lined up on the deck. The instructor introduced himself to me and moved me to a spot of my own. As the teacher began outlining a schedule on the poolside blackboard, Mr. Tomita appeared.

"There has been a mistake," he told me. "You are not supposed to be swimming. This is a regular physical education class; it has nothing to do with Class Match. Swimming for Class Match will take place during noon recess. You should come with me now to soccer."

A feature of the Japanese national personality—

amusing and puzzling too—may have been revealed by something that happened to me while playing soccer today.

Mr. Tomita delivered me to a group of students, among whom I spotted Bobby. Unsurprised at my reappearance, Bobby asked, "Are you good at soccer?"

I responded truthfully, "I'm poor at it, and I've played only in gym class, not on a real team." To Bobby and the others who were listening, my answer meant that I must be good, and modest too. Naturally they put me in the main position: center forward.

Deep down inside I dreaded playing team sports. I was always bad at them, much preferring solo efforts like karate, track, swimming, and sailing. I never played well with others and usually found myself shut out of the game. I wondered whether I'd be good compared to the kids here, but I doubted it.

In my experience on teams, there's usually a super player: someone who 'makes' the team, a player to watch, someone always there to pass to and to attribute the success of the team to. There was none here. The boys were of varying abilities, but no one took the spotlight, or seemed to want to. There was also a lot more teamwork on offense than I was used to, or else just a pronounced lack of individual assertiveness.

Homeroom classes worked as a unit throughout the school year. At my U.S. high school students were separated by ability, but here each student was expected to compensate for, and work with, students of all different ability levels. So, too, in sports.

Bobby had lousy scores on his national sports proficiency test, and he actually made us lose our first game when he twice bungled a defensive play. In America you'd drop someone like that. Not here. The other students helped and encouraged him.

Our class didn't do well, but no one seemed to care. They had more fun just playing than I'd seen anyone have in a long time. They had fun skinning their knees and tripping and losing and crashing into other players.

I felt satisfied, which meant I hadn't tripped over my feet or the ball, or walked into the goal post during any of the three games I'd played. Everyone said I was great. I wasn't, but they said this so profoundly it made me suspicious: if saying I was bad told them I was good, what did it mean to be complimented?

Mr. Tomita drew me aside as I left the field. "Steven, I'm sorry, you are not supposed to be in soccer after all, but in softball!"

I put up an exhausted hand and said "soccer," so he let the matter drop.

Now, of all the *kumis* (teams) in the school, I was a member of the purple *kumi*. By sheer coincidence, there were two purple *kumis* that day, but I didn't know this. Mr. Tomita later explained, "Two purple *kumis* today was a mistake. It was caused by lack of togetherness planning."

Returning to my team, I spotted a group wearing the familiar purple headbands and socks and attached myself to them. While we sat together, I grinned at a few students and they grinned back. I chatted with one or two. Then we headed toward the field. I don't understand why I didn't recognize that they weren't my *kumi*. No one gave me a hint either.

My wandering into the other purple *kumi* was easily done. Japan is known to be a society where everyone feels they must belong, and membership is sometimes jealously exclusive. Being different here is sometimes akin to being wrong. Indeed, the Japanese word for "different" is also the word for "wrong."

As the only foreign student in the school, I seemed to

be able to fit into any group. Paradoxically it was my differentness that allowed me to attach myself – if
inadvertently – to this other class team, a class that had
been working together for several months now.

We marched onto a soccer field. I took up center forward, which means that, without being aware of it, I
bumped someone – probably the class leader – out of his
spot and off the team. He must have simply accepted this
state of affairs and left the field. The team and I played
well and had fun. We won and retired, patting ourselves
on the back and joking.

My real team was waiting for me as I came off the field.
They never asked me where I'd been or why I'd just
played for a rival team. They never broke it to me that I'd
been lost. I just figured that softball had ended early and
the students I was now joining were the softball players
from my class, waiting for us soccer players.

Instead, this group of purple players immediately took
me onto the field with them – to play yet another game of
soccer! Now this would be my fifth soccer game, out of
four. I spotted Bobby again. "How many games were we
to play?"

"Four."

"Are you sure, Bobby?" I quizzed him. When he nodded yes, I had him count the number on his fingers, then
draw it in the sand. It was entirely possible for him to
mean one thing and say something else – it's happened.
Then I realized I hadn't seen Bobby at all last game.

I didn't play well after that. I was trying to pierce the
persistent haze of confusion that surrounds the foreigner
in Japan. When I thought I'd figured out what had happened, it worried me. It wasn't funny at the time.

No one had challenged me. It may have been that the
students were too polite or too shy. Perhaps everyone was
just playing along with me, or no one was willing to take

the first step, preferring to let the whole matter slide. It was unfathomable.

There was one other remote possibility. They could have thought *I* knew what I was doing. Incessant confusion can bring about its own state of confidence. But if they thought I knew what I was doing, it means that, without exception, *they* didn't know what they were doing.

I still wonder.

Contests in swimming—my best sport—were held at noon. When I stepped onto the diving block for our 200-meter relay, I heard cheers from behind as well as from the windows of a nearby classroom building. For all the butterflies in my stomach, I pulled our team from a lousy start to second place in both races.

The first-place team was way ahead of us though, having practiced for this event for months. They deserved to win.

The club swimmers—the top people in swimming—asked me to join their club right away. I demurred. To demur in Japan is to say "yes" halfheartedly, while being vague about what you are "agreeing" to. Then the other side politely lets the matter drop. Don't specify a time or place or say you will actually *do* anything, but agree in principle. Saying "no" is the height of bad form.

I demurred for practical reasons. I could swim anywhere. There were some things I could do only here, like judo or shogi (Japanese chess). Besides, my schedule was not my own. In fact, I didn't even know what I was doing that evening.

As we were about to leave the swimming event, I beckoned Johnny to follow me toward the pool. As the announcer and leader of the swim meet, he was dressed in his sports uniform. I was in trunks, not yet dried. I took his megaphone, clipboard, and towel, placed them on the ground, and quickly tried to toss him into the pool.

A judo expert, he easily twisted the situation around. The next thing I knew, he was laughing and I was whirled off balance and headed for a dunk. I grabbed him to try to pull him in with me. But he had amazingly good balance, and with a twist he slipped out of my hands as I went splash.

When I climbed out, I hugged him all over to get him wet. He ran around in a circle like a cartoon character on fire, hooting and getting roars of laughter from the swim group and the classrooms facing the courtyard, where students were watching us from windows.

I caught him, spun him around, and gave a big shove. Anyone else would have gone right over the edge, but he still didn't. Finally, someone from the audience that had gathered took pity on either Johnny or me and, coming from a weird angle, gave Johnny a shove that sent him, arms flailing, into the pool. He surfaced to uproarious laughter. He loved it. As he got out, he ran over to a group of girls and shook his wet hair like a dog. I called out, in mock astonishment, "Johnny, you are all wet!"

Later, as we gathered for the closing ceremony, Teacher Tomita appeared again and said, briskly, "See me directly after this is over." My immediate thought was that maybe not everyone had been impressed by that pool stunt.

Dutifully I trotted to the teachers' room, full of misgivings. Mr. Tomita was in a jovial mood, however, and apologized for leaving me in confusion about the events of the day. Then he invited me to attend an English seminar and help teach it.

The seminar would be a major event, with native English-speakers from Australia, Canada, England, and America, and Japanese teachers of English from all over

Kyushu, plus 400 Japanese students selected from a large pool of candidates. He invited me to teach at two of these seminars, in fact, but I decided to tackle only one. Because each lasted three days, I felt that two seminars would take too much time from my schedule and family.

He also asked if I had any questions, so I inquired about something that had been on my mind a while. "I—was wondering—could I teach your class sometime?"

He stared at me, then beamed. "Good! Good! Tomorrow! In fact, if you like, you can teach another of my classes, too. I would like that."

Back in homeroom, I paid Diana about $2 in yen for the purple socks and the headband she'd sewed for me, embroidering a delicate "Steven" in black thread.

"Is it OK to go home now?" I asked Diana and Bobby.

"Yes," they chorused.

As usual, however, I couldn't. When I started off, Bobby called me back, "Where are you going? You must stay here now." School dragged on for hours. Until 5, and sometimes 5:30, like today.

Our homeroom teacher, Suzuki-*sensei*, appeared. "On our last day of school, I will hold a going-away party for you," she told me and asked me to prepare a speech for it.

Next, she asked Bobby, Kendo Kid, and me to buy drinks for the class with money she gave us. We hurried out to the corner shop, but other homerooms had been there first and bought up all the packs of soda. So one by one, we purchased 45 cans from the drink machine outside the shop, emptying a whole Pocari Sweat machine. The operation took close to a quarter hour.

Okāsan asked if I'd like to go for a haircut now. I said yes, so she drove me to one of their barber shops. Shika came along to describe to the barber the sort of cut I wanted. There were no other customers, so the two young barbers both worked on me. It took over an hour: they washed my hair twice, trimmed it three times, and shaved my sideburns and chin with a straight razor. I took a photo to commemorate the most deluxe haircut I'd ever had.

That evening, with Shika's help, I prepared what I hoped was an entertaining and useful lesson plan for tomorrow's English classes. Much of it revolved around games and skits.

Week 2: July
Friday
Yesterday, in the excitement of Class Match, I'd left my lunch box at school. I still felt bad about it. Okāsan didn't ask me for it after school yesterday, as she always did. This morning she said, "Please to get lunch at school restauranto" (the school had a small cafeteria) and handed me some coins.

When I walked into school this morning, I found that Teacher Suzuki had wrapped up my chopsticks and empty *obentō* and left them on my desk. I never had to admit to Okāsan that I'd lost my lunch box because she already knew, thanks to a call from Mrs. Suzuki.

The night before, as we left Class Match, I told Diana I was going to be a teacher tomorrow. This morning, as I walked into the room, I heard whispers of "Stibu-sensei." All during the morning the girls and some of the boys called me Stibu-*sensei*.

I was nervous, but became quite calm as I strode to the rostrum in English Readers. I'd planned nothing complicated and was sure they'd have no problem with my simple sentences.

On the spur of the moment I decided to both say *and* write all my sample sentences. It was good that I did. It made it look to Mr. Tomita as though I was teaching them something sophisticated. (I gave examples of three tenses and explained why one says "I swam," not "I played swimming," as more than one student had said yesterday.)

Next I divided the class down the center into two teams. This in itself caused considerable wonderment and murmurs from the students, who glanced up at Teacher Tomita for his approval. He too was curious and didn't interfere.

Johnny was to have been the leader of one team, but as president of the school he had to preside over the seniors' Class Match today. In his place I picked the class's own leader, the serious Satoshi. He had trouble managing his group, which was not very responsive. To uproarious laughter, I picked Mister Sumo as the leader of the other group. He was able to get his group together better, even though—or maybe because—he was the class clown.

The game "Hangman" —Shika's suggestion—became the ice-breaker I needed. I started off by writing on the board :

American city:

— — — — — — — — — —

Satoshi's group called out "Washington" without ever guessing a letter. The same happened for "sashimi" and for "Disneyland" after someone guessed the "L."

Next, I offered the easiest one of all: the clue was "Name of Steve's country." Satoshi's team guessed the "A." I was certain that Mister Sumo's team would now get the whole word: A _ _ _ _ _ A. Mister Sumo became excited, blurted out "Australia!" and lost it for everyone on his team. Australia?

After explaining my skit exercise, I gave the teams a few minutes to work out among themselves a dialogue between exchange students and hosts. Everyone wrote their individual part on paper, except Mister Sumo, who ad-libbed his, to everyone's amusement. He got stuck on the simplest English and went dumb after such questions as "What is your name?"

The lesson went well. Even though I gave homework, they all said I'd done a good job. At the end of class, Satoshi shouted his usual, "KIRITSU! KIOTSUKE! REI!" and the class rose, bowed to me, and sat down. I bowed back from the rostrum, my chest tight with pride. This was an unforgettable reward.

Kendo Kid composed his first letter to his American host family, and during lunch he asked me to read it to see it if was suitable. It was fine and needed only a few corrections.

I told him to embrace American culture wholeheartedly when he arrived in the U.S., because that way he would learn most, experience most, and truly become American. But I was thinking about myself, too. It's difficult for foreigners to adapt to life here; it's unheard of for a foreigner to become truly Japanese. A century ago Lafcadio Hearn became the first Westerner to gain Japanese citizenship, and today he's beloved by Japanese for the folktales he preserved in his writings. Eventually, though, he gave up trying to be Japanese in heart-broken defeat. Kendo Kid can actually become American, and America is unique in that respect.

I recalled what Larry Radner, a returnee from a previous year's exchange, had told me in Seattle. "When Japanese students go to America, it puts them under great stress. On returning to Japan they must immediately fit back into a regimented society and into a high-school system that's pumping the students into universities and careers. They'll be behind in their subjects. They'll be different because of their experience. They'll have to act more reserved than the rest of the students because any side of their nature that they expose will immediately be ascribed to the questionable influence of America."

I wondered about this advice, though, because I didn't see that Shika was experiencing any of these problems as a result of her year's schooling in the U.S. Quite the opposite, in fact.

Mr. Tomita's six-period English class was weaker than the earlier class, but there was no problem.

After school, when I arrived at the teachers' room for my regular visit with Mr. Tomita, he said, "I like your idea of giving everyone in the class an English name. Would you please give me a list of the names so I may continue after you leave for America?"

He'd asked me earlier in the day to correct some English exams for him—essays—and I'd begun them. "I need them back today," he now informed me. As I sat down and hurried to finish them, five girls took seats at the table opposite me and softly oogled and laughed at me the whole time.

When I finished the papers twenty minutes later, Mr. Tomita checked them, handed them—"bloody" with my red correction ink—to these girls, and began to go over their mistakes with them. I blanched. They'd watched me cut up their papers, slash their serene prose, and never let on or whimpered!

As I left the teachers' room, Johnny leaped out from a doorway, "Stibu!" He was bright red, having spent two days in the sun at both junior and senior Class Matches. I made as if to hug him (it would have been painful), but he ran circles around me. Then I showed him my own sunburn, holding my strawberry arm next to his. We rejoiced in our newfound kinship, made as if to hug each other, then simultaneously backed off. Johnny chuckled, then looked serious, "You are my brother."

Late that afternoon, Mākun and I left the house to try again to see the concentration-camp display at the museum, this time with directions to the place.

The exhibit was deeply sobering. A woman spotted me and directed me politely, in good English, to a map on the wall that had the only English in the room, so I could read something. The map depicted the location of the camps. She was so pleasant and helpful that I paid her the biggest compliment I know, "Are you an English teacher?"

She blushed and waved me off with a "No, my English is very bad." Later her class arrived, and I saw that she *was* an English teacher.

When we left the museum at dusk, Mākun took me through the busy town center to pick up Dai at basketball practice. On the way home we passed a festival with lots of booths and activities. Dai wanted to stop because some of his school friends were performing on drums and cymbals in the main event. Dressed in a motley mixture of traditional regalia and Western clothes, the young boys all drummed the same rhythm, competing for style and assertiveness.

Dai held my elbow as we strolled through the festival. At first I thought he was leading me, but it turned out I was leading him. He was very responsible and attached himself to me for safety because I'd become a figure of respect. To him, I was a big brother and could do no wrong. Although the festival was action-packed, his face maintained the idle, distant look that he wears when tickling my leg.

Otōsan came out from the house to meet us with a scowl, displeased that we were late, "If you out past 8 again, phone home first."

My Secret and Relax Place

Week 2: July
Saturday
As I pulled in late to school, three teachers were stationed at the entrance gate. While I walked my bike down the long aisles of bike racks in front of the school, I tried to think of ways to slip through the gate without being seen. I couldn't.

The school buildings were well organized to prevent late-comers from sneaking in. Hunting out a hole in this system and trying to sneak past the hydra at the gates would just have made me later, so I parked the bike, put on an air of confidence, and casually marched past the teachers. One shook his head, "You are late."

"I'm sorry," I responded contritely, "I'll try not to be late again."

The halls and yards were a ghost-town as I walked purposefully to my classroom. My classmates were envious that I could be late (this was not the first time) and just walk in, no questions asked. They thought I had some influence above. I expected a dressing down each time, but it never came.

Today the geography teacher introduced himself to me and asked me to visit his family at their home. He said he was teaching English to his own young children and they'd very much like to meet me. He lived near the Andos and knew them, so perhaps I'd be able to go. He said it'd make him happy if I stopped by. I got a lot of offers like this one.

I also found myself in confusing conversations. This morning, for example, a loud, shrill bell went off, but it wasn't the bell to change classes. It was piercing, as if someone was blowing a whistle in your ear, but my fellow students ignored it. It went on and on.

Me: "What is that?"

A blank stare from Bobby.

Me: "Nan desu ka?"

Bobby: "Oh . . . It is a bell."

Me: "What bell?"

Bobby: "Fire."

Me: "Fire?!"

Bobby, still perfectly calm: "No, no fire."

Me: Hopeless sigh. "What . . . Oh, forget it."

A blank stare.

If the bell was for a fire drill, no one was responding. Still puzzled, I put it out of my head.

Mr. Tomita had told me several times that I was welcome to skip any class if I had something I would rather do, but that I should be sure to leave before the class began. I could go to the library, which I wanted to see at least once, or I could go to the teachers' room, where he'd be available to talk to me anytime he wasn't teaching.

I usually spent the time writing in my diary, which made teachers and classmates curious. What would you think if the *gaijin* in your class wrote in his notebook all the time? All the teachers and most students—from those I didn't know who saw me in the hall, to the shyest ones in the class—leaned over my shoulder to see what it is I was writing that was so fascinating. They need only have looked around!

School was said to be a half day on Saturdays, but it

was longer than that. Before I could leave at noon, I was dragged to a meeting of the school's English-Speaking Society by Julie, who'd invited me several days earlier. The Canadian was there, and my impression of him improved greatly.

His little group of students were like a family, and he knew all of them by the English names he'd given them. As they entered, he asked them what they'd been doing this week and directed a conversation back and forth among them. He was totally in control, patient and kind. You could tell his students liked being here.

In the hall today I was handed a thank-you note by one of the girls whose tests I corrected yesterday. "It was a pleasure to read your corrections," she wrote.

"Thanks for your letter," I nodded.

"Thank you for thanking me, but you shouldn't thank me," she replied sweetly in a high, little voice. She'd seemed extremely shy from the moment I first met her. It must have taken a lot of courage to write that letter.

Back home by 1 p.m., Shika and I got ready for a party she was holding tonight for her basketball team. The preparations took all afternoon. I swept the cement areas of the yard and set out folding chairs and washed them down. Ojisan and I erected a large square contraption of logs for more people to sit on.

Shika and three of her basketball friends organized an enormous amount of food, washing cabbage, cutting watermelon, preparing fresh squid. Ojisan and Otōsan set up three pits with grills over them.

Ojisan was delegated to build the fires, and he was the right man for the job. For wood he scavenged branches from the park across the street and scraps of building material. He set about constructing the fires as if they were his new kids, cooing over a branch here, patting a 2×4 there, and stowing a bottle of kerosene nearby, just in case. He was obviously relishing his role as firemaster. Shortly before the party began, he found himself unable to light one of the three fires. He soaked the wood with kerosene, then tried to set a magazine ablaze with a lighter to touch off the pile. After several tries he threw up his hands in chuckling disappointment.

Otōsan laughed and patted his chubby sides, then asked me to light the fire. I ripped the magazine along its binding and tossed away half. At one end I tore several strips part way down, then rolled what was left into a torch. I kinked this "chimney" so the fire wouldn't leap up onto my arm. Lighting the magazine from one of the other fires, I touched off the kerosene-soaked wood. Ojisan and Otōsan laughed appreciatively, "Boy Sukauto" (Boy Scout). They'd remembered this fact from my Youth for Understanding bio.

About 40 people arrived as we set out the food on the grills. The team members were varsity-level players, but now that they were seniors, the school wouldn't allow them to continue basketball on account of the need to study for exams.

Not only were the boys' and girls' teams there, but also family friends, neighbors, the coaches and their families, the PTA president, community leaders, and more. Shika played songs by Billy Joel, one of her favorite singers, in the background.

I savored each kind of food, picking morsels off the grills with my chopsticks. For hors d'oeuvres there were strips of raw and dried squid, tiny dried fish, seaweed, and potato chips. Roasting on the grills were cabbage, squid, slices of fish, chewy cow intestine, egg plant, large and small strips of beef, and a type of vegetable jello that everyone said was healthful but no one touched.

While we ate, each team member gave a speech. They

were all good friends and had a grand time heckling each other and laughing as they took turns climbing onto the "stage" formed by a raised portion of the driveway.

At the end they asked me to speak. "No, no," I said, feeling unprepared and not really part of this team celebration.

"Yes, yes, you must. Stibu speak!" came the enthusiastic reply. They cheered me as if I'd been a star player. I thanked everyone for their kindness and hospitality.

After the party ended at a late hour, I spent a long time in the Japanese room staring out at the city. I knelt and watched the shimmering, blinking lights below. For nearly an hour I didn't want to do anything but hope that the summer wouldn't end.

The children of the family saw me and respected my silence. I heard the family going about its routines. I could tell who was passing by the kind of footsteps, and I knew exactly what each person was doing in preparation for bedtime.

Week 3: July
Sunday

Mākun's alarm went off at 4 a.m., after we'd gone to bed at 1. He was eager to take me on an insect hunt, and I somehow managed to shake myself awake.

Silently he led me by the hand out the door and into the shrouded forest across the street. The way he did it, it wasn't just a spur-of-the-moment activity, but a carefully planned and executed expedition.

We explored the jungle-like park, people's yards, and the backroads. We shone our flashlights at trees, rocks, and utility poles, and under earthen overhangs. It was tough going because of the pitch-black underbrush. To Mākun this was a great adventure. He hid behind bushes as cars appeared, skulked past houses and other relics of civilization, and scouted around trees as if searching for treasure.

We must have probed for about a mile. We hunted everywhere that could be a hangout for insects but didn't find a single bug, although some mosquitoes found me. I pulled my arms up into my t-shirt in an unsuccessful attempt to protect them. Coming up empty was odd because often, when I least desired them, Kyushu's giant insects sought me out to pester me.

That summer locusts were everywhere, apparently hundreds in every bush, but not this morning. Locusts like to congregate and buzz incredibly loudly. Often I couldn't hear myself think.

A plague of locusts gives children the chance to indulge bug-catching. Locusts are special fun because they don't sting and can be played with and collected in pockets. They can also be kept in a cage for weeks by the forgetful without needing care.

Back home at 6 a.m., Mākun flicked on the TV to the U.S. Women's Open Golf Championships—the only thing on—but soon tired of it. Next he played the family's videotape of Chaplin's "Modern Times." It was my first time watching an entire Chaplin film, and I had to come to Japan to do this! Afterward I tried to sleep but failed.

A neighborhood festival procession took place in the late morning, featuring Dai and his peers from Sakuragaoka. The event used to be just for young boys, but nowadays girls were included. Dai and I donned *hapi* coats and colorful headbands and, carrying festival fans, we accompanied Okāsan to a nearby shrine.

Nearly every neighborhood in Oita has a shrine. They are prominent gathering places, and while no one lives in them, they receive constant care to keep them in good condition despite their age. This shrine had a packed earth floor and a few rough-wood pagodas and tent-like structures, in addition to a well for the purifying ritual of hand-washing.

On the way, we met lots of the younger neighborhood kids and their fathers, all dressed similarly and forming quite a parade by the end of our walk.

Dai was proud to show me off. The children all oogled at me and ran around me, fascinated yet afraid—that is, until they found I could pull coins out of the air to put in their collection boxes. The festival was also a fund-raiser for youth activities at the community center.

I was asked to lead the procession, which would meander from the shrine into the neighborhoods of our community. My job was to haul the heavy, carved-wood drum-and-cymbal wagon. Three kids walked directly behind me, playing traditional rhythmic music by beating on the cart's huge drum and two cymbals. After a sweaty hour of providing the cart's locomotion uphill and down, I was replaced by one of the fathers and invited to beat the drum while the kids played the cymbals, then play the cymbals while the kids beat the drum.

In addition to the cart, there was another contraption in the parade: four of the fathers carried on their shoulders a palanquin-like platform supporting a miniature shrine. I'd originally been designated as one of the "pallbearers" for this platform, but my height tilted it out of alignment. The consensus was to give me the cart instead.

Everyone wore *hapi* coats, except Okāsan and the other mothers, who followed at a distance with cameras. The girls' coats had a flower pattern; the boys and I wore coats with an oblique, geometric design. Dressed in the same colorful festival clothes as their young sons, the fathers behaved giddily, like kids having a lot of fun.

Our parade cruised up and down all the streets, pausing in alleys and at shrines, schools, and hospitals. A mental hospital's residents, dressed in pajamas, crowded at barred windows to nod, wave, and clap. At every stop the four fathers gave their portable shrine a big spin, each holding an edge and jogging around in a circle.

Spectators dropped money into the children's coin boxes, with the children leaping after potential donors like squirrels after nuts. An elderly woman in a light purple kimono appeared from a tiny apartment, merrily holding up a coin. Four or five kids rushed at her, thrusting up their coin boxes to beg for the money and threatening to topple her.

After lunch, Ojisan, Mākun, Dai, Okāsan, Shika, Ojisan's two cute little daughters, and I piled into the Andos' van and drove about 15 miles out of Oita to a small, secluded, and crowded beach. Oita's harbor was too polluted to use the beaches that were closer in. I changed into my swimsuit in the back of the van, while Ojisan marched to the beach with an umbrella to plant in the sand.

The beach was pleasant, except for a five-foot-wide tidewash made of shells, sticks, rubbish, and stones. Ojisan had chosen the exact middle of this strip for the umbrella. Everyone else started setting down the cooler and blankets. When I pointed out the debris, he tapped his head and said, "Boy Sukauto," before shifting the umbrella to a better spot.

Mākun and I played underwater tag, then frisbee with the Aerobie I'd given him. An Aerobie flies far and doesn't float. This made our game livelier because the Aerobie disappeared below the surface if we failed to catch it.

Freighters, tankers, and fishing boats passed along the coast, so close I could have swum to them. I spotted a starfish and some small fish. Whenever I found something slimy floating on the water—a piece of trash or seaweed or flotsam—I showed it to Ojisan and said "Oishī!" (delicious), a casual poke at the foods he likes to eat.

Ojisan liked nothing better than to feed me some Japanese specialty, like roe or raw meat or sea urchin, to see my reaction. He always added, "Oishī, ne" (Isn't it delicious?).

Shika hadn't brought her swimsuit but jumped into the water anyway in her casual clothes. It was very hot, despite a stiff breeze.

Driving back, we listened to the Beatles, whose music both Ojisan and Otōsan enjoyed. We stopped for ice cream and octopus from a roadside vending truck that had been altered with wood to resemble a super-sized octopus. The octopus snack was a family favorite – spiced balls of meat inside steaming, moist, spicy dough – gobbled up as soon as it was served.

The road ran alongside extensive rice paddies. I was constantly reminded by the paddies of this country's reliance on rice. Watching the plants whizzing by in military columns, I asked Shika, "How does rice grow?" She thought for a while, then shrugged, translating my question for Okāsan, who also shook her head. I was laughing hard by then. These people live on rice and close to rice. Ojisan was laughing as hard as I was, his chuckling shaking him like hiccoughs. He didn't volunteer any answers, though.

Then one of Ojisan's daughters spoke up. Chika knew, and Shika translated: "Rice grows in clusters on stalks, like wheat. The grains' green husk is turned brown by the sun, and later the brownish exteriors are removed. The result: white rice."

Chika was all of six years old.

Week 3: July
Monday

Last night Okāsan gave Shika and me two 500-yen coins to buy something to eat at the school cafeteria because she wasn't going to prepare *obentō*s today.

Mondays were her holidays, and she did no work. Otōsan chuckled when Shika translated this for me. Today was Okāsan's time for herself. I asked her what she'd do. Last Monday Otōsan took her and her friends, and me too, to lunch. "I will rest today," she replied. As far as I knew, Otōsan didn't have any days off.

In English Readers class, I collected the homework I'd assigned the class. Only one student did it, which was a bit humbling.

Afterward, Mr. Tomita asked me to help the class read a lesson titled "How To Study for the English Exam." That was what classes are about at this time of year: studying for national exams. The schools have much to gain or lose: they're judged by their students' performance.

Kendo Kid had received a letter from his new American host family. They'd adopted a Vietnamese child, an "Amerasian." I explained that word to him. Unfortunately, Kendo Kid was caught red-handed reading his letter instead of following the lesson. "Ohhhhhh," went the class. Mr. Tomita didn't seem too upset at the transgression, though.

Kendo Kid's English was so good that he should have been in a more advanced class. Mister Sumo's English didn't extend beyond a few memorized phrases. He fidgeted in class, passed notes, played with his handkerchief, and made life miserable for the girls who sat near him.

"Steven," Mr. Tomita said to me later, "I teach three English courses. So far you have taught two of them, and I would like you to teach the third tomorrow." I felt honored. It meant he liked what I'd taught; my appearances hadn't been just a freak experiment or something he let me do out of politeness or a desire for novelty.

On the notebook that the girl in front of me used for

her English class notes was the slogan of its manufacturer, "Lets studious," written in English and illustrated with a merrily studying cartoon character. It reminded me of the Andos' vase of silk flowers made by "Living Decolations." Stores holding sales hang banners announcing "Summer Casual Last Off" and "Hyper Off" (meaning a Super Sale). This mangled language is called Japlish. From a festival vendor I saved a decorative paper plate called "Country Collection," made in Japan for Japanese. I liked what it said. (In English:) "Shall we go with me? Your relaxed place. One day I walked on the mountain path with feeling gentle breeze. Under the green hill I found a small lake surrounded by many flowers. On the water surface parents and children of bird enjoyed playing. What a wonderful place here is compared with my crowded town. This place is like heaven. This is my secret and relax place."

The paper plate's inspirational message recalled to me the times I'd spent alone in the Andos' traditional tatami-matted room, and I understood the special function – in crowded Japan, but also anywhere – of this quiet, empty space.

Somebody passed me a curious note in class: "CUL-TURE FESTIVAL. What is Japan remind?" I was baffled, but never found out who'd sent it.

School technically ended at 4, but regularly continued until 5 or later for one reason or another. Clean-up time seemed to have no set end, and many students hung around afterwards to work or socialize. If there was a special event, students were there until dinnertime – making school their one activity of the day.

"I study for the rest of the day," Kendo Kid told me when I asked him what he usually did after school. Other students had their hang-out groups, like Heavy Metal,

3-D, and their sidekicks, who frequented record stores. Some kids worked after school in their parents' small businesses. Ordinary jobs—non-necessary, non-family jobs— are sometimes prohibited by schools, which can regulate many aspects of students' extracurricular life, like curfews, hair-length, permissible shops, and sports.

Leaving school with Shika took quite a while because she had to wave and say good-bye—"Baibai" —to everyone she met. Shika was friends with everyone in the school, it seemed.

During the day today we were handed pages and booklets of material—homework for the summer holidays that started next week and lasted only three weeks. Some students would go to exam-preparation school during this time, too.

I wouldn't be attending exam-prep school, but Shika would, and those two weeks would be like regular schooldays for her.

On the way home, Shika talked about her college plans. "I have decided that I want to go to Jochi University, and my second choice is Meiji. Both universities are private and excellent. Meiji gave me a special chance to skip the usual exams and admission procedures. I have thought a lot about their offer, but finally I turned it down so I can take the exams for Jochi." Jochi was founded about a century ago by Western scholars, she said, and she liked this aspect of the school.

Tokyo University, a public university, is considered the best in Japan—or at least the hardest to get into. "Why aren't you considering Tokyo University?" I asked.

"I haven't taken all the right courses for Todai, as we call it—not enough science and math, among other things." She explained to me that a child had to get into the correct channels of schools and courses right from elementary school in order to have a chance at the top universities and jobs. This need to be admitted to the best schools provided the impetus for parents to push their children and for students of all ages to work themselves silly.

After dinner Otōsan asked what I might like to do for a special family trip. He added, "Do you want to see the atomic bomb at Hiroshima?"

The question startled me, but I managed to nod and act unfazed by this innocent reminder of our countries' awkward past association.

"Good," Otōsan said. "I want to see it, too."

Monday was the barbers' day off. The staff were like family to each other. The young women were a close group, as were the young men. They spent their free time with their group.

I didn't much notice the presence of Otōsan's staff. They got up earlier than I did and left. They took care not to impose in any way. They ate after we did. Next to the Andos' cars on the abbreviated driveway in front of the house there was a little shack where the barbers stored their bikes and moped.

Today I played ping pong against the three female employees. One had played in the ping-pong club in her high school and was highly skilled. Then I played Otōsan. Since he often beat the female employees, they merrily ganged up on him. Whenever I scored a point, I got cheers. Whenever Otōsan scored, no one cheered, so this chubby, bearded fellow cheered himself in the same high-pitched, spritely way the women had cheered me, prancing around in mock exultation. "Woooo! Wheeeee! Hurrah!"

He won, as usual, playing with a rare combination of Eastern and Western styles that I tried to emulate. Fast and hard like me, yet with plenty of spin and subtlety, almost delicately at times.

Otōsan soon left for the evening to catch up on work at one of his hotels.

To celebrate their day off, the female staff set off fireworks and invited Shika and me to join them. They introduced themselves by name to me for the first time; there'd been greetings and smiles at dinner time, but never introductions. They told me their ages: 16, 17, and 20. This surprised me. I'd expected them all to be over 20 because they looked older. I thought they were joking until Shika confirmed what they said.

"Why aren't they in school?" I asked. "Are they apprentices?" She said that by law only the ninth grade must be completed. Most students go on to high school, but some take up trades, like these girls.

When we left after an hour, they were still lighting fireworks.

At midnight Shika got a call from the police. A neighbor had complained, so she and I had to tell the employees to keep the noise down. They giggled, like children being caught with their hands in the cookie jar, and went to their rooms.

Before going to bed, we watched "USA Express." Last time the subject was "Prom." Tonight it was "Heavy Metal." The show took us to Long Island, L.A., and other places where punk rockers congregate. It was perhaps the only TV show that all four kids loved. They were spellbound. After the beginning of a dating-game show, I went to bed.

Game shows are among the most common TV programs. At least once a week I saw an American or two on a game show. The Americans always spoke Japanese fluently, and that annoyed me because I found the language impossibly difficult. I commented to myself, "Who are these people to shatter my misconception!" Americans who spoke Japanese well were a big hit and were all over the networks. They gave America a good name.

The most popular of these Americans hosted "USA Express." Teenagers, especially, liked him. A blue-eyed blond Mormon, he spoke Japanese better, Shika said, than she did. He was polite, knew all the Japanese jokes, and was clearly interested in the culture. He might talk about beaches in both countries, new fads, and what different classes of people do here and there. He had the kind of wholesome image that foreigners don't always associate with America.

Week 3: July
Tuesday
English Readers
Yesterday, in Mr. Tomita's class, I asked all "friends of Steven" to write a letter to Harvard University to "please admit Steven Wardell," and to make up their own reasons why.

"Steven, this is strange that you ask students for references," Mr. Tomita commented afterward with a whimsical smile. He told other teachers about my request, and when I walked into the teachers' lounge this morning I found them grinning at me from ear to ear.

Only three students gave me their letters today, though all had promised to. I wasn't surprised because only one student had done my assignment when I was their "teacher" — an even more respectable position than "friend." So I brought out a pad of paper of my own, and between periods handed a sheet to everyone who hadn't responded.

Physical Education
At kendo I made the mistake of grabbing the *boken* (bamboo practice sword) hard for the duration of the prac-

tice, and it hurt my fingers. For a long time afterward my hands still instinctively closed on an imaginary sword.

After the teacher taught me stances, holds, and the parts of the *boken*, we practiced attacking people's heads for the rest of the period. The teacher was skilled and commanding, but when his attention was elsewhere, the students fooled around, pretending to be samurai and laughing at each other.

World History

Mister Sumo stumbled in late to class, looking untidy as usual. Everyone let out reproachful cries of "Ehhhhh."

Bobby helped me understand the situation. "Boy too long lunch. Class telling sensei he with girlfriend or asleep." Mister Sumo had to stand there and accept the jibes he usually hands out. The smile gradually wore off his face. He looked relieved when the teacher let him collapse into his seat.

I didn't do well teaching Mr. Tomita's other class; I couldn't get anyone to ask questions. I felt I'd let them down. "I am sorry for their shyness," said Mr. Tomita, as if he were responsible.

Meanwhile, two other English teachers, Mr. Nakasone and Mr. Kanda, invited me to teach classes for them. In Mr. Nakasone's class I had to prod and coax the students half the time, but generally things went well.

Mr. Kanda's students were a rare pleasure to teach. As I approached the rostrum, I was greeted by a roar of giggles, exchanged comments, and hoots. I took charge with an "Ohayo gozaimasu" (Good Morning). But I'd gotten my salutations mixed up: it was now afternoon. Some laughed, some cheered. The ice was not only broken, it was smashed.

My homeroom students secretly passed around a card for Kendo Kid, who was leaving soon for his year in the U.S. I wrote on it, only partly in jest, "Dear Ken, I know you'll have fun and learn English, and when you come back no one will know you because you will be American." My classmates finally came through with their letters to Harvard just as we were about to leave for the day. I was deeply touched. Their letters looked similar, because the kids had been copying from each other. The handwriting, as always, was precise and attractive.

Here are a few excerpts:

"Dear Harvard University. Hello. I am a Japanese high school student. Steven is a good friend. He usually works hard. He seems to be interested in Japanese culture. He is almighty, as you can see." (This superlative was from Kendo Kid.)

"Dear Harvard. Steven speaks Japanese very well. He knows many things about Japan and he knows the knowledge of the world. He will be a Harvardian student. Please admit Steve." (Diana was more than generous in her praise for my dexterity with a Japanese phrase book.)

"Dear Harvard University, Steven was a very good boy in Japan. He is a clever and humor boy . . . By the way, July 4 he hoisted the Stars and Strips. It means his patriotism, doesn't it? Good-Bye." (This letter came from Bobby.)

"He can speak Japanese, to say nothing of English." (I still don't know where this concept of my language abilities originated.)

"He is not only hard working, but also motor nerve well. Especially he is good at swimming. There is something noble about him." (This one was Johnny's.)

"Steven is very serious and effort student. He is very good at do card tricks." (Thanks, Satoshi.)

I had to blink a few times to finish the letters.

After school, Shika and I headed to town to get my camera fixed and find a fax machine to send my columns to *The Ridgefield Press*. Curiously, we never did find a fax machine available to the public.

The commercial area of the city was fragmented, full of specialty stores. There were few supermarkets or discount stores, but instead a profusion of small shops that sold just one product, such as fish, vegetables, or curtains.

Because these shops were staffed to the brim with service people, many young women could find work there. Shika stopped frequently to say hello to old school friends behind the counters. The friends we saw today mostly graduated last year, Shika told me. She'd been in their class but had stayed back a year because of her Youth for Understanding exchange to Kansas. "These girls don't like their jobs," she added.

I thought to myself, "You need only look at them to realize this."

"They're all in low-level positions, clerks and helpers in shops or bow-ers at the fancier stores," she said. "There's nowhere they can go, no place up for them. There's only marriage."

While the girls in my homeroom were happy and studious and very much a part of the class, these shop-assistants did indeed seem lonely and sad.

"What are your plans for after college, Shika?" I asked. "What do you want to be?"

Without hesitation she replied, "I want to work for a big company with international connections."

"You're ambitious," I remarked.

"I am," she continued. "I want to work in America or Europe, where I can be valued for speaking English as well as Japanese. Perhaps an American company would be the best."

Week 3: July
Wednesday
Today's highlight for me was Required Club.
As I exited from one of my visits to Mr. Tomita, the young English Grammar teacher, Miss Hamazaki, and some girls from my class were waiting for me. "Stibu, would you like to join us at the Tea Ceremony Club?" Actually, this was an event I'd been looking forward to.

The tea ceremony room in the crafts area of the building was furnished with *shōji*, a niche for a shrine, and tatami, including a special tatami mat with a hole in it, where you lit charcoal to boil the iron teapot.

A complete tea ceremony takes nearly two hours, and the club met three times a week to practice parts of it. We sat in perfectly straight lines and, after the first half-hour of the ceremony, were served some super-sweet cakes.

Miss Hamazaki explained: "*Ocha*, the traditional thick green tea, is bitter, so you eat something sweet beforehand, to balance your senses. Drinking tea is not the point of the ceremony: it is to practice and appreciate the beauty of the process. A premium is placed on simplicity, grace, cleanliness, and naturalness. Sometimes the ceremony is performed without the tea."

Throughout the ceremony, the school jazz band could be heard rehearsing in the background. Talk about clash of cultures!

The girls giggled at their mistakes. A hand movement out of place was a serious error. A twitch was reprimandable. A giggle? Well, let's just say that giggles fed on themselves and were so universal as to need a blanket pardon. Even the teacher, whom the girls looked to for a nod each time they made a movement, laughed at the mistakes all the way through.

The tea ceremony is a precise art, and proficiency comes only after about three years. The girls meticulously measured their movements and their placement of the implements by means of the reeds in the tatami flooring. After witnessing their condensed ceremony and drinking some tea, I was allowed to make tea myself.

They had me mimic each step. While they almost never corrected me, I felt clumsy and ill at ease. The sleek, simple ladle became an earthmover in my hand. My tea wasn't as hot or frothy as theirs, but at least I did make tea in an official tea ceremony, and I was pleased at the accomplishment.

Week 3: July
Thursday

This morning a student handed me some pages of calligraphy, a gift sent to me by the school's calligraphy teacher, whom I'd never met. I asked him to thank the teacher for me. Because this was my last day, I wouldn't have a chance to see her personally.

In homeroom, we performed a major clean-up before the holidays. While some students washed the windows, others mopped the floors and cleaned the walls. The loudspeaker broadcast Tchaikovsky. Out the window I watched students grooming the plants and bushes in the courtyard below.

I was mopping the hall when I encountered Johnny. He wasn't working, so I asked, "Are you on holiday already?"

"No!" He began grabbing girls as they passed, and asking me, "Shi isu kyuto garu (she is cute girl), true or false?" He let out a silly staccato laugh.

"True," I said each time. Julie, the girl he'd just grabbed, giggled, put her hands over her face, then rapped Johnny on his crewcut to show her disapproval.

Afterwards, I read a *Japan Times* scavenged from the teachers' lounge. My faithful guide Bobby interrupted to show me a packet of Kairo hand-warmers. "We use in winter," he said. "This is very warm. We carry in pockets." I wondered why he brought up the subject of camping-style handwarmers now, when the temperature was constantly over 90 degrees.

Okāsan once told me that she, and most Japanese, can't sleep unless they have something over their chest and abdomen. "Without something on the chest, you catch cold," she told me, with Shika translating. "Some people put a bath towel cross-wise over the chest to absorb perspiration, even on the hottest nights."

Now Bobby wanted to tell me that there's a superstition that children who bare their navels are robbed of them. I asked, "Who steals the navels?"

With a straight face, he answered, "The horribles. Children must not sleep with baring their abdomens not to catch colds," he explained, continuing his chatty, if curious, commentary on Japanese bodily customs. I appreciated his enthusiasm for adding what he must have considered some finishing touches to my knowledge of life in Japan.

Home Room

Back in class Mister Sumo played the fool with his sunglasses and multi-purpose handkerchief, then chased the boys who called him names until they apologized. Donning someone's swimming flippers, he unbuttoned his shirt and goose-stepped around the room.

The rest of us re-arranged the desks to make an oval amphitheater. Kendo Kid and I sat at the head table with Johnny.

Soda and snacks were provided by the cheerful Mrs. Suzuki. The snacks were mostly potato chips and candies, but the girls in charge of distributing the food made sure I got a sampling of some traditional sweets, like fried dough and sweet bean paste. They hastily shooed Mister Sumo away from these goodies, as though they'd be wasted on him.

Mrs. Suzuki sat among us. No one was eating or drinking yet, although they'd all been served some soda. They were waiting a signal. As usual, I didn't know what it was. It turned out to be Mr. Tomita. When he entered, we popped open the drinks, "Kampai!"

Official farewell remarks were now in order. My classmates passed the duty like a hot potato, eager for the attention to move on to someone else. Each addressed Kendo Kid and me together, since we'd both be leaving for America soon.

"I hope you are good luck," said Julie.

"Please not forget me," said Bobby earnestly.

"See you again," said Mister Sumo, slicking back his buzz.

"Come back to Japan," said Diana with an emphatic bob of the head.

"I want you success in the university," said Johnny.

3-D threw in a special farewell for me: "I like your blue eyes. I hope you succeed."

Johnny presented me with an attractive gilt-edged, white-cardboard plaque that displayed the signatures of the class members. Kendo Kid got one too. The kids had added greetings above their signatures:

> Don't forget us, please.
> All must again.
> "Where there is a will, there is a way." See you again.
> It was fun to talk with you. Especially American movie stars.
> I never forget you.
> You must speak Japanese in Japan. I wanted to speak more and more.
> Life will never be the same as it was again.

I want to your good friend. Please remember life of this class.
I am sure you will be writer or doctor. I never forget you. Good friend forever. See you again.

Teacher Tomita began a speech about me to the class. It was going to be flattering, I could tell; I told myself that with luck I'd be the only one who understood the English.

Because he'd been like a father to me as well as a teacher, from the first day, I acknowledged his opening remarks by bowing and addressing him as "Otōsan," Great-Male-Honorable. This caused such a hush in the room that I thought for a moment I'd made a big mistake. But Mr. Tomita seemed pleased.

He said he'd become more sophisticated since meeting me, that I'd brought with me qualities money can't buy. He listed the qualities, but I was so embarrassed and emotion-filled by this time that I barely heard them. He concluded, "I hope that someday Steven will come back to us in an official position, as ambassador or maybe president."

I addressed my own farewell speech to the class. I didn't try to use Japanese this time, but proceeded to thank everyone and be seated as expeditiously as possible so I could get past my mixed emotions of pleasure and sadness and let everyone get on with the party. On the board I wrote, "Class, you are very kind."

Week 3: July
Friday
Mākun so enjoyed a *hora* show he watched on TV last night that this morning he invited Otōsan to watch the videotape he'd made of it, then later he watched most of it again. That's three times!

Today we were off to a camp in the highlands of central Kyushu for Youth-for-Understanding's event-of-the-summer. Ojisan drove Shika and me to the camp, with Mākun and Dai coming along for the three-hour round-trip. Ojisan chose the challenge of the backroads, though it would have been shorter if we'd taken a highway, and shorter still by train.

The camp's first event was a reception to greet our fellow YFU exchange students staying in Kyushu and Okinawa and their hosts. The Aussie contingent seemed most at ease because, unlike the Americans, they were spending an entire year in Japan.

Social life for an exchange student is easy, because the Japanese are such good hosts. They *want* to be friends, and they do everything possible to make you feel welcome. Therefore I was surprised when I heard some Americans laughing in a superior, petulant tone. For the first time I heard complaints.

"Couldn't even speak English good . . ."

"The teacher criticized the students so harshly; I'm glad I'm not Japanese . . ."

"Rice, rice, rice."

"We all live in one room on the 13th floor. You have to take the elevator down to burp . . ."

I love these differences, but suddenly sensitive to peer-pressure, I didn't speak up. I was conscious again of my luck in having the Andos as my hosts.

Then we saw our accommodations: eight people on bunk beds in a room the size of a college-dorm single, each bunk equipped with a tatami mat and a cupboard at the foot of it for clothes and backpack. I unpacked all my things, fitting them neatly in the cupboard. We had plenty of time, so I made a thorough job of it.

Then I discovered that, with the cupboard now full, my bed was too short. The solution was to remove and repack my clothes in my backpack so I could stretch my legs into the cupboard.

Several of us played cards. Four of the exchangers said they didn't like Japanese food at all. While I did enjoy Japanese cuisine, I must admit I didn't like the food at the camp so far. "Eat lots of rice," they'd said during the opening announcements. We grumbled about tonight's tofu, weak tea, broth, excessive amounts of soy sauce, tasteless boiled cabbage and onions, raw eggs, and plain rice.

The next day, when we *gaijin* met again downstairs, we found we shared many observations:

- When the Japanese seem to be waving you away, they really mean "Come here," but to *gaijin* it looks like "Go away."
- The Japanese nod when you talk to them in English, but these are blank nods—they don't necessarily agree or understand.
- All *gaijin* get stared at and are the center of attention.
- The word "international" is so overused and misapplied as to have become meaningless.
- Ads attempt to put a "foreign" and "Western" aura on domestic products.
- Commercials can be so simplistic as to be mentally painful if you actually pay attention to them.
- The Japanese like to ask your age, height, blood type, and star sign. It matters.
- Japanese kids seem young, in behavior, for their age. Refreshingly so.
- Japanese teens are more polite and less cynical than our peers.
- The students don't study as hard as we've heard.
- Our English has deteriorated. This is partly because the Japanese understand our deteriorated English better than if we spoke correctly, and partly because we are constantly exposed to Japlish.
- The Japanese like overly cheerful music.
- The night life is pretty wild and intense. (Clearly, some

kids had been given a freer nocturnal roam by their host families than I had.)
- Japanese kids work together, and there is less social friction than we'd expected, much less than in America.
- Japanese international news focuses on America — enough to put it in a class by itself. That is, there are three categories of news: domestic, foreign, and American.
- Felix the Cat appears on many consumer goods, like chopsticks, pens, pencil boxes, t-shirts, keychains, and sunglasses. We can see no point to this.
- The Japanese appreciate many American institutions — for example, Disneyland, cowboys, NASA, and the Statue of Liberty — just as much as we do, and in some cases even more because they don't take them for granted.

We ate an unappetizing breakfast of a rice, hard-boiled eggs, and iced wheat tea before we divided into groups for an orienteering contest.

After a visit to the camp's tiny planetarium and observatory and some craft work with "Shrinky Dink," we broke up for pleasant, communal, single-sex baths and a dinner of curry on rice with weak tea.

The evening's candlelight service celebrated "friendship among different peoples." Three students in the center of our circle represented the Japanese, Aussies, and Yanks. Their candles were lit first, and they spread the flame to the other 200 of us as we sang Japanese and English songs about peace.

A Western-style dance followed, with the usual American pop music. The dance was stilted, and almost no one danced because we didn't know each other well enough. When it broke up, my friends and I rounded up a posse of a dozen eager hands and played cards in my room until late.

Poker was the game of choice, and we bet in yen. We called them "dollars" to sound important: 20 yen, about 12 cents, became "20 Big Ones." The night's grand winner was a Japanese boy who spoke almost no English and was playing for the first time.

Week 4: July
Sunday
I slept through the usual all-camp meeting by the flag-pole, but no one noticed.

Our couple of days here had been full of hiking, group games, and lecture-discussions about our experiences in Japan. During the final tidy-up, we separated our room's trash into glass, metal, burnables, and non-burnables to take to the camp's recycling depot.

At our volleyball game, some Japanese little-league kids who were sharing the camp sought our autographs in special little books, alongside their favorite Japanese base-ball players' signatures.

At the closing meeting, the teenage Japanese leader of my team was called to the front to receive our orienteering prize, an attractive hand-made pottery bowl. "I rode my bike many miles to get here," he later told me, "and now I have to ride back. I can't carry this bowl on the bike, so I want you to take it, Steve."

I tried to give it back to him, but he said, "No, it is in exchange for the happiness you've given me in teaching me magic tricks."

The bus from the camp to the train station had two employees on board, the male driver and a young woman about the same age as Shika. Dressed in a neat uniform with white gloves, the woman bowed us on and off. She stood behind the driver and stared at the wall of the bus the entire ride. None of us wanted or needed someone to bow. "What a job. I feel sorry for her," I heard an American boy say. She may have heard him and understood.

The camp had been a refreshing break—as it was meant to be—from the sometimes solitary life of an exchanger. One boy, I learned, had wound up in a rice paddy with a lonely grandmother who spoke no English. He had to bike to a telephone. Another had arrived at the time of a family emergency and needed to fend for himself for a while.

High up on the mountain it was cool and sunny all the time, and comfortable, unlike the city. And it was good, I had to admit, to speak English with fellow *gaijin*. We were no longer Americans and Australians, simply *gaijin*.

Matchmaker

Week 4: July

Monday

"Tell me," I asked Shika, "how do you say 'Happy birthday, Obāsan'?"

Today was her grandmother's birthday, and Dai and I were about to take her gifts and wish her a happy birthday. I was going to give her some New Zealand kiwi-fruit jam that I'd brought from the U.S.

Shika frowned at my question, which puzzled me, since I was sure she knew the answer. She explained: "Wait a minute. I want to get the wording correct. I mean, for maximum courtesy."

She went to ask her mother, then came back and recited the best wording for me. The sentence immediately slipped my mind, and I repeated back a hopeless mess. She wrote it down.

I felt a tugging and found Dai beside me, pointing forward. We were late. In my hurry I left Shika's paper behind and promptly forgot the words again. As we walked up the hill, Dai insisted on rehearsing the birthday greeting. When I recited what I remembered, he squawked and reprimanded me with a hurt look as if his trained monkey had started forgetting its tricks. So I set myself to relearn the words from Dai, and we practiced them a few times before we entered the grandparents' house.

Eight or nine cars lined the edge of the road by the house, so I thought Obāsan must be having a birthday party. The cars, it turned out, belonged to friends visiting the grandfather. The grandmother spent her day cleaning the house and looking in on her husband and his friends, who'd turned the upper floor into a workshop for making Noh masks.

Dai and I skipped around this group to join Obāsan in the kitchen, where I blurted out an impressive "Happy Birthday" in the most respectful Japanese.

She and Dai had great trouble understanding what the fruit in the jam was. When I drew a rough map of New Zealand, she thought it was a map of Japan. Finally she connected "kiwi" to the fruit. I explained that my Dad was from New Zealand, and thus was a Kiwi, too. She came to the conclusion that my Dad had made the jam in New Zealand.

She served wheat tea to us in delicate, thimble-sized cups. I sang "Happy Birthday" in English. Dai knew the words and sang along, and his grandmother knew how to hum it. When Dai and I applauded her, she gave us a broad smile, a big bow, and a long thank-you.

In the tea-ceremony and dining rooms, ten serious men were painting, crafting, and chipping away at wooden masks. They wore craftsman shirts, or gi, of blue or dull-yellow with sleeves sewn on loosely to let air in at the seams.

Each "station" was equipped with special tools for the different stages of mask-making, and the grandfather moved among them, consulting with his friends about their works-in-progress. They listened to him closely.

Obāsan carried in a tray of snacks for Dai and me, and picture books of Noh masks for me to look at. There seemed to be two schools of thought about how to make the masks: overly-simple or very gaudy. The grandfather was making the simple ones. He and his friends were teaching themselves how to create Noh masks by examining the works of ancient masters.

There are many Noh characters, including devils, heroes, gods, samurai, geisha, and slaves. Each has a myriad of expressions, and each expression can be modified, a slight twist on the classic portrayals, in order to fill a special role for the character. The masks are supposed to convey every emotion, even the most subtle.

As they worked, the old men listened to baseball on the radio.

Obāsan continually refilled my tea cup as soon as it was empty, and the grandfather showed me each step in making a mask. He wanted me to appreciate the time and care the masks represent. Something about the atmosphere today, like the previous time I was here, made me feel humble. While I was trying to behave perfectly, Dai was hopping around for attention, playing with all the art treasures on the walls and making faces at the serious men, who didn't look up from their work. "Frog!" said Dai, pointing to himself.

"Fish!" I mimed back at him, because I liked to swim.

Gradually the craftsmen departed, one by one, each paying homage to the grandfather, the guru on the dais.

After all the visitors had gone, we entered his real workshop, a tiny tin shack built off the side of the house, with a massive air-conditioner, bright lights, and no windows. He kept many sharp tools there, and used band-aids littered the floor. He was re-painting a mask he'd sanded after its most recent painting. The sanding had caused nicks in the previous layer, and he spent about an hour listening to baseball, the Noh mask right in front of his nose, giving each nick a delicate dab of paint.

As I left the workshop for home, I saw his wood blocks and masks in various stages of completion. I pointed to them and said, "Isogashī" (busy). He nodded and smiled. "I appreciate your work," I said, and knew he understood my sign language. As I left, Obāsan handed me a thank-you note she'd already written for my gift of the unusual jam.

When I got back I found I'd left my camera behind, and Obāsan called to tell Shika that she'd drop it off later. "Steve," Shika called to me, "Grandmother wants to know if you'd like to go to a baseball game tomorrow. Grandfather said he'd like to take you with him because he liked meeting you." I was all for going, but Shika covered the phone and whispered, "I have to tell you that going to a high-school baseball game means sitting in the bleachers and watching from 9 a.m. until evening." So Shika declined for me and conveyed my thanks for the invitation.

At dinner I felt so good and so much a part of my Japanese family that I slurped my soup for all to hear and ate two refills on rice. Okāsan was pleased that I was eating lots of rice.

Proudly using my chopsticks with greater dexterity than ever, I picked every rice grain from my bowl, as I'd often seen Okāsan take care to do. When my bowl was clean, I lifted it to compare it to hers. She gasped and began to pick further at her own, saying, "Stibu very Japanese."

Afterward Ojisan and Otōsan played ping pong. I could beat nearly everyone in the family at ping pong except them. "Who is better?" I asked them.

"Same," responded Ojisan, grasping my meaning.

Almost simultaneously Otōsan said, "It is the same, donchyu?" I'd expected each to say that the other was better.

Otōsan and Ojisan seldom played a match but enjoyed

volleying. They didn't want to compete because they didn't wish to find out who was best. They had such a strong friendship that neither wanted to show up the other by winning. They played so fast that I couldn't tell who actually was better. They probably knew but didn't say.

While they were playing, dizzyingly fast, they started using English interjections: "Ouch." "Wow." "Whee." "Go for it!" "Oh boy!" Both got a big kick out of this. They chuckled so much that more mistakes occurred, which led to more English.

"How did Otōsan and Ojisan become such good friends?" I asked Shika.

"You know," she said with surprise and paused, "I don't know."

She asked Ojisan, who immediately broke into a grin. He clasped his hands and began talking rapidly in Japanese while Otōsan beamed and nodded.

"It started many years ago," Shika translated, "when Ojisan designed and built Otōsan's building in the middle of town. In return, Otōsan was matchmaker for Ojisan and his wife."

It was becoming clear to me how different the two men were, and how they complemented each other—Otōsan the hefty "Westerner" and leader, and Ojisan the diminutive and reserved traditionalist and craftsman. In his outlook and actions Otōsan seemed to belong more to his children's generation than to that of his peers, I mused. The contrast was even sharper between Otōsan and his parents—in particular his father, the Noh-mask maker.

In telling me the family's story, Shika had previously mentioned that her grandfather didn't approve of the risks Otōsan had taken when he parlayed his one inherited barber shop into his present business empire. Shika felt that it probably was too much of a foreign way of life for the old gentleman, who focused on the past as he crafted his masks, even though his ears might be tuned to a ballgame.

That same evening Shika revealed something about herself that didn't come as a complete surprise either, though I hadn't thought of it in the way she put it.

We were by ourselves in the Japanese room, the only room in the house that had an air conditioner. We'd gone there to cool off. She looked lost in thought.

After a few moments she said, "I love my family, I love my mother—we all have great fun together." Then, after a pause: "I don't want to have the kind of life my mother has. I want to work and use my skills and be out in the world. I'm—what do you call it? It slips my mind. You know, what women are—it's not the word 'activist'."

I said the first word that came to mind. "You mean 'feminist'?"

"Yes. A feminist. My father, he's so American in style, but my mother is in the kitchen. I'm thinking more and more of the United States, that that's where my future may be. I wish I saw more hope for women in Japan."

Wink was coming to Oita! Mākun invited me to attend their forthcoming concert, and I accepted. He'd taped them whenever they'd appeared on TV, and today we watched one of his tapes. The duo was cute but not one of my favorites. Like most Japanese groups, they didn't move their bodies much. Instead, the girls usually stared blankly at the screen, without a smile, and recited their song. That made them a crowd pleaser here, though.

There's a pop-chart countdown on TV every day. American music is always among the Top 10, but seldom first. On this countdown show, which invites Japanese groups that make it onto the chart to perform, the lyrics are also televised as subtitles so the TV audience can memorize them.

The #4 hit, a Japanese song with a good, all-male Japanese dancing group, was shown with English subtitles, but the translation made no sense. "Put a good shape front" and "Want to happy!" were among the fragments. But why were they translating the song at all?

Another song, today's #1 hit, featured a live act involving a crew of young Japanese boys in snazzy, sequined clothes performing an elaborate roller-skating routine in front of a huge American flag.

Tonight we also watched the country's most popular soap opera, about a Japanese military officer and his lover during World War II. It was full of men making sacrifices for their country and doing manly things in the face of overwhelming odds, while the women, pretty and emotional, clung to their soldiers. Shika knew all the American soaps from her stay in Kansas, and she judged this one better than those.

I was practicing "Watashino Nihongo moto warui desu" (My Japanese is very bad) out loud to myself, when Mākun poked his head over my shoulder to add, in serious tones, "Very yes."

A few days before, as I was leaving the house, Otōsan asked me to tidy up my room, and Mākun overheard. Otōsan had said it in a kindly way, but it was a well-deserved rebuke: my stuff had been spread all over the floor. Since then, Mākun has told me to clean up the room—"Kuriin za ruum!" —with annoying frequency, even though the room was in the best shape it's been since I got here.

Strangely, that behavior—and his criticism now of my Japanese—only made me aware of a change that had occurred in him. At first he was shy, eyeing me warily from the top of the bunk and repeating, "Sankyu for your letter." Now he could be assertive, even zany. And we enjoyed doing things together.

Like brothers.

"Who?" Makun demanded that night, from the top bunk.

"I don't know," I said, looking up at him. It was late, and I wanted to get to sleep.

"Don't know? Don't know? *Know*—you know!"

"I don't."

Makun was trying to get me to tell him which of the two Wink girls I liked more. (Because I said I'd go to their concert, he assumed I liked them.) Not only did I not know, but I couldn't even remember their names. So I simply referred to them as *Hidari* and *Migi*, "Left" and "Right," the way they always stood during concerts and photo sessions.

"Yes. You know!" he bobbed his head insistently.

I stared at him, then decided to turn the question around. "How about you? You. Wink—you!" I often lapsed into a combination of sign language and shorthand. "Which? *Hidari*? *Migi*?"

He looked flustered. I kept prodding him, and he finally admitted he liked both—hardly a surprise since he had a huge poster of them on his wall.

"But which *best—Hidari*? *Migi*?" I insisted.

"Oh," he shrugged, adding tentatively "*Migi*."

I agreed with him, but only so I could finally get to sleep.

Week 4: July
Tuesday

In the late afternoon, Ojisan, Shika, and I went bowling. Entering the alley we walked through a video-arcade full of race-car-driver and spaceship-pilot machines. We signed up for two games and rented shoes.

The alley itself was a high-tech blow-out. Two TV monitors overhead played American heavy-metal videos – male singers wearing women's underwear and studded leather. Two TV monitors in front of us showed our tally on touch-screens that switched, as we played, to video images of each ball's success at toppling pins.

The attendant, a punk-rocker, bobbed his shaved head to the music. Shika had registered herself as "Louise," her English-name in Kansas. The attendant typed her name onto our video scoreboard as "Rouise."

Shika and I tried to make Ojisan laugh and mess up whenever it was his turn, but he nevertheless ended up with the best score. I came in third each time.

Japan drives on the left for a reason that goes back to the days when samurai roamed the island. They wore their long swords on the left hip, so they could draw them with their right hands. The bulky swords would catch or knock together if two samurai passed each other on the right. If they strode past each other with their swords on their mutual outsides, they didn't have a problem. Or so I was told.

On the way back from bowling I was astonished to see a *left*-hand-drive (American-style) Jaguar. Now Jaguars are manufactured as right-hand-drive (British style) cars, and Japan too is supposed to have right-hand-drive cars. So a left-hand-drive Jaguar must have been made for America or continental Europe, and shipped from there to Japan. It must have double the cachet!

We stopped at Ojisan's town office, a mobile home with a rice paddy on one side and a tall apartment building on the other. The neighborhood's rice paddies were slowly being drained and built on. Inside was heavy air-conditioning and a big desk for his architectural drawings.

After dropping Shika at Ojisan's house to study, he took me to see the famous "Monkey Mountain," where wild monkeys lived and where we'd get spectacular views of the city.

We turned onto a rough mountain road, less than one car wide, with the hairpin turns and chills of a roller-coaster ride. Jade-green bushes clutched raspingly at the car. At one turn, some branches reached in Ojisan's open window and tore off his sunglasses, tossing them onto the road. We retrieved then, then stopped again to look down at the sprawling city creeping its way across paddies and up hillsides. Ojisan pointed proudly at one area, "Mai hausu" (My house).

We never saw any monkeys but we did look down a beautiful, white cliff face, its vines and gnarled trees reaching perilously over the edge for light. The cliff dropped into a deep, waterless gorge, with frothy, shimmering green jungle on all sides. Stopping on our return trip at an ancient Shinto shrine, a large castle-like building, we each bought a fortune—a wrapped piece of calligraphy paper—but didn't open them yet.

Before we left the shrine, we visited a three-tiered stone pagoda about my height. As Ojisan directed, I took a stone from the ground to place on the first tier. Next I moved another stone from the first tier to the second, and balanced one from the second on the third, a small pinnacle. Ojisan didn't know the English to explain the purpose of the tradition to me, so I simply contemplated with awe the fact that people have been performing that small rite here for hundreds of years.

Just outside the shrine a refrigerator and smashed vending machine lay in shared desolation by the side of the road. The dumping of heavy appliances is common because disposal is expensive.

A reservoir stocked with fish made Ojisan hungry, so at the next village he bought us each a cold baby squid-on-a-stick from a vending machine and two bottles of "FIBE-MINI, Daily Fiber Drink."

Back at Ojisan's, we rejoined Shika for dinner, but not before I got a tour of the house, which Shika, too, was eager to see for the first time.

Ojisan's house was a beautiful, blond-wood house in a purely Japanese, pagoda-roof tradition. Stunted trees and bushes surrounded a garden and pond. Stepping stones led up to the house, down to a river behind, and over to an ancient temple across the street.

Inside were traditional lacquered wood floors, tatami mats, and *shōji* walls. The main room served as dining and living room and displayed on one wall a Shinto shrine, its black lacquered wood dazzlingly decorated with gold, frills, and lace.

Ojisan eagerly watched me admire his house. Shika translated for him: "Stibu, if you ever build a home, please contact me, and I will design you a traditional Japanese room for it."

I made the mistake of looking interestedly at a conical peasant hat made of fine, woven strips of cedar. Ojisan promptly took it down from the wall where it was displayed and gave it to me.

His wife had prepared a totally Japanese meal, and we ate in one of their many Japanese-style rooms. The room was decorated in creamy tones—ivory *shōji*, wheat-colored tatami, and unvarnished pine wood. Most of this house was in the old style, whereas the Andos had only one traditional room in an otherwise modern house. It was hard to believe Ojisan had designed both.

As dinner began, Ojisan excitedly opened his fortune

from the shrine. "Mi richi!" (Me rich!), he exclaimed. Mine turned out to be a good fortune, if not the best: I would get over my hay-fever.

During dinner Ojisan called to his wife through the paper walls to fix this, or refill that, or bring the next course. She scurried to fill his requests, cooked, and cleared off the table, but didn't sit down to eat with us or even set herself a place at the table.

"How special and delicious this food is!" Shika complimented both of them.

Ojisan's parents ate in a different room, after we'd finished. His wife served them, too, before cleaning up the kitchen and eating her own meal. It took her well into the night.

Ojisan's home, his sense of humor, his food, and his manner were Japanese and traditional. Otōsan, in contrast, not only considered himself very Western but tried to speak English whenever he could, even to his own family. Ojisan ate with his daughters, while his wife and the grandparents ate separately. At the Andos' everyone waited for Okāsan to finish cooking so she could eat with us.

I was grateful to have the opportunity to observe these two best, and contrasting, friends.

Ojisan sat back from his meal and sighed with content. I thanked him for showing me the mountain and shrine. "You are a good boy, but too skinny," he told me through Shika.

"I'll fix that," I told him. "I'll see if I can work out in the Harvard gym." The remark pleased him.

Ojisan gave me a present after dinner, a polo shirt. When he dropped us back at the Andos', I gave him my flamboyant Hawaiian shirt, a gift from Dad many years ago. It had a wide collar and bright oranges, greens, and yellows.

It fit Ojisan well. He liked it because it was loud. "The new Ojisan!" I announced, adding that I knew he'd make many friends because of it. Clasping it to his chest so he could see how it looked, he threw back his head and roared.

Week 4: July
Wednesday
Minori, Mākun, and I stayed up until 1 this morning to watch a beauty contest. She was doing work in front of the TV, but he was watching raptly. It was a pretty exploitative beauty-contest—just bathing suits. Even though I already knew the answer, I kept asking Minori what the show was: "Nan desu ka?" She grew more embarrassed, and said at first that she didn't understand, then that she didn't know.

My parents called this morning for the first time since my arrival. They liked my postcard but were annoyed with me for not sending my columns to *The Ridgefield Press* yet. They read me my SAT scores. I was so happy that I dropped the phone and hugged Okāsan and Otōsan.

I passed the phone around. I was surprised to hear Mr. Ando say, "My house is very big." But he was modest in his own way. When I held the phone again, I confirmed that the house was indeed "huge." In the background I heard him say, "No, no."

Because I did well in my exams, Otōsan started introducing me to his friends as though I were already a Harvard student. I hoped I wouldn't disappoint him.

I helped Minori sweep every time I saw her cleaning the driveway. Today Okāsan asked me to pick a chore for myself. When I said I'd continue to sweep, everyone was pleased, especially Minori, whom I replaced. She clapped her hands and thanked me.

With Mākun I made the rounds of the house and yard to learn about collecting the trash, separating it into bags of glass, metal, burnables, and non-burnables. There was no trash pick-up; the Andos carried their sorted trash to the neighborhood collection center a block away. This wasn't a heavy job because, for a big family, they created little trash.

Week 4: July
Thursday

Because I woke up yesterday around 11:30, Okāsan announced a new rule. I must eat by 8 with everyone else. After that, I could go back to sleep—except for today.

After breakfast, Okāsan took me and Mākun by taxi to the city newspaper offices. Through YFU they'd known about my part-time job as reporter for my town newspaper, and they'd thoughtfully arranged a special tour of theirs.

The Oita newspaper is thin because many people read the larger, big-city papers, but it nevertheless rates two daily editions.

An employee who spoke English diagrammed for me how the newspaper was put together, the steps in producing a story, and the actual printing. The evening edition had just gone to bed, so we found the reporters watching the Oita High School Baseball Championship on Oita TV. All activity in the cavernous, partitionless newsroom had stopped; they were entranced. From the TV emanated the words to the fans' enthusiastic cheer, "Who's the leader of the pack that's made for you and me? M-I-C-K-E-Y—M-O-U-S-E."

I had often wondered how the kanji were printed, and I found out today. Instead of having 2000 or so keys, one for each character, each of their typewriter keys has 12 related characters on it. You hit one of these keys, but you must also simultaneously hit a number from a 12-number pad, to select your specific character from among the 12 — a slow and highly skilled process.

The typesetters weren't watching baseball with everyone else, but were working intently. Because their computers weren't connected with the reporters', they had to re-key all the news — click, click, click all day. Their kanji keyboards were hooked up to machines that spat out ribbons of punched paper, like a really old American computer. The paper was then fed into a laser printer.

The layout was done by six big IBMs with joysticks and large monitors, then printing presses whipped the editions out to the waiting trucks.

As we left after many thank-yous, it began to rain hard. "Taifun," said our newspaper host.

"Taifun, yes," agreed Okāsan. Well, at least I wouldn't have to sweep the walkway today.

Okāsan, Mākun, and I dashed down the street to an Italian restaurant. The waitresses didn't look as though they appreciated the overdone atmosphere of painted grapevines and loud opera music. My fish and steak covered with spaghetti sauce was tasty.

Mākun cut his meal with his knife, omitting any use of a fork. Next, holding his knife in one hand and fork in the other, he picked up a piece of veal as if with tweezers and managed to get knife, fork, and veal all into his mouth at the same time. A modified version of chopsticks.

Okāsan had better Western table manners than I did. She said she'd learned "American manners" in school. She learned English in school, too, and though it had become rusty, it had improved considerably since my arrival. If only my Japanese would improve . . .

An attractive young woman in a crisp uniform bowed us into Tokiwa, the most elaborate department store I've ever seen, and one of the few places I found that took credit cards. It was like a Macy's, A&P, and antique store all in one. Its service was perfect, and the prices were sky-high. It's so high-class, I was told, that people save its paper bags so they can walk around carrying them or put other stores' goods in them. As a result, Tokiwa changes its bag every few weeks in an effort to keep people coming.

Other doll-like young women stood by the escalators on each floor, bowing and reciting a long list of the floor's contents. At each escalator stop, competing with the bow-er for the customers' attention, was a TV screen suspended from the ceiling and broadcasting baseball. When people spotted the game, they'd get off at that floor and stand watching in total absorption.

Okāsan wanted to show me the kimono section: 180,000 yen (about $1,600) for a patterned silk fabric. Then 398,000 yen, 580,000 yen, 680,000 yen for varying degrees of radiance and abstract pattern. You can pay 980,000 yen ($8,500) for a hand-made patchwork kimono by a famous artist.

She gazed at them in awe and envy. She was sensible, though. Her feet carried her past the displays, though her eyes lingered. She didn't really *want* them if it meant paying so much, but for a moment she was caught up in their glorious tradition and beauty.

In the pet department there were four customers, including the three of us, plus four staff who just stood there. Tokiwa sold mice, hamsters, and lots of large bugs. Beetles were the choice pet for small kids because they need little care or space. As we walked past the bugs, I said to Mākun, "Oishī-neh" (Delicious, isn't it?). He grinned wanly at this old joke. But the bow-er girl, whose job it was to stand next to the bugs all day, erupted in laughter and clapped her hands over her face.

As we strolled through the store we encountered a performing magician, and I stood entranced as he displayed his tricks. He sold many generic tricks, all simple hand-held ones, plus some of his own invention. I showed him some of my tricks, all of which he knew, and he improved on my coin-disappearing tricks. I bought some of his tricks, and he taught me how to do them.

At home Okāsan searched in a closet for a few minutes before retrieving her wedding picture, in which a frail-looking young woman—unrecognizable behind her pale, heavy make-up—wore one of the expensive kimonos we'd seen at Tokiwa. She stood stiffly but slightly bent at the shoulders, as if weighed down by her decorated, piled-up hair.

Looking up from the photo, Okāsan giggled, puffed out her cheeks as she often did when she imitated the round-faced Otōsan, and laughed, "Okāsan fat now." Her smile faded slightly as this still-petite woman focused wistfully on her doll-like former self. "Not fat then."

She returned to the storeroom to haul out all the old family pictures. Skinny Mākun was a fat baby. About the time Mākun was born, Otōsan grew a beard and added a cheerful, bold look—a big change from the serious, preppie-looking young man in his high-school pictures. His bohemian look was more handsome, we all agreed, and fit his personality better.

Shika too changed a lot after her trip to America. Now she stood straighter, was less shy, and had a more intense look in her eyes.

Week 4: July
Friday

This morning I was surprised to see Shika at home. I was sure today was her first day of extracurricular school. "Don't you have school?"

"Yes," she said. "But I am skipping it because I did not do my homework."

I went into the Japanese room to read a book; I would have read in bed, but my sweat-covered futon was being aired. Shika and Okāsan were cleaning with mops and vacuum cleaners, but they refused to let me help.

The mail arrived early, and Okāsan shouted to Shika that there was a letter for her. Otōsan materialized from another room, pretending not to be paying attention.

Shika nervously opened the envelope and read slowly. Suddenly her eyebrows lifted and her face broke into a wide grin. "Very good!" she announced, holding out the letter. Okāsan took it, and her husband looked over her shoulder.

"Aah," said Okāsan, beaming and hugging her daughter.

"Aah, good, very good, very excellent," Otōsan said, embracing both Shika and Okāsan. They were ecstatic.

All A's—high and low A's.

That morning held a surprise for me too. I didn't think I'd made a good impression on my stern judo teacher. Kuriyama-*sensei* had invited me to four sessions, but because of my schedule I'd attended only one. I figured he'd assumed that I turned down his offer.

But at 9:30 today he dropped by during more of the heavy rain, just long enough to give me a wonderful and unexpected present: a judo uniform and—I guess because he knew I was interested in all the martial arts—an expensive kendo sword. What generosity, I thought, and in the middle of a taifun.

Okāsan had perfected social salutations. She spent her days greeting Otōsan's friends, entertaining guests, caring for children, holding her own parties, cooking, and managing the house. In a day she might greet dozens of people. Each time she bubbled the traditional series of greetings and compliments, then laughed with the person whom she was addressing as if to say, "We're really friends, so isn't it silly how we feel constrained to be so formal in our greetings?"

She also saw off the family's guests when their visits were over. Otōsan preferred to walk in after the greetings were finished, and his good-byes were sincere but brief. He'd rather let Okāsan represent him. She would introduce him after the greetings, and he could therefore make his remarks more directly, more straightforwardly.

People were always coming and going at the Andos'. Otōsan was an open person who liked socializing and entertaining. He decided to name his house, which is unusual in Japan. "What name house, Stibu?" he'd asked me early in my visit.

When I finally understood the question, I didn't have any suggestions because I didn't know what he wanted to convey to passers-by and the community. Ever resourceful, he soon came up with a name that thrilled him and touched me deeply.

Ojisan spent this morning constructing a handsome, big wooden sign in order to "name house today," as Otōsan explained to me with a mysterious air. Using a gas torch, Ojisan burnt the wood's surface, then scraped off the charred part. This left a durable, natural-looking, jet-black finish. On it he nailed the stark white letters that he'd carved from a sheet of heavy-duty plastic, copying a sample painted by the calligraphy teacher.

INTER NATIONAL
(several kanji letters here)
DE A I NO MURA.

The third line is a rōmaji transcription of the kanji on the second line, so as to make pronunciation of the kanji easy for anyone, especially foreigners. According to Shika, the words DE A I NO MURA and their kanji mean "House of Friendship." Too late, I pointed out to Ojisan that "international" is one word. He scratched his head, commenting that international should really be two words anyway.

Otōsan and I hauled the heavy sign up the long, curved driveway and strapped it to a small tree by the roadside. "This is the first time I've seen you in a business suit since our meeting on the plane," I remarked, noting his out-of-place attire.

"I wear bijines suit often, Stibu," he responded, tilting his head to one side in mock rebuke. "You don't know because you sleeping!"

Ojisan, Okāsan, Otōsan, and I ate sliced apples and tiny dried fish in the courtyard to celebrate the naming of the new house. Ojisan rubbed his hands conspicuously, an expression of satisfaction on his face, as he scanned our faces for approval of his handiwork.

"I want day to come when House of Friendship is so well known that anyone can say 'De a i no mura' to a taxi anywhere in the city and be brought to my home," Otōsan boomed with a sincerity that was greeted with equally fervent nods from Okāsan and Ojisan.

Ojisan and I practiced martial arts in the basement for a while. We'd gone there to play ping pong, but two of the barbers were already using the table. "Judo Masuta" (judo master), he called me as we circled to perform judo half-moves on each other. I called him "Ninja."

He began moves that would have sent me crashing to the floor, then he'd stop, playfully, at the last minute. I attempted a few throws, but he successfully blocked them all. Later he admitted he was a *shodan*. First-degree black belt.

I was getting better at ping pong against Otōsan—I'd never beaten him—and Mākun was getting better against me. Mākun and I played a lot. When anyone asked, he always said he was #1, but I beat him in perhaps 11 of 12 games.

Various members of the family played ping pong at weird times—after breakfast, late at night, or in the wee hours of the morning. We played for a long time, and the whole family would trickle down, getting involved on the sidelines. One night our games lasted from 10 p.m. to 2 a.m.

Mr. Tomita stopped by in the afternoon. As I'd requested, he'd written a reference for my college applications and wanted to have me correct the draft he'd produced on a word-processor. There was only one minor flaw: he was missing the final "do" in the "When in Rome" quotation.

"The English teachers at school are now busy preparing for the English seminars they will lead in Beppu," he informed me. "I'm glad you will be able to accept our invitation to teach at one of them. I won't be able to go myself this year, but after the seminar, I'd like to take you to visit my home."

I accepted his renewed invitation, then took the occasion to express to him my concern that I didn't have anything to give Mr. Kuriyama that could possibly repay him for what he'd given me—the judo lesson and, today, the costly sword and uniform.

"I don't believe Mr. Kuriyama expects anything in return," he counseled. "Just write a thank-you letter from

America." He paused in thought, a small smile brimming at the edges of his lips. "Some people give a gift only for the satisfaction they see on the face of the person they give it to. I think Mr. Kuriyama is like that."

Shika had been invited to a party tonight. Because she'd skipped summer school today, her friends thought she was sick and cancelled the party. When her friends found out she wasn't sick, they reinstated it.

Before she left for the evening she said in a hollow voice, "You can come too, Steve, if you wish, but it's just me and my friends, all girls." So far I'd regularly accompanied Shika to her activities, few though they'd been beyond her intensive studying. By now, though, I'd been in Japan long enough to distinguish an invitation from a polite gesture, so I crossed "party tonight" off my schedule and caught up with my hiragana.

Week 4: July
Saturday
The city of Beppu is really just a big festival built around any occasion. It's a glitzy resort famous for its hot springs. Today I went with the Andos to Beppu's annual Fire-Sea Festival, famous for its *hanabi-taikai* (fireworks display).

Ten of us packed into the Andos' van: Ojisan, Okāsan, Otōsan, Mākun, Shika, Minori, me, Ojisan's two daughters, and a family friend. As usual, Ojisan drove.

The road took us over a mountain and around a bay. As we rounded the turns, Otōsan deliberately slid from side to side, squashing the rest of us on the wide bench-seat. Finally, those of us who could, ganged up and, at the next turn, squashed Otōsan into the farthest corner of the van. This drew applause from the other occupants of the car.

While Otōsan was pinned down, Chika and Miyuki, Ojisan's daughters, tugged on his beard until he roared with laughter and mock-indignation and promised to quit. The passengers in the front seat leaned back to try to push Otōsan even farther into the corner. "Ohhhh, ahhhh, owww," he groaned, loving it all.

We stopped at a precipice overlooking Beppu's inlet. The other cars on the road were pausing there, too. Staggering like a queasy sailor back on dry land, I debarked to see why: across the water, elaborate fireworks were exploding in beautiful patterns over the town.

I said "Ojisan wa kureizhi" (Ojisan is crazy), referring to his race-car style of driving. Pressing down on his nose, he laughed and repeated, "Kureizhi?" When I nodded, he pointed down at Beppu, twinkling afar, and announced, "Stibu walk!"

The fireworks were being launched from a narrow beach that halted suddenly where hotels, apartment buildings, and shopping centers sprang up. The Tower of Beppu, the city's neon-needle landmark, shone out among the flashes.

After parking the car in the town, we made our way through a dense forest of seafood vendors to reach the actual festival-site on a strip of sandy beach.

Myriads of red and gold paper lanterns lit up the seaside promenade and floated in random patterns on the surface of the bay. I met some students I knew from Uenogaoka High School hanging around the beach in groups and drinking bottles of festival soda. They waved and offered me some of theirs.

I bought a squid-on-a-stick, licked the now-usual drips of soy running down my fingers, and ate every bit this time, suckers included. At a nearby stand Shika bought spiced balls of octopus baked in dough and shared these favorites with Minori and me.

When we reached home long after midnight, Mākun flicked on the TV while we awaited our turns in the shower. A Japanese drama came on. I said to myself, "That looks like *Macbeth*, like Banquo being mugged and killed." It was *Macbeth*! In Japanese. The nobles wore an anomalous mixture of flowing silk robes and traditional Scottish garb, and Macbeth wore a golden kimono and silk headband tailored to look like a crown. Just the sort of show—lots of *hora*—that Mākun loved.

Week 5: July
Sunday

After breakfast, Otōsan strode into the Japanese room shirtless, clapped his hands, and proclaimed that in five minutes he'd take Dai and me to the country. "We visit old lady's home in rice paddies and drink tea," he explained. "My job to visit many, many people, donchyu? Come see country, old houses and farms." Ojisan joined us.

As we arrived at our destination, the children of the tiny farming community went wild. They'd been catching the butterflies that their golden retriever flushed out of the reedy brush. All dropped their nets to form a half-circle around my side of the car and point at me. Dai winked at me as if to say "I'll take care of this," and made grinning, pointing gestures back at the children.

Ojisan sauntered off in another direction because this was Otosan's friend.

Business-suited Otōsan greeted an old woman who wore a plain, calf-length, gray silk dress. After gracious bows and hellos, she turned aside to shoo away the children now trying to poke my heels with straws.

She invited us to kneel at a small, low table to share pickled onions and tea in her spartanly furnished but immaculate dining room. Here I made another of my big mistakes.

Otōsan was obviously friends with the woman on a formal basis. As he had intimated, this was a business as well as social call. Observing that he was more serious than usual, I tried to behave perfectly, and he helped me by demonstrating the proper etiquette: I was to remove a pickled onion from the tray with a communal pair of chopsticks and place it on my left hand, replace the chopsticks for the next person, then drop the onion into my mouth with my right hand.

After serving myself correctly several times, I instinctively put the communal chopsticks to my mouth. Realizing too late what I'd done, I jerked them out. This caused me to drop my onion onto the table, where it skidded onto the elderly woman's delicately embroidered placemat. Reaching out to retrieve it as unnoticeably as possible, I knocked over my full glass of iced wheat tea.

Otōsan and the hostess pretended they hadn't noticed, and Dai smiled at me consolingly. I was horrified and practiced all my words of apology. Our hostess calmly fetched a cloth and mopped up, never breaking off her conversation with Otōsan or acting as though she were really cleaning up my big mess. I made motions to help her, but she gently refused. Her imperturbability made me feel all the more guilty.

Her large, old house had been modernized inside so that it looked like my 1960s Connecticut house, without furniture. During the tour she gave me, she paused longest at her fancy, plastic-crystal chandelier. "Made in America," she beamed with pride.

While Otōsan, Dai, and I were inside, Ojisan had sketched some old houses in the village and picked a sunflower head from the woman's garden. On the way home he sat next to me to show me what to do with the flower. After stripping it down, he tossed the husk out the window and plucked the ripe seeds from their tombstone-like rows. He passed around handfuls of seeds for us to snack on and slipped a few into his pocket for another time.

We ate lunch at a small restaurant back in Oita. Some friends of the family walked in after we'd ordered and joined us. During the entire polite conversation, Dai crawled all over his Dad, hugging him from behind, sitting in his lap, racing around him, running his fingers through his father's hair, tugging at his beard, and hanging on his arm. Deftly and discretely Otōsan played with Dai, managing at the same time to carry the lead part of the conversation. No one showed signs of noticing Dai's playfulness. No one criticized or stopped him.

Then it clicked. That was why Dai—who didn't fit into any of this trip—was here. To be with his Dad, to share experiences and play with him.

I remembered that Shika had told me she felt sorry for Dai. "My father had become a very busy man by the time Dai was old enough to miss him. Otōsan and Dai have had little time together over the years. Dai loves attention, especially Otōsan's."

Today might be the last time for days that the two could enjoy each other like this.

There were no locks on the inside doors of the Andos' house except for the toilet—not even on the shower-sink room. Its door had frosted windows, though, so you could tell if someone was in there by whether the light was on.

That evening Okāsan was first in the shower. Minori passed by and—to play a joke—flipped off the light on Okāsan, which was easy to do because the switch was in the hall. Okāsan had to step out of the shower stall and change in the dark.

I wanted to brush my teeth and inadvertently walked in on Okāsan. I slammed the door shut as soon as I opened it. We both shouted "Sumimasen" (Sorry). Otōsan wasn't there, but I could hear Mākun, Dai, and Shika laughing hard. For the rest of the evening they giggled whenever they saw me.

Minori didn't laugh. She ran to her room and barricaded the door with her feet. When Okāsan finished changing, she forced open Minori's door and scolded her soundly before stalking across the house to her own room. I followed and apologized, but she said it wasn't my fault. Later that night, Minori emerged for a snack and apologized to me.

With that, things returned to normal in the house.

Around lunchtime I'd mentioned to the family that I'd brought some brownie mix from the U.S. for them, and Shika jumped at the word. Brownies were her favorite food in America, she said, and made me promise to bake them that day.

Around midnight, when the family was preparing for bed, she remembered the promise she'd extracted – and she and I baked brownies. Their smell drew everyone from the farthest reaches of the house.

Tragedy Strikes!

Week 5: August
Wednesday

Today Shika and I took the train to Beppu for the four-day English seminar. Two dozen English-speaking *gaijin* would serve as "teachers" to several hundred of the best students of English in the prefecture.

At the hotel where the seminar was taking place, I learned that I was to be teacher's aide to a college student from New York City, Danny Roberts, who'd be the *sensei* for the 30 students of Group F. I received my room assignment and hauled my stuff to a bare tatami room smaller than the bedroom Mākun and I shared. As at the YFU camp, the room was meant to sleep eight people.

Our classroom, also in the hotel, was a large room with four kneeling tables that formed a square. The students, I learned, had been bombarded all morning with instructions by the seminar's Japanese organizers, called "tutors," on the importance of their behavior in front of "foreign friends."

Soon after I entered the classroom and met the students, an incident occurred that, better than anything else I'd seen, highlighted for me some of the subtle yet significant differences between Japan and America.

Today was the birthday of one of the students, a girl whom Danny named "Sharon." Danny soon arrived with a birthday cake he'd bought for her—his own idea. After we all sang "Happy Birthday," he groped in his pocket for his Swiss army knife, then proceeded to cut the cake and signaled for the students to line up. Shy and confused, they remained kneeling at their places, staring at their fingernails. It was several moments before the boldest ones began to line up; the others slowly, cautiously followed.

As the students filed past, Danny plopped a piece of cake in each one's hands, a big slice for Sharon and tiny ones for everyone else. The students were noticeably flustered. American kids wouldn't have been, but the Japanese are perhaps the cleanest society in the world, and from the expressions of surprise on their faces, I knew many had never held cake in their bare hands before.

I took the last place in line. The Japanese "tutor" assigned to our class, kindly Mr. Sudo, approached me and insisted on having the last spot. Bobbing at each other and pointing, we came close to an argument over who'd be last.

The line moved slowly past Danny, who talked to himself about his own recent birthday, the cake he'd had for it, and the fun he always had slicing cake. Instead of returning to their seats and eating the cake, the students held onto both their cake and their place in line. Danny went on talking to himself, handing out cake, and licking icing off his hands with great show of relish.

When my turn came, Danny kiddingly asked the class to vote on whether I was to get a piece: "Thumbs up, Steve gets a piece. Thumbs down, he doesn't." The students stood in line, cake perched on their hands, and smiled nervously back at him. I gave the thumbs up sign to everyone, and they gave it back. I got some cake.

I turned to Sharon, the birthday girl, who'd been first in line. She was holding her big slice, and everyone was watching her. I prompted her: "They" —I motioned at the line—"wait for you." After I pantomimed for her the eating of cake, she took a bite. Down the line, the rest of the group dutifully ate too.

Now another difficulty arose, but it took a while to dawn on me. I'd been served last, and I ate promptly. But the rest of the group, who'd had to wait with the cake in their hands, now had a serious problem. There was icing and maybe a few chocolate crumbs on their palms and fingers, and they didn't know what to do.

Take the average American kid—like me. They'd deal with the problem summarily, licking their palms or wiping them on their pants. Polite American kids would've wiped or licked inconspicuously.

Now these students had no towels or water to wash with. They began wandering around, palms up, painfully distressed, but too polite to call this to the attention of anyone else.

The Japanese, from what I've observed, are very self-conscious, and this cake on their hands paralyzed our group. I saw one boy turn to fish a handkerchief out of his pocket. After a clandestine brushing of his hands, he slipped the handkerchief back into his pocket with a relieved look. If he'd been seen, he would've been asked to share his handkerchief, and politeness dictated that he couldn't refuse. The Japanese graciously share many things, but not their expensive handkerchiefs.

Danny wanted to slide full-swing into a number game called "Buzz," to give the students a feel for using numbers in English. The game started to fall apart, however, because no one could concentrate: "Buzz" required holding hands, and no one—but no one—would do that now.

I'd viewed this developing crisis from a detached perspective. Who, I wondered, was going to help? Someone should say or do something.

The handkerchief gave me an idea. I slipped out to the bathroom and returned with paper towels. As I ducked from person to person, handing out the towels, the tension melted with an audible sigh of relief.

Danny was annoyed; I'd broken the flow of the game he'd managed to jump-start while I was gone. "Don't pass those out NOW," he said. He hadn't caught on.

"But," I said sheepishly, "they have cake on their hands."

We settled down after that. I felt that someone should have just asked for napkins, but students here have great respect for teachers, and no one was willing to question or correct Danny.

The game went well now. Everyone appeared to be fluent in the numbers in English. I didn't do at all well, because the game required concentration, and my mind was elsewhere. I was frustrated at being scolded, but relieved that the crisis was over. If I felt I'd learned a lot during my stay in Japan, that notion was shattered now. No one had voiced any distress or objection. I felt bad and responsible, somehow. I felt dirty: I'd never wiped my hands. Had they noticed? What were they thinking?

When I returned to my seat, I found an anonymous gift: a delicately crafted origami crane made of paper towel—slightly stained with chocolate cake.

According to the seminar brochure, the reason hundreds of high-school students gather each year for the Beppu seminar is that "it feels so good to communicate with foreign peoples." No Japanese was to be spoken here; for four days English was constantly pounded into their heads. I tried to picture myself in their place, being pressured into learning a foreign language, having the language drummed into me every waking hour. They had to be feeling every bit of that pressure.

At night, with classes over, the students became fun-loving kids—at least my seven Japanese roommates did. In fact, on the first night of the seminar, they gathered around me before the 10:30 official bedtime, and laughing and clapping their hands in delight, tried out their English slang, dirty words, and gestures. They had them all down pretty well.

Many "popular" expressions that you wouldn't find in English dictionaries are meticulously defined in English-Japanese dictionaries. But that doesn't mean that the definitions are really understood by the populace at large. American dirty gestures and swear words don't mean the same thing, or perhaps even anything, to the Japanese because they're used often and out of context here in order to be American and therefore "cool."

If you called someone a pig-head in the Japanese language, he'd be offended. But if a Japanese person called someone a "pig-head" in English, even if the victim looked it up and understood the definition, it wouldn't have the same derogatory meaning. It would seem just a cute and facetious Americanism.

As another example, on popular teen shows, the TV camera pans the excited studio audience at every convenient break in the action, and they thrust their middle fingers into the lens, en masse. I've also seen middle-finger salutes exchanged among members of my polite class at Uenogaoka, everyone thinking it clever and funny.

The teen audience of "Genki TV" likes to yell "Fahkyu" at the on-stage performers. "Fahkyu" is by far the most popular swear word that the trendy Japanese have adopted.

I was up almost all night because the students were running amok at all hours. You could hear the pad-pad of slippered feet running in the hall, and my roommates had the TV going all night. They sat in a corner with the light on, slicking their hair up and back with mousses and gels, drinking soda, eating cup-o-noodles, and joking. They didn't sleep at all.

It was impossible to get mad at my roommates, though. They woke me up again and again with their noise. I'd wander over to show them my sleepy visage. "Here soda, Stibu," one would offer his bottle. Another handed me his roll of candy. "We want to go to America," another added, as if in explanation of their noisy chatter.

"Why," I demanded, "you no sleep?" I was too tired to wince at my bad English.

"Because . . .," one boy whispered, as he proffered his cup-o-noodles (How do you get mad at someone who wants to share his cup-o-noodles?), "because I am exciting."

Despite the pressure the students were under, I thought that, all in all, most of them were gaining something from the seminar and even having some fun. But the night before the seminar was to end, tragedy struck.

That night I went to my room early, spread my futon on the floor, and fell asleep. Only two of the seven students were there at the time, both asleep.

About 1 a.m. I opened my eyes to bright light.

"Sorry to bother you," a tutor apologized to me softly. "Just a bed check." Dazedly I heard him reading out names before I fell back to sleep.

A half hour later, the light flashed on again. Another bed check.

Around 3 o'clock I heard more noise and felt some kind of movement above me. I slept closest to the door, and noticed five kids slinking over me. They took their places in the corner around the TV, murmuring things like "Pocari Sweato," "Super!" (pronounced "Supah"), "Wonderful" and "Fantastic" (pronounced perfectly), and a few salacious expletives from American movies.

Someone turned to a travel channel that took viewers to the topless beaches of French Polynesia. An ad came on for a local spa resort with scenes of nude women soaping up for a Japanese-style bath. A few minutes later the kids switched off the TV and hit the sack.

Shortly before 4, a group of tutors entered and busted them all. All I remembered was the harsh light, loud voices, banging noises, and dull thuds of many feet on tatami. After perhaps half an hour of this, sleep overcame me again.

It turned out that my five roommates had gone into town against the rules and had drunk beer and sake. They were thrown out of the seminar that night, that instant. The seminar leader stood over them (and over me, literally) as they packed and departed into the night.

These boys had been friendly, polite, and amusing, and had readily admitted me to their circle. They'd opened up to me like no other group of Japanese I'd come across – except the Andos – and I felt grateful and attached to them.

It made me feel very sad, and guilty somehow, because I was their friend.

Week 5: August
Saturday

My first sight, on waking, was of papers scattered around the usually super-tidy room. My roommates – with the two exceptions who had not gone to town – would be home by now.

Strewn among the papers were pajamas, a mirror, some brushes, and a Donald Duck pillowcase left behind in the rush. Casually picking up one of the diaries that the seminar required each student to keep, I read, "I am happy for the first time because I am very English." I almost cried.

The seminar ended in the early afternoon, so I packed my things. I'd slept through breakfast because no one awakened me—a mixed blessing as I needed both sleep and breakfast.

Mary Alonzo, an English teacher at the seminar whom I'd first met at Minori's school, mused aloud, "This disgrace will hurt them in innumerable ways." I talked with her about the incident while sitting in the breakfast room even though there was no food left. Their futures had been dealt a severe blow. None would now go to America on official exchanges. They were in trouble with their parents and schools, and the stigma would probably follow them into college.

"Personally, I'm all for the students," she remarked. "Those boys had been the most spirited I've seen in Japan. The Japanese should really encourage, rather than squelch, this characteristic."

Mine wasn't the only group to be kicked out that night. My roommates hadn't been alone, and several other boys got booted. A few girls had left the seminar separately and returned with sake for a party in their room. They were caught and tossed out, too.

This morning no one spoke English. The students were sick of the seminar, though everyone said they loved it.

At our final Group F meeting, the students circulated small notebooks to collect signatures. Below their kanji names and addresses, most wrote messages in English, like, "I'm gonna miss you," "Please remember me," and "See you again." To their own names, they added the English names that Danny had given them.

At this moment, because they were not being graded

or checked, the kids were using English among themselves—this time for fun.

When Shika and I arrived home, we learned that an appendix problem had landed Dai in the hospital for an operation. His parents were constantly at his bedside seeing to his needs.

Otōsan's mother stopped by the house to help out while Okāsan was at the hospital. Noticing her high energy-level, I told her she was *genki* (spirited). She shook her head vigorously to say she wasn't, but she looked pleased. She made herself right at home, sweeping and doing the wash.

Tomorrow night would be one of the biggest festivals of the year. I'd met another American exchanger from Oita at the seminar, and as a result of some elaborate arrangements that Shika helped me with, we'd all watch the festival fireworks from the roof of his host-family's apartment building.

Shika said she'd wear her *yukata* (a cotton, summer kimono) to the festival, as it'd be the last occasion for this traditional garb before I went home. I'd planned to purchase a *yukata* for myself ever since the returnees in Seattle said it was the best thing to buy. I decided to make the purchase tonight so I could wear it to the festival.

The family wanted me to wear Otōsan's *yukata*, so I wouldn't have to buy one, but his was obscenely short on me. Obāsan, who was helping with the household, said she'd find one at home for me. She measured me, then searched her house, but couldn't find one long enough. "Depāto" (department store), she declared on her return.

Otōsan dropped Obāsan, Shika, and me at Tokiwa, where we were waited on immediately. Very much in charge, Obāsan sent the female clerk scurrying and shrewdly judged the costumes until she determined that I finally had a good-looking one that was long enough.

The whole outfit—*yukata, obi* (belt), and sandals—was a gift from Obāsan, a big present that she insisted on making. I was grateful, and she was gratified that matters were being handled properly.

Week 6: August
Sunday

Today was Hiroshima Remembrance Day. On TV I saw some of the ceremonies, which included much gong-ringing, and people—mostly elderly—praying and releasing doves to fly around the skeletal hulk of a building that's been preserved as a memorial.

Minori got a lot of calls, I'd noticed, and she took them on a distant phone, speaking quietly, sometimes for a long time. Shika had told me she thought the caller was Minori's boyfriend. "But Minori doesn't have a boyfriend," I said. Wrong!

This afternoon Minori brought a boy home for the first time. Mākun and Shika watched at the window next to my bed, unable to suppress excited giggles as he walked down the driveway. Dai and Okāsan were at the hospital, or they would've been watching too. I had to pull Mākun and Shika away.

Otōsan was entertaining business guests in the living room. Upon hearing that the boyfriend was approaching, he changed his seat a couple of times until he settled on the one closest to the hallway that the boy would pass through.

Minori's friend Tomo was nice-looking but really skinny. He said a polite good-day and introduced himself to Otōsan, who managed to look pleasantly surprised and greeted him with the utmost friendliness. Minori made her appearance shortly after Tomo arrived, as if she hadn't been waiting for him, and both exchanged a polite nod with Otōsan and his business friends.

Tomo followed Minori to her room, where they talked and listened to records for a couple of hours with the door open. It had all seemed so under- and yet over-played, so casual yet important.

We left for Timothy's host-home at 6:30. Shika and I wore *yukata*. As Otōsan drove us through the people-packed streets, I got stares through the windshield and pointing fingers.

"I like this yukata," I remarked to Shika, in part to reiterate my gratitude for the trouble her family had taken to clothe me in festival garb. To myself, I admitted that a *yukata* is an uncomfortable garment.

"Well, I don't like mine," Shika rejoined with candor. "It inhibits your movements, making it impossible for a girl to sit back in a chair because of the large belt-bow in the back. And the loose sandals make walking difficult."

Timothy's host brother studied English fanatically and owned a shelf-full of English-language tapes, including a BBC language course. His English was good, but not nearly as good as Shika's. He was to leave for Hawaii next week for a year's exchange, and because no one else in the family spoke much English, Timothy would be more or less on his own for the last couple weeks of his stay.

Tim's host-brother also had an American starlet's poster tacked on his wall. He'd clipped dozens of other shots of her from magazines and pasted them neatly all over his mirror and cabinets. It reminded me of Mākun's infatuation with Wink.

The family had clearly gone to extraordinary lengths to make space for an exchange student in their tiny apartment. There was no living room for socializing, so tonight the kitchen was cleared to make space.

Later, on the roof, we ate a Western-style meal of fried chicken and egg-salad sandwiches, plus sushi, before the fireworks began. It wasn't a big display, but we enjoyed one of the best views in town from atop this building near the launcher. We watched the chrysanthemum shapes and streamers at their most spectacular, at eye level.

Tim's host-father must be a person of some importance because we had the roof to ourselves. At one point during the fireworks, the younger son of the family joined us, but the father told him he had to study. Without protest the boy turned around and went back down. The family seemed rather formal; I noticed they didn't use nicknames, the way my own family and the Andos did.

After the fireworks, Mākun and I excused ourselves and headed off to the long-awaited Wink concert in the courtyard of Oita's castle.

The area was jammed with people. Some had been camping at the castle for nearly two days to get in. Standing against the mammoth gates, we could see that the courtyard was 100% full. No, more like 200% full, like Tokyo subway trains. There was no way I could squeeze through the gate. We had no hope, so we left. Mākun was downcast.

Shika had acute senioritis. She'd already told me many times how hard she must study for the important college-entrance exams. Students attended extracurricular cram schools to prepare for them and studied elaborate preparatory books. Now was a critical time for her because her college exams began soon, but now she didn't want to study.

Instead she pondered her future. "On the one hand, I'd like to go to college in America. And I wouldn't mind leaving for the U.S. right now, to avoid these terrible exams," she said, listing her options for me. "On the other hand, if I pass the Jochi exam, I think I might go there now, and later to an American college. If I fail this exam, I might go straight to an American college." At the moment she seemed to prefer the American-college-immediately option.

I had attended only one of two available English seminars in Beppu. I avoided the second because it would take too much time away from me and my family. My decision also meant that Shika, who'd accompanied me to Beppu, wouldn't have to take more time away from her studies.

Today the seminar organizers requested her back for the second seminar; they needed a "returnee" from America for their discussion groups, so for a few more precious days she wasn't able to study — not that she was in any mood to do so.

Week 6: August
Monday

Otōsan hauled home a large karaoke set today. *Karaoke* means "empty orchestra" — empty because your voice is missing. Its voice-enhancing electronics go a long way towards transforming even the most reserved of Japanese *bijinesumans* into Elvis or Ol' Blue Eyes.

Otōsan carted in dozens of 8-track cassettes, a microphone, and an expensive-looking player. He liked social events and parties, and often invited the neighborhood to his house, so that's how his new set would be used.

Week 6: August
Tuesday

The Japanese like massages, and I got the impression that just about anyone will give one to anyone else. Today Mākun gave Ojisan one, by walking slowly over Ojisan's lower back. Ojisan looked as though his back had been hurting him all his life and now, through the wonders of Mākun's feet, he was getting instant relief and pleasure.

After Ojisan stood up, his face expressing how good he felt, Otōsan announced that we were going to visit the family grave today.

"It—is something we do this—" he gestured expansively, trying to grasp the right words out of the air—"this time of year, Stibu. All Japanese do. Japanese visits grave often.

"It's a good time," he added, reassuringly. "Family gets together and has good time. It makes us feel—closer to people who die, the people who died. And also to whole family here living." Another sweep of his arm took in everyone in the house. "Feel even closer to people living, donchyu?"

I said we generally don't like visiting cemeteries in America, a sad experience that calls our attention to the emptiness that exists when people we love have left us.

"Japanese more practical," he countered. "They feel filled up after a visit . . . not empty."

Ojisan, Otōsan, Mākun, and I made the trip, along with Otōsan's mother. Borrowing a broom and pail of water from a rack of equipment near the gates, we swept the outside of the altar-like stone grave that held the ashes of several family members. Obāsan washed all the surfaces with a cloth and water, while she talked to the grave, cooing over it. We lit incense by the gravestone.

"We come also so grave clean," said Otōsan, admitting to a second purpose. "Don't want people who come here to think this grave dirty, not visited by family." We knelt and meditated.

A third purpose emerged. "Sometimes I bizhito gurandofaza," Otōsan said, mystifying me. Stuffing some dried flowers into a vase on the grave and clapping his hands, he explained about his "visits to grandfather": "If I have important decision or business problem, I come here to talk with gurandofaza. I know I already have the answer inside me, but maybe if I come here, it will come out easier, donchyu?"

He looked at me to check that I understood before bending down to give the flowers a final pat.

The other graves had been tended with flowers, wine, bottles of orange juice, and cans of Coke. What the deceased liked when alive—or what the family thought they would have liked—was ceremoniously deposited at the graves' built-in altars.

We stopped to visit Dai on the way home. I had wanted to take him his favorite hat to help relieve his boredom, but I couldn't find it. So I asked Mākun to pick out some comics to take. Otōsan too had grabbed a comic for Dai on the way out. Comics are the Japanese panacea for boredom. I knew, though, that my comics were more appealing to Dai; Otōsan had meant well but didn't know which to choose. I felt bad about this. I didn't want to take the spotlight off Otōsan when he visited his son.

I needn't have worried. Dai didn't want to read the comics or play with any of the many toys he'd received in the hospital. He wanted to hug Otōsan, and he did.

After his appendectomy, Dai had developed a fever, but he seemed all right now. He said he didn't like hospital food and wanted Okāsan to cook for him. At this, Okāsan leaped up to hug him, while the ancient women who were his roommates clicked their tongues affectionately. To their delight, Dai introduced them to us as "Obasan" (Aunt) and "Obāsan" (Grandmother).

A tiny, drab building crowded among little shops, the hospital mainly served chronically ill old people. As long as Dai was there, Okāsan left home early each morning to spend the day with him, returning late at night.

It was almost dinnertime when we returned. I decided to watch TV, where a movie called "The Final Countdown" was in progress. An American aircraft carrier was transported back in time and had the power to stop the attack at Pearl Harbor. Ultimately the time-travelers decided against this, so as not to mess up history. It was eerie to watch American F-14 fighter-pilots dogfighting while conversing in dubbed Japanese, then shooting down two Japanese Zeros, all to Japanese patriotic music.

As a little kid, one of my favorite TV animations was "Star Blazers." At the end of the world, the last human survivors raise "The Yamato," an enormous World-War-II Japanese battleship and convert it into a starship to carry them to a new life in some distant world. I'd always wondered why the scriptwriters chose to raise and refit "The Yamato," in particular, and why the characters' lips were never in synch with what they were saying. The reason, of course, is that "Star Blazers" is a Japanese cartoon.

From the Andos' windows, Oita was a pretty city, but it wasn't quite as attractive close-up. It was constructed of dirty-looking concrete, a hodgepodge of varied-purpose but similar-looking buildings. Many were apartment buildings, their outsides latticed with balconies – with similar patio furniture on each and laundry flying in the wind.

A broadcasting tower, a multi-level golf complex with vast nets, and a big, white natural-gas tank added variety to the otherwise densely packed buildings on the skyline. There seemed to be no method or plan to the city. It was built wherever it fit. At night the city looked like Las Vegas. Big, blinking neon signs filled the air, creating a technicolor halo over the city.

We got to bed early for the Ando family, at 11:45, because, amazingly, everyone was tired.

Week 6: August
Wednesday

I didn't get an early night last night, after all. Mākun left the light on to play cards in his bunk. Next he read comics or wandered back and forth to the TV in the living room to watch late-night baseball re-runs. Perhaps I wasn't the only one being driven to distraction by the intense heat.

With only $20-worth of yen in my pocket, I needed to cash a travelers check. A trip to the bank, Mākun leading the way, turned into an exhausting run-around. At the first bank they were out of money, or were too small a branch, or didn't want my business: all this was conveyed to me by the plastic smile on the manager's face as he pointed us in the direction of a larger bank.

On the way to the larger bank, I spotted a couple of young Americans also heading that way. From their bearing, I thought they must be with the military, though they wore casual dress. I nodded hello to them, and they nodded and returned a friendly "Hi!" These exchanges between strangers must make the Japanese think a foreign conspiracy is afoot. In reality, *gaijin* are just surprised and relieved to meet other people in the same confused state.

The bank was packed with American soldiers in civilian dress, waiting in a long line for the only English-speaking teller. When I saw this I knew I wouldn't get anything done today. It was 2:30, and banks close at 3. "Here! Here!" Mākun wanted me to wait in the line, but that was out of the question.

I approached one of the Japanese-language tellers—no line there—and motioned Mākun to come help me. I had, I thought, one of the simplest transactions in bankdom to make. In contrast, some of the GIs were setting up bank accounts and engaging in other financial complexities. Since I had a Japanese friend with me who knew what I wanted, I figured I could have the Japanese teller serve me. Mākun wouldn't participate, though. He ran to the farthest corner of the room, shaking his head violently. It would've caused a scene for me to drag him over, but I nearly did.

I figured I'd try to cash the check without his help. When Mākun saw this, he rushed over, pleading, "No, Not, Not, Noooo!" He tugged at my shoulder, frantically trying to pull me away from the Japanese teller and back to the English-speaking one. Why couldn't he let me do the job on my own?

I had no alternative but to leave the bank, no checks cashed. My conclusions about Mākun's new confidence were apparently premature. He was inexplicably shy.

Another example of his inhibition occurred whenever I sang or whistled while biking, as I liked to do. He'd furiously motion for me to be silent and get distressed if I didn't. What was I doing? Calling attention to myself? Whatever it was, he didn't want that.

Mākun and I biked to his favorite book store. While we waited for a light, a busload of Japanese tourists drove by and clicked photos of me. I felt like a lion feels when a safari pulls up.

Books Bungo was more than five miles from Sakuragaoka, but near where the Andos used to live. I could see why he liked this store so much: it was full of comics, flashy teen magazines, and *hora* videos. I couldn't find anything in English, so I browsed while he read comics.

Most of the magazines were for teens, and this week all of them seemed to have "Wink" written somewhere on the cover.

I bought a *manga* as a souvenir, a relatively small one that would fit in my luggage. Its title was "Young Champion," but it was written mostly in Japanese. It cost about $1.00 and was numbered as part of an ongoing series.

In America a comic might be 40 pages; in Japan they're 500 pages but still relatively inexpensive because of the ads, cheap construction, and mass production. They're as fat as the publishers can physically make them. Inside the brilliantly illustrated, attention-getting covers, the newsprint pages are coarse and thick—probably deliberately so, because some kids just grab the biggest. New volumes for each series come out every week.

What's most amazing is that people buy these comics twice: they read them in this big form when they first come out, then throw them away because they're too big to store. They buy them a second time in reduced size and on better paper for their collections.

Kids, and adults too, become addicted to *manga*. On a commuter train you'll see impeccably dressed *bijinesuman*s reading them. *Manga* are extravagantly illustrated and loaded with machismo. The men are dashingly handsome, and the women are adoring. *Manga* reek with major violence: faces torn off in fights, whole cities destroyed, blood everywhere. More explosions and karate throws but less gunfire than in American comics. Clearly *manga* offer an outlet for the controlled emotions of the notably nonviolent Japanese.

There are comics for young and old, nerds and jocks, specialty comics, dirty comics, and history comics. They're meant to be read fast. I've seen Mākun complete one the size of a small phonebook in one sitting. His was about sports players, all imaginary, performing superhuman feats in soccer and baseball to impress the female cheerleaders.

I browsed through the magazines. They're expensive—one of the ones I bought cost $8. Kids must spend a lot of money on the many teen-idol magazines that line the long racks.

The movie magazines focus on American movies because there don't seem to be many major Japanese ones, and some American stars are possibly even more popular in Japan than they are in the U.S.

Above them all towers that resident *gaijin*, Mickey Mouse. Tokyo Disneyland, complete with castle, characters, and dreams, has been a smash-hit since it opened. Mickey attracts all manner of Japanese, and presumably, evokes the same feelings of happiness and fun.

The other magazine I bought, *The Computer* (or—according to its katakana subtitle—"Za Konpyuta"), read American-style, from front to back and left to right, because it was a progressive magazine and took its lead from the U.S. The words "MS-DOS," "microchip," "ROM," "IBM," and "Toshiba" were dropped frequently, in English, into the Japanese-language sentences. The magazine was full of articles about American computer experts. While people here might think the future of computers lies in America, we Americans worry that it could be the other way around. All the ads in the computer magazine were in English.

Many of the things I brought from the U.S., like my pens, watch, and camera, were made in Japan. Otōsan and Ojisan were always curious about where things were made, and it surprised and tickled them when they found something of mine that was "Made in Japan." Some of the kids in school were like this, too. Why should they be surprised? Didn't they realize how phenomenally successful they were in the business world? Some under-dogism seemed to persist, and I often felt like responding, "Of course this is made in Japan. We don't make these things anymore."

In America, you get the impression that no two products in a store are made in the same country, but in Japan everything seems to be "Made in Japan." Nearly everything in the Andos' house was made in Japan, though you'd expect some of it might come from other parts of Asia. Their air-conditioner, for example, was a Mitsubishi. My diary was made by Kokuyo, which also made the chair I sat on to write.

Japanese culture is a different story. It's frequently invaded, if not overwhelmed, by outside influences — neon signs, Kentucky Fried Chicken, rock music, Marilyn Monroe, and James Dean. Inconsistently, perhaps, I grit my teeth. I even felt guilty talking with the Andos or my classmates about this invasion, as if it were my fault that English regularly appears in ads and on storefronts and marquees. I tried to overcome my own sense of loss by making these cultural incursions seem perfectly natural. "International," I called them, taking my cue from Otōsan.

The Japanese like to consider themselves "international." They love the word so much that I added "You are very international" to my compliments, along with "Are you an English teacher?"

Every home I visited had an English-Japanese dictionary handy. The Andos had four or five of varying sizes and composition, and they left them lying about, whereas they cleaned up everything else fastidiously. Maybe such dictionaries are prestigious. They say, "I understand English enough to use one of these." Or maybe they lend an international flavor to a house when casually left on the coffee table.

I saw dictionaries lying around a farmhouse and a one-room apartment. I suspect these books are necessary for the Japanese if they want to find out what's happening in their own country because so many of

their products, signs, and tourist areas display their information in English. You might miss out if you don't
know English.

When Mākun had had enough of perusing *manga* in
Books Bungo, he said what he always said when he was in
a hurry, "Very go." Whenever I had to wait for *him*, he
squinted and pinched his fingers together, "Small minute."

On the way home from Books Bungo, my foot slid
off the bike, and I mashed it between the road and the
pedal. Mākun was solicitous, wondering how he could
help, as I sat on the curb to let my agony pass. When the
throbbing lessened, he insisted on carrying my omnipresent backpack, now heavy with its purchases as well
as my diary and camera. He slung it over his arm and
partly over his own shoulder bag full of huge comics. I
was grateful.

On the news today I saw another ceremony of remembrance, this time for the Nagasaki victims of the bomb.
Bells rang out at the exact time of the explosion almost a
half-century ago. TV commentators talked about promot-
ing the ceremony among the young because the survivors
were now so old and the young seemed not to care. Somehow I felt grateful that the Japanese remembered and re-
told the stories of these disastrous days, turning what
could have been bitterness into the long strings of origami
cranes – a symbol for peace – that decorated their ceremonies, and into hopes for a war-free world.

Week 6: August
Thursday
Mākun kept me up until 1 again. He had the light on to
play cards or read magazines about Wink, as usual, then
he whistled. Why did he whistle? He could sleep later in

the morning these days—until 8 instead of 6—because it was summer vacation and extracurricular school had replaced regular school.

Mākun made up a name for me. "Stibun" is how Japanese usually say Steven. But because this family stayed up so late with the result that I was always sleepy, he now called me "Sripun" (Sleepen). He was tickled with his linguistic creation. Painstakingly he wrote it out time after time on my notepad, so I couldn't miss the message.

Most of the morning Otōsan worked at the living-room table, heaped with an old calculator, a stack of money, and a big pile of bills. He was methodically peeling through them, completing everything, keeping records. I told him that in my family Mom took a course in finance and handled the money. He said he handles so many transactions in his varied positions and deals with so many people, that he's the only one who could tackle the Andos' finances.

He'd been working for a couple of hours already, and these were only the transactions that had piled up this week.

Some workers painted the house white today. When they finished, they burned all their plastic coversheets and materials in a bonfire that gave off clouds of noxious black smoke.

The Japanese burn much of their garbage. There's an incinerator smokestack on nearly every city block. Ueno-gaoka High School has its own. Land is scarce for landfills, so perhaps half the non-recycled trash goes to incinerators. Because of the high cost of garbage disposal, illegal dumping is a chronic problem, and a public garbage can is often stuffed with someone's home garbage.

The TV news reported that crime is surging in Japan,

especially among unemployed juvenile delinquents. Violent assaults topped the list.

Oita's very safe, Otōsan told me. Anyone could say that, but it was corroborated by the fact that nearly all the local policemen appeared to be in their late 50s or even in their 60s. Their main job was settling arguments, giving parking tickets and directions, directing traffic, and – so it's said – drinking tea in the ubiquitous street-corner police boxes that they inhabit.

Mākun found a postcard in his new *manga* for applying to join the Wink Fan Club, so he did. I went to town with him to mail it.

The post office excursion, as usual, turned into a major expedition. As we left the house, Mākun performed the elaborate procedure of shutting all the many windows and sliding doors and locking them since we were the only people left in the house. It took him a long time.

I cast a backward glance and saw a closed and locked house, and this was one of the rare times I'd seen it so.

Before we set off, Mākun gently but firmly removed my backpack from my shoulders – I couldn't figure out what he was doing – and wore it on top of his own again. I protested that he needn't – my foot was fine – but he waved with a smile, released his brake, and sailed downward, leaving me to catch up.

When we passed the playground that marked the start of the Sakuragaoka hill, the children ran after me as far as they could. As a group, they made faces and called for me to come back and talk with them. They were using Japanese with some English, and their meaning was pretty clear.

After Mākun mailed his fan-club application, we

stopped for refreshment at a big bank of vending machines. Whenever I used these machines, I tried to pick a soda I hadn't had before. NCAA Sport Drink was sold out. So I chose American Soda. When I hit the button, out came a can of West-brand iced coffee.

Pocari Sweat from a Vending Machine

You can buy anything from a vending machine in Japan. The first vending machine I saw sold suntan lotion. I thought that was amazing, so I had my picture taken beside it. I should have saved my film: that particular machine was tame for a land where automatic vendors seem to dominate every street corner, from modern city thoroughfares to rice-paddy country roads.

A vending machine will serve you whatever you need at the moment—any moment—from band-aids and hot face cloths, from salads to aphrodisiacs.

When I say vending machine, I mean VENDING MACHINE. Imagine the biggest one you've seen in America. Now picture two or three, add flashing lights and a video or *jan-ken-pon* (rock-paper-scissors) game in the center, and say, under your breath, "This is a VENDING MACHINE."

The machine near Uenogaoka High School consisted of three Double Vending Machines. The soda section of this conglomeration was especially popular. Drop in your coins, and bright, multicolored lights flash, a high-pitched siren goes off, and a "Wheel of Fortune"-type wheel spins. If the flag lands on the slice marked "LUCKY," written in

English, you get another item from the machine free. I was never LUCKY.

You choose from 15 brands of soda. The Japanese like soda as much as Americans do. Their market isn't dominated by a few megabrands, as in the U.S. In addition to Pepsi and Coke, there are three varieties of honey-and-lemon soda, all the major Japanese soda brands, and wheat tea. There are several unusual fruit drinks such as Apple Squash and Melon Squash. I didn't get through all the choices during my stay.

There was a popular new phenomenon called "isotonic" drinks—uncarbonated "sports" sodas much like Gatorade, with brand-names like Aquarius and Sports Drink, and C. That's its name, C.

My favorite was the "ion supply drink" Pocari Sweat. It describes itself on the can as "a health oriented drink which supplies water and electrolytes lost through perspiration. POCARI SWEAT is quickly absorbed into the body tissues due to its fine osmolality and contains electrolytes for replenishing body fluids. POCARI SWEAT is thus highly recommended as a beverage for such activities as sports, physical labor, after a hot bath, and even as an eye-opener in the morning."

All the drinks are made in Japan, including Coca-Cola (under license), yet they have labels in English in order to be stylish and international.

Coke's much more popular than Pepsi, and it dominates the soft drink market. I once saw a Pepsi truck on its way to service Pepsi machines—its drivers were drinking Georgia iced coffee, Coke's best-seller in Japan.

I never saw anyone drinking Pepsi, although Madonna advertised it on TV.

Kendo Kid once explained Coke's nonsensical motto to me: "I feel good" is one of the most widely known Americanisms in Japan; therefore the soft-drink's motto, "I feel

Coke," comes to mean "Coke is good." Come to think of it, Coke's American motto, "The real thing," doesn't make much sense either.

The big-brand sodas are offered in two sizes – the U.S. size and a smaller can – yet you pay the same 100 yen for each. So why buy the smaller one? Kendo Kid again shed light on the issue, "Many Japanese are accustomed to small drinks. This goes back to when they sipped tiny cups of tea, and they hate to waste anything, like a can still containing soda."

Traditional Japanese tea is also available in vending machines, in waterproof boxes labelled (in English) Green Tea.

A lemon drink can declares, "Good morning, dear lemons. How juicy you look today."

One of the drinks calls itself "the classic elixir."

A popular soft drink states on its can, "There is a gallon of deliciousness in every drop."

Another drink can says, "Any soft drink makes you feel refreshed, and presumably relaxes both your mind and your body. Yes, PRIO serves you with drinks of more fresh, delicious taste and higher feeling than any others." Can this be so? All this in English, of course.

A soda vending machine bears the cryptic label "PHARMACEUTICALS."

Tiny bottles of pick-me-up tonics – probably laden with caffeine – are popular drinks obtainable from these machines. One of them, Regain, was causing a sensation. It's designed to get businessmen going and keep them going during their long, gruelling, and perhaps boring days. It became an overnight success through its offbeat advertisement – a catchy song sung to a lively march. Kendo Kid translated it for me:

The Sign of the Courage
Yellow and black are the sign of the courage.
Can you fight 24 hours?
Regain, Regain, our Regain.
Attaché case with the sign of the courage.
Can you fight all over the world?
Businessman, businessman, Japanese businessman.

With hope to the paid holiday,
Peking, Moscow, Paris, New York.
Regain, Regain, our Regain.
With hope to the yearly income up,
Cairo, London, Istanbul.
Businessman, businessman, Japanese businessman.

The fire in the pupils is the sign of the victory.
Do you smile to the cloud in the morning glow?
Regain, Regain, our Regain.
The pledge of the heart is the sign of the justice.
Can you shine above a starry sky?
Businessman, businessman, Japanese businessman.

The up-and-coming drink isn't a tonic, sake, tea, or even beer. The drink is coffee, particularly iced coffee. It's a "cool," fashionable drink. Somehow it's all called American coffee, although we grow none of it. There's a Georgia brand iced coffee as well as American, West, and American West brands. While coffee consumption is declining in America, it's skyrocketing in Japan.

Surprisingly, the biggest machine at the street corner nearest the high school sells beer and liquor. You can buy a keg of beer, a one-liter bottle, and large, regular, small, and trial-size cans. Whiskey comes in one size but many varieties. Suntory's label displays a short poem in English, "Our brewmaster's inspiration/Bottled in draft through microfiltration."

Beer's what brings people to this machine. Budweiser's

sold, along with Kirin, Suntory, and Asahi. There's even room for a trendy beer. Called Penguin's Bar, it's decorated in pastels and shapes out of "Miami Vice."

Kendo Kid assured me that a school and a beer-machine can make comfortable, if strange, bedfellows. That's because vending machines that sell alcohol display a sign saying "Minors are not allowed to use this machine," and therefore none do. Even in Tokyo hardly ever do kids take liquor out of the machines, he said. I didn't notice a sign on this machine, but I never saw a minor using it either.

You can buy cigarettes, gum, dried fish snacks, and dinner from vending machines. I saw spiced squid and eel as well as pop star pictures and porno magazines. The machines deliver frozen steaks or names of prospective dates into your waiting hands. Truly a marvel of instant gratification, these ubiquitous machines provide just about anything anytime to satisfy the wants of the increasingly acquisitive Japanese consumer.

The pen shop near the school always caught my eye with its display of *hanko* (plastic seals with kanji engraved on them). A family name – Matsumoto, Kaifu, or Honda – is pre-carved inside a circle in handsome calligraphy. I thought this store might carry the complete line because it had racks upon racks – hundreds – of the different *hanko* that some Japanese like to use for signing checks and other documents. You pick your own pre-made *hanko*, but you can also carve it yourself a bit afterward to make it unique.

When I couldn't find a *hanko* there to express "river valley" – a generic version of my surname – Shika told me I could order one at Tokiwa, where a craftsman on the staff did custom *hanko* carving.

Mākun bought an expensive quill pen. The question is why? How would he ever use a quill pen? A better question is why did I want to buy a *hanko*? Could it be that the mysterious attraction of orient to occident pulls both ways?

Back home, he used his pen to write his English signature and the statement, "I can speak in English," on every piece of paper he could find. He'd probably drop the quill for a ballpoint when he went back to school tomorrow, in the same way I'd probably put away the *hanko* I planned to get.

Shika arrived home from her second seminar. She said she'd had a great time and this seminar had worked out much better than the first—much more relaxed. No one got busted for drinking either. "My enjoyment was diminished," she said, "by the idea that I was missing my extracurricular school and falling below my classmates here."

"You mean 'behind'," I said. On the rare occasions when Shika said something in awkward English, I corrected her, and I often volunteered tips on English to her because I felt this was a reason the family had invited me. She was generally very receptive, but sometimes—not unexpectedly—it seemed to wear on her and she'd look annoyed. Today she got mad.

"Why," she demanded, "do you do that?"

"Well then I won't anymore," I said as casually as I could. "But that's what you said you wanted."

"I'm sorry," she said, with a little sigh and a shake of her head. "Please, I want you to. You should, you must. I do appreciate it."

She looked exhausted, and she couldn't afford to be. She stayed in her room all evening, studying. I think this was the first time she did so since the school's exam-time just after I arrived.

Mt. Aso was active again. I saw TV shots of the picturesque valley covered by a sulfur haze that looked like rain.
Even the haze couldn't hide the valley's intense greenness
though. The eruption mustn't have been too bad because
camera crews were peeking into the mouth of the volcano,
helicopters were flying close to the rim, and no one was
being evacuated.

The news-translation commented that many of the fa-
talities in earthquakes result from the toppling of walls
made of thin, unreinforced concrete, perhaps a couple of
meters in height. That made me wonder how many walls
here fit that description. The answer is: very many.

Walls are everywhere, surrounding everything imaginable. Between our house and the high school, there was
a section of the neighborhood where walls lined every
road and divided every house from its neighbors.

They're all the same kind of wall. Picture some cin-
derblocks, about half as thick as the common American-
type, stacked and glued with cement and with no rein-
forcement within or without. They couldn't stop anything
bigger than a bicycle, and they fall on people during earthquakes.

Yet these walls appear to be wanted and needed, so
people can say, "This space is mine," and neighbors' eyes
will stay on their own tatami. The Japanese are communal
about many things, but their land—like their handkerchiefs in more ways than one— is not one of them.

We aired our futons every day or two. For sleeping,
the futon is tied inside a wrap-around sheet, like a pillow
case; to air it, you remove the sheet. I aired mine regularly
now, since Okāsan delegated the job to me when she had
to drop everything to care for Dai.

Because of the humidity, bedding can become smelly
even after a single night. During the day the futons hung

on the porch railing along with the laundry. At night I gathered up the pieces of my bed, tied the futon back inside its case, and tried to sleep . . .

I had to shower early tonight because Okāsan would be doing some special wash—sheets, tablecloth, and blankets—in the bathtub beneath the shower. Whenever she did the wash, she was generally in a hurry, especially now with Dai in the hospital. If I handed her, as I did last night, a suspiciously small quantity of clothes, she'd demand, then and there, the shirt off my back and, of course, the socks off my feet.

When Okāsan cooked, she really cooked. She shopped every other day and needed two rice cookers. Often she started on dinner around mid-afternoon, from scratch. She made hearty, big meals because she had so many mouths to feed. There was the family: Otōsan, Okāsan, Dai, Minori, Shika, Mākun, and Stibu. Then two, single-sex sittings for Otōsan's six barbers. Mākun and I were sometimes asked to set the tables or carry, but never to help cook.

When dinner was called, you moved quickly or you found everyone waiting for you. If Otōsan reached the dinner table first, he announced in a business-like tone, "I am waiting."

Okāsan would say, "Hari apu" (Hurry up), if you didn't show yourself promptly.

If Mākun beat me to the table (and he usually did), he sought me out, "Stibu . . . Stibu . . . Stibu, Stibu, Stibu, Stiiibuuun!" in my ear while I finished writing in my diary, until he got so annoying that I dropped my pencil and followed.

The World's Best Wink Fan

Week 6: August
Friday

Even though we had a relatively early night last night, I couldn't sleep. The house was fully open, the windows and *shōji* spread apart, yet it was still too sultry. Mākun got up several times to pace around our room or watch TV. I couldn't blame him.

After breakfast I made my way solo to the big bank to try again to cash my travelers checks. I didn't see a single computer there; it was all paperwork, official-looking stamps, and carbon copies.

There was a long line for the other tellers today but not for the English-speaking one. I was his only customer. He spoke English well and recognized me from my last attempt. The yen had fallen slightly in value since then. "You are good bijinesuman," he chuckled.

I told Otōsan a week ago that before I returned to the United States, I'd beat him at ping pong. Today we played for a long time in the basement. We didn't play a match or keep score, but I was in my best form, and he was in a particularly jolly mood.

We volleyed for over an hour, with crescendoing speed. When we finished, he said, "OK, you beat me." I objected, but what he said was final. So I've "beaten" him after all. I still hoped to play him in a match, just to be sure.

With only a week and a half remaining, I wished I'd somehow accomplished more during my stay. I didn't arrive with any special plan for my visit; I just wanted to see and experience as much of Japanese life as possible.

Some *gaijin* I'd met at the English seminar were intensively studying judo, karate, origami, tea ceremony, calligraphy, or Japanese palm reading. I did all of these, but none deeply. Somehow this made me feel as though I'd really done none of them. With so little time left, I felt I'd missed out on something, and though my days up to now had been packed, I wished I'd done still more.

Another disappointment was that the English seminar didn't work the other way around: I thought that somehow I might learn Japanese by teaching English. While that sounded like a good idea, it didn't happen. This was one more thing I didn't accomplish during my stay, and it was too late to start now.

"Stibu," Mākun called, motioning for me to come to our room.

After a whole afternoon pouring over teen magazines, Mākun had discovered a calendar in one of them displaying a girl model's photo for each month. He flipped the pages for me.

"Who—best?" he grinned.

I shrugged noncommittally. "Each is pretty."

"Ah, but *best*?" he probed intently. He then came up with the idea of using a points system and hovered next to me until I assigned the most points to one of them.

I thought this might mean that his infatuation with Wink was over. But no. Later he watched a tape he'd made of them from the TV, then he rewound it, and gazed, entranced, at it all over again.

He had Ojisan get his camera. While Mākun paused the tape, Ojisan took a photo of him with Wink on the screen beside him. He put his arm around the TV as if embracing the rock duo, held up the fingers of his other hand in a "V" peace symbol, and gave a big smile. Ojisan shot nearly a whole roll.

Ojisan proudly showed me some photos of his two cute young daughters taking turns riding a unicycle on his driveway. I replied, appreciatively, "Cute. Like Wink." He beamed and handed the pictures to me as a gift. I thought he gave them to me because he thought I liked Wink. Mākun informed me later that he gave them to me because Ojisan likes Wink and was complimented by my comparison.

On the TV news we saw that the police have caught a suspect who could be Japan's first mass murderer. For several months someone had been kidnapping and killing young girls in the Tokyo area. The person they caught has admitted to one murder, but not to the others.

The key words in the reports about him were "loner," "anti-social," and "non-social." Everyone who knew him labeled him this way.

Because I'd told Shika many times how tasteless and violent I thought *manga* were, I said to her now, with a sarcastic grunt, "I'll bet *he* reads *manga*." The truth was stranger than fiction, however, because it later turned out that he *wrote manga*! Also he was addicted to violent Japanese cartoon serials. The news showed a picture of his room: a small, square, spartanly furnished room, its walls filled with racks of video cassettes. Shika gasped as the camera panned around the room, "There . . . are . . . no . . . windows."

The thing that drove everyone nutty about this case was the handwriting on the murderer's notes found at some of the crime scenes. The notes were written with a refined skill far above that of the average layperson. That means that the perpetrator was highly educated, and if that was so, then a murderer proceeded a long distance within Japanese society without being filtered out by the social system that the Japanese put so much faith in. This was the real shocker.

Week 6: August
Saturday

This morning the grandfather's frail sister came to visit the family and greet me. She'd been Otōsan's nurse when he was a baby, and he loved to see her, take care of her, baby her. She wore a 1960s-style flowered magenta dress, like the ones my own grandmother sometimes wore.

After she left, I talked to Otōsan for a long time. The TV was blaring in front of us, but by now I'd learned to shut it out the way he could. We spoke about the differences between Japan and America, and I told him how different he seemed from most Japanese.

"*Me?*" He said it with a kind of astonishment, but you could see he was pleased and amused.

Otōsan liked to talk, and he rolled out English in a confident way that was at first difficult to understand, but when you caught on to his accent and free-wheeling use of words, it became easier. He was a fast learner and liked to embark on ambitious quests for knowledge—English, Spanish, saxophone, and his long-standing enthusiasm for international friendship.

"You," he pointed at my nose, "cowboy."

"I'm a cowboy?"

"*Like* a cowboy," he corrected himself, then pointed at his own nose. "Japanese is like a farmer, donchyu? Always plant rice. Sometimes no good, sometimes hard, but always plant rice. It is ancient ways and long job in small paddy. Planting rice and waiting and picking and planting again. It is what we know. It is different in America, don-chyu? Cowboy, John Wayne. Draw!" He used both index fingers to do a quick-draw, then laughed and nudged me in the ribs for approval.

At first, I thought he was being literal. Finally he connected the images and ideas, "Cowboy is fast and individual and runs free. I think everybody must be friends, so I want to be like cowboy, too." Somehow I wasn't surprised at this ambition. Otōsan did remind me of a cowboy – free-spirited and adventurous, a real buckaroo. He concluded with a shrug, as if in an afterthought, "But anyway, Japanese always plant rice."

Baseball suddenly came on TV, and everything stopped. Ojisan's old high-school team was playing again, and everyone gravitated to the set. It was fun just to watch Ojisan's face because he was so excited and even more jovial than usual. His team had won the finals for Oita Prefecture and was now competing for the national championship. We all had to watch – even Shika, who'd studied all morning.

The cheering in the stadium never stopped during the breezeless, baking summer afternoon. The boy students sat in one of the stands, the girls in another, everyone wearing their team's colors.

There was a "Mickey Mouse" cheer and a "Popeye" cheer in English. Japanese words were sung to the tune of "Take me out to the ball game." Air horns were saved for big moments, whereas the cheering lasted from the starting siren to the end of the game. I asked Shika why spectators cheer throughout the game, and she replied, "*Because this is important.*"

The groups swayed to their cheers – back and forth and around in well-coordinated yet apparently spontaneous visual cheers. The cameras regularly panned in on the fans, especially toward the end, when the rigid order of the school-uniformed students finally broke down, and they became a noisy mob. Their faces were red, their voices hoarse. Past exhaustion, they never stopped cheering, waving, and swaying for their team.

As a siren went off to close the game, the two teams bowed opposite each other in long lines, doffing their caps. The members of the winning team—unfortunately not Ojisan's—trotted around the field bowing and taking in the cheers of the crowd. They hammed it up, acting delirious, pompous, and zany, and playing out their crowd-manipulating fantasies on the field.

The losing team's fans were swollen-faced from crying. Ojisan too looked glum—the first time I'd seen him dispirited. Trying hard not to break into tears themselves, the losing players shuffled back to their dugout, scooping up handfuls of dirt from the playing field to drop in little sacks that they held.

I asked Shika why the losers gathered dirt.

"To play on that field, *the* national baseball field, is the dream of every high school baseball player," she said. "And because of sudden-death eliminations, a team can lose only once. So they'll never play on this field again, and they want a souvenir. Getting even this far is a great accomplishment."

We tried to console Ojisan with this fact.

Nightly Mākun asked me if I liked Wink, and I usually replied, "Perhaps," or "Yes . . . and no." Tonight, so I could get some sleep, I gave him a firm "Yes."

"Which better, right or left?" he pursued the subject.

Until now I'd always said, Wink *Migi*, when we reached this level of our perpetual discussion; it was a safe answer because the girl on the right was generally held to be the prettier and Mākun had indicated she was his favorite. Tonight, desperate for sleep, I decided to try the stun approach and reversed myself: "Wink *Hidari*!"

"Really, Stibu? . . . Really?" he demanded with a quizzical tilt of the head.

"Yes, but it can be our secret, OK?" I answered, knowing Mākun would find it bizarre for me suddenly to like the less popular singer. I just wanted, by any means, to bring some closure to the matter.

He agreed to keep my secret, "OK, OK." But now he had to know "Where? You like Wink *Hidari* . . . where?"

This Q&A session was taking place during his usual prepared monologues with me in the wee hours of the morning. His monologues used to be about America and Disneyland, but lately they were only about Wink.

"Stibu, where?" He hopped out of bed, flipped on the bright overhead light, and hurried over to the life-sized Wink poster on the wall. "Where? Eyes? Mouth?" He looked like a general pointing at a tactical map. I'd had enough of these questions, so I told him to shut up, then rolled over and played dead.

But Mākun continued the assault by leaving the light on. For an interminable time, he pondered both the poster and my change of heart. Finally I flipped my weary body over again and groaned, "Eyes."

"Good-o," he said quietly, soothingly. With a victor's magnanimity, he lowered the light to its usual night-light glimmer and hopped back into the upper bunk.

In my mind I said, "Count sheep," though I knew it wouldn't work. Count Wink duo's? The idea so amused me that I chuckled and relaxed. I could finally get to sleep.

"Stibu, Stibu," Mākun's voice pierced my fog like a match in a tent. "Stibu . . . Me, too."

Week 7: August
Sunday

Chūgen, or "giving time," is the season when people who are indebted to others present gifts—not to repay them, but to acknowledge their help. Otōsan received several deliveries every day now, mostly cases of beer, little cakes, and coffee. Otōsan was good to a lot of people.

Today Mākun "gave" too, in a sense: he joined the Wink Fan Club. It cost him 4,000 yen, about $35. He had access now to taped phone messages from Wink that cost him a hefty sum per call, and he'd receive a t-shirt and membership card. He danced around the house. He must be the world's *best* Wink fan.

Today he and I went to town to deliver some important papers to Otōsan's office building and do some shopping. He was very responsible when dealing with his father. He promptly dropped off the satchel and waited silently for the manager, in case he needed us for anything.

Our next stop was "College Station," a section of teen magazines and stationery in the Parco department store. Parco's like Tokiwa, but more diversified and not as high-class. Today being Sunday, the store was packed with people and the aisles overflowed with mounds of new comics and magazines.

I wanted to get a photo of the amazing stacks of *manga,* with me pointing to them the way Vanna White points to the letters on "Wheel of Fortune." I handed Mākun my camera, but he shook his head vigorously and wouldn't take the picture. So I tried to take his photo there. Again, he wouldn't let me. He didn't want to stand out. Against his advice, I took a picture of the stacked-up aisles.

Mākun bought an expensive book called *Double Tone*—yes, it's "The History of Wink." Mostly a picture book, it told stories about the girls' lives before they were a duo and before their first hit single.

At a record shop, I browsed while Mākun stood starry-eyed in front of the pop-fluff section. He bought a life-size Wink poster, although he already had one. He also came away with one of their cassettes, "Wink—Especially for You," costing nearly $20, as well as a wallet-sized card with Wink's photo and a sticker with their picture on it.

For lunch Mākun insisted I choose between Kentucky Fried Chicken and Makudonarudo. What's that? It's an American business that came to Japan when everyone warned it would fail, wouldn't catch on, wouldn't work. Now it's the most successful fast-food chain here. Mc-Donald's! Or, as it's affectionately dubbed, Maku.

Mākun wouldn't go to a Japanese restaurant, which was where I wanted to go. It was a tough moment, so we flipped a coin: it came out McDonald's. This was the last place I expected to eat at in Japan, but it was bound to happen, I guess. "Unavoidable," as the Japanese say to console themselves.

Maku was packed. Located on two floors of a narrow building, this small restaurant was staffed by about 20 people, including a young woman outside to say hello to everyone passing by, a manager to watch the lines of customers, and another manager apparently assigned to keep the first one company. Eight lines of customers fit in a space where there'd be three in the U.S.

As soon as the manager saw the *gaijin* walk in, he ducked behind the counter to find an English-speaking cashier to take my order in English, even though I could easily point to what I wanted on the laminated photographs on the counter. He stood next to the English-speaking cashier, watching over her shoulder and smiling at me the whole time.

While waiting for Mākun's order, I managed to forget

my Big Mac, which I'd parked on a shelf next to the watcher-managers.

"Very sorry, very sorry," shouted the managers, as both chased after me outdoors, holding aloft my meal between them.

It was mid-afternoon when we picked up our bikes to start for home, but Mākun had an idea. We should visit Dai. During our long ride to the hospital, Mākun raced me several times. When he got ahead, he'd disappear down a back street, so I'd think I was lost. Then he'd pop out, grin impishly, and we'd take off again.

Okāsan was keeping Dai company, as usual. He'd be home tomorrow. He proudly showed me the small row of "x" stitches above his right hip.

After we arrived home, a huge flock of birds landed in the yard. Otōsan called us to see them. The dense cloud of birds had arrived in a rush and took off in little groups, circling around in the courtyard playing tag. They looked like small sparrows, about 200 of them fluttering about.

Otōsan considered the birds an omen. "Birds mean that this is a nice, friendly place, where everyone welcome," he beamed.

While Mākun was visually caressing all the things he'd bought today, he told me that next he wanted to buy Wink's video, even though he taped their TV performances every chance he got.

He begged me to watch his master Wink videotape. On it I saw a clip of them dancing in front of a *papier-maché* winter-wonderland, another of them dressed in hornet costumes in front of an abstract, geometrical background, a clip of them dressed in futuristic robot-like outfits in front of a cosmic set, and one of them dancing in ridiculously bulky designer dresses with a laser-light background.

When we came to the last of these scenes, I thought I heard voices crack, a note missed, and maybe even some lines forgotten. I glanced at Mākun, who was studying me for my reaction with a scrunched-up, sympathetic look on his face. In the last scene Wink had had a rough day, he said, awake too early, singing too much. "Uinku machi taiado, very, very taiado" (Wink's much tired, very, very tired), he concluded, defending their poor performance.

Shika said that before Mākun liked Wink, he liked Mozart. Not in the same way, I'm sure, but he owned several Mozart tapes. Shika said she likes Mozart and eagerly borrowed my "Amadeus" soundtrack. When I offered it to Mākun, he said he wasn't much interested anymore.

Minori had some Beethoven CDs in her room. I asked Shika if it's typical for children to listen to these classics, and she said no, not really.

I had no idea what Mākun's favorite school subject was—or if he even had one. Tonight, while I watched him slogging away at some English grammar multiple-choice questions, he mentioned casually that he liked English best. Shika confirmed this, and Otōsan said Mākun had liked English for a long time. So that wasn't my doing.

In the short time I'd been here, Mākun's English had become more fluent. He used to be timid about speaking English, but now he really was more self-assured. He knew enough to add phrases fairly easily, and he tried hard to participate if the conversation was about something he liked. He'd make up his own English in the middle of a conversation rather than stop dead for want of a memorized phrase, as he used to. I thought to myself that this may be the greatest thing I've helped him with. Otōsan, too, has remarked on Mākun's new confidence with English.

That evening we ate outside—always a big event and lots of fun. Ojisan and Okāsan barbecued chunks of beef, cow intestine, squid, and cabbage. I heaped a load of squid on my plate and was content.

As it grew dark, the fires from the barbecues lit up the house and the neighborhood with a spooky, flickering light. The kids wanted to watch "Genki TV," but Otōsan wouldn't hear of it. Tonight was the Japanese version of Halloween: part of the *Bon* festival, the Festival of the Dead. It's the day people offer food and other items to their ancestors and pray for the happiness of the deceased in the next world. Otōsan told me that the ancestors, in response, might pay a visit!

Mākun organized the VCR to tape "Genki TV," then we kids were divided into three groups for what Otōsan would only call "ceremony."

Minori	Shika	Mākun
Miyuki	Chika	Steve

Otōsan next launched a contest to see which pair of kids could walk through the cemeteries on Sakuragaoka first, following a route that encircled the hill. Ojisan took off on a bike so he could lie in wait for us somewhere along the way. Otōsan held a stopwatch to time the groups, dispatching us at two-minute intervals, Mākun and me last.

After the first two groups had departed, I got an idea. Surreptitiously I removed some cold charcoal from one of the firepits to streak my face, one big gash running diagonally from temple to cheek, just to add to the ghoulish atmosphere. Mākun gleefully congratulated me on my transformation, "Good. Good hora."

At a signal from Otōsan, Mākun and I set off at a clip into the darkness. It was actually scary. I began to whistle "Whistle a Happy Tune" because whistling was a proven way to embarrass and annoy Mākun, and also because it helped keep my skin from crawling. Mākun whispered softly but authoritatively, "No, no, Stibu." I figured he wanted me to stop; instead he wanted us both to whistle "Heart on Wave," the hit Wink single—which we did.

Our groups had gone opposite ways around the hill, and soon Mākun and I spotted a group of four approaching. From their voices we could tell that Groups 1 and 2 had combined. In this they were breaking the rules, but it was so spooky they must have needed each other for comfort. Mākun and I nodded to each other conspiratorially before darting for cover at the side of the road.

I crept around behind the group, and Mākun rolled a stone into the path in front of them. Jumping out from behind a bush, I hugged someone and screamed "Rahhhh!" as loud as I could. Chika dropped to the ground, Shika went wild with fright, Minori nearly bit me to get loose, and Miyuki emerged from hiding only when we began to beat the bushes for her.

This encounter took place in the dark. No-one got a good look at my face, though they knew it was us because ghosts don't go "Rahhhh!" in Japan.

The others arrived home first. As Mākun and I finished our circuit a few minutes later, I gasped, staggered down the driveway, doubled over, and collapsed under a spotlight, where they could see my face in all its ghastliness. They just laughed.

Ojisan had biked past the girls and scared them but never got around to us because he'd stopped at a vending machine to buy sodas for our return. Now we broke open the drinks, relit the fires, and had another party.

There was no sleep for me this night. I thought that since Mākun was going to buckle down and work on his English homework at 1, he'd let me put on my eye-mask and sleep.

"No, Srippun. Not to sleep," Mākun announced. "Finish soon. Then talk about Wink." For the next few minutes he painstakingly searched his English-Japanese dictionary for words for tonight's monologue.

He'd found a confidant in me. His other siblings kidded him about his crush on Wink. Shika was at the point where she said she couldn't *stand* Wink. My own opinion was that Wink was OK in small doses, and I liked them as a popular rock group, but I couldn't tell Mākun that or he'd burst with disappointment. Actually, he reminded me of myself three years ago.

Last night I teased him by switching my choice, making it a big-deal secret that I liked Wink *Hidari*. Now, while he was preparing our conversation, I removed his new Wink megaposter from its place of honor over his bed and stuck it on the wall over my bunk. When Mākun turned around and saw this, I could tell he was distraught, but he didn't say anything.

Next, I hooked my mask onto Wink *Hidari*'s face—his favorite—so she didn't show. I didn't know why I did this, but I was bored, driven silly, and he wouldn't let me sleep. So I thought I'd have fun with him instead. The next time he turned around, he immediately protested this indignity, threatening to move the poster back over his bed. I removed the mask.

Mākun's monologue went something like this:

"Uinku is not a two-sister team, but a duo who look alike. When Uinku born? Uinku *Migi* born February 22, *Hidari* February 23. Mmmmm. My happy birthday? My happy birthday is February 26."

I told him we simply say "birthday," and he nodded, correcting the notepaper he was reading from. He concluded our Wink talk by telling me his ambition: "When I to grow up, I to live with Wink in Tokyo."

Week 7: August

Monday

Today I made a long-awaited trip to Tokiwa to order my *hanko* and buy some other uniquely Japanese souvenirs I'd seen during my trip.

First, Minori, Shika, and I went to the music section. I wanted to get a Japanese tape to take home, any tape. I asked Shika to pick out the best one for me from the many racks of music, mostly pop fluff. She couldn't decide, but Minori knew exactly which one. She picked an album by a raucous and totally outrageous head-banger so she could copy it from me for her own collection. I was content because I could show my friends in America that Japan was hip and swinging.

I bought a special, traditional-paper notebook at the next stop. I wanted to get more, like a calligraphy set or pieces of calligraphy paper, but Shika said I should wait and get these when we went to the resort of Yufuin.

At the next stop in this ritzy store I bought a fan and fan-case. Made of delicate, flexible pieces of bamboo and paper, the fan displayed Buddhist scripture in handsome calligraphy on one side.

I didn't have to find a cashier because an old woman had been watching me discretely from a distance and seemed to know exactly when I needed her. Each time I made a purchase, she took my credit card with both hands and bowed, "Okādo."

Then she and the two counter attendants disappeared for a long time. It couldn't possibly have taken them that long to prepare the bill, so I presumed they were checking the validity of the card and were too polite to do it in front of me. The fan came back wrapped and in a bag, both wrapper and bag sealed with a Tokiwa seal. The credit card receipt, packaged in its own special wrapper, was presented to me with both hands, the old woman holding it by the corners and bowing again.

When I signed the credit card receipt, everyone who had played a role—about six people by now—gathered to watch me sign. They'd already returned my "okādo," so they weren't checking my signature, just watching me write. When I left the register, they bowed me away with a long string of thank-yous in English.

In the food-filled basement, I bought seaweed crackers, candy in clear, rice-paper wrappers, and dried squid.

I'd come to enjoy dried squid; we'd had it often for a snack. It's a delight to handle. Because of the way a squid moves, by contracting jets of water out of a funnel, its muscles run in parallel rings around its body, making it easy to peel off horizontal, bite-sized strips, and impossible to tear any other way. Eating it is like chewing thin leather or bungee cord that's slightly salty and mildly, pleasantly fishy. After masticating for a while, you just swallow. The trick lies in tearing off strips small enough to gulp down.

To leave Tokiwa, we walked past a bank of four elevators. In front of each stood an immaculately uniformed young woman, and all four bowed to us in turn. These trim young women paint their faces white, apply deep red lipstick, then don white gloves before taking their places— one outside each elevator and one at each escalator-landing. Their only job is to bow and thank you for shopping. I wondered if a promotion would raise the best bow-ers to the relatively rarified role of announcer, the young women who ride inside each automatic elevator to list in a singsong chant, the wonders of every floor.

At home, Ojisan showed us the photos he'd taken of Mākun hugging Wink-on-TV. Mākun cheerfully demanded some of the prints and quibbled over who should get the better shots. They gave the rest to me.

With his *kama* (sickle-like machete) Ojisan quickly cleared the grove outside my bedroom window of the tall, fast-growing grass bamboo that had sprung up since my arrival. Most of the water-logged, celery-like stalks took only one stroke to hack off.

His daughters, who often tagged along, were interested in the cuttings. It's hard to believe that this "grass" is thicker than your finger. Ojisan made spears for them out of three-meter-long sticks, and they raced around with them, playing an old lady who needed a cane or a pole vaulter or a samurai brandishing his sword. (Teri the dog was, I'm afraid, vanquished.)

Ojisan wanted to show me his word-processor ("wapuro") in the office section of the Andos' home. Made by Canon, it was rōmaji-, kana-, and kanji-capable on its screen as well as on the printer. A lock key could convert its QWERTY keyboard to kana. Or you could get kanji or kana to pop up by typing their rōmaji equivalents. All highly complicated.

Eleven-year-old Miyuki knew how to operate the word processor, and Ojisan didn't. He got a big kick out of holding her head, as if he were deriving spiritual power from it, and referring to her as a "konpyuta."

Laboriously I typed in hiragana: "Chika to Miyuki Uinku desu" (Chika and Miyuki are Wink). (Having left this printout on my desk, I later returned to find that Mākun had inserted in the middle of my sentence, in bright red ink, "NOt.")

The two girls really did remind me of the pop duo. Resembling twins, they had giant, laughing eyes that dominated their delicately pretty faces and petite bodies.

Ojisan asked Miyuki to log off and shut down the computer. It had been too much work for too little result, I decided—no wonder this wasn't a noticeably home-computer-oriented society.

For a long time Ojisan had wanted to take me for an overnight visit to his house. Later this evening he announced, "OK, rest go," so I threw a change of clothes into my backpack and took off with him and his daughters. Maybe he'd been planning this visit for days, or maybe it was as spontaneous for him as it was for me. I'd never known my schedule more than a few heartbeats in advance, and I was beginning to like it that way.

Ojisan's old car had been driven hard and bore lots of scratches on the outside. He'd removed the door to the glove compartment to add a radio. I could understand why Ojisan liked to drive Otōsan's new car.

We picked up his wife at a supermarket. As I jumped out of the front seat, she protested "No, no, no" and scooted into the back with the girls. I would've gotten out for Okāsan or my American Mom, but this was not the traditional way here: I should sit in the front.

"Japanese boys are not chivalrous," Shika had told me earlier, casting a different light on the front-seat, back-seat relationship between the sexes. "When I returned from Kansas, I found Japanese boys very impolite. I miss that part of America, Steve, and like the way you open doors."

Ojisan's home was in a suburb that still retained some rice-paddies. Tonight the reflections in the paddies doubled the light given off by the lanterns set out in front of the homes for the *Bon* festival.

As we sat around the TV, Miyuki and Chika, who'd also been to Tokiwa that day, presented me with gifts—toys they'd bought there for themselves: a rubber stamp of a googley-eyed dragon, a pen with Japanese comics (in English) down the side, a pencil with a big-eared space-alien on the eraser end, and a bunny that hopped if you wound it up.

They were important gifts in the girls' eyes, and I found it touching that they wanted me to have them. Ojisan thought it funny that I showed such enthusiasm for the dragon. In his turn, he gave me an expensive pair of short, black *ohashi* with a gold label on them—for keeps and also for use at dinner that night.

Ojisan's wife, whose name I never learned (Shika didn't know it either), had gone shopping that day to buy the food for our big dinner. A graceful, quiet woman in housedress and sandals, she spent her time at home in the kitchen, cooking for a long time before we ate and cleaning up endlessly afterward. Again, she didn't eat with us. And as before, Ojisan's parents watched us from the next room but were not served until after we'd finished.

Dinner was an assortment of Japanese delicacies. In my hunger I impressed the family by consuming three bowls of rice which, though normal at a Japanese meal, was not a particularly *gaijin* thing to do.

Ojisan was strict with me and his daughters about a 9:30 bedtime, and I was relieved to get to bed this early.

As he slid open the doors to the guest room of the house—the Japanese room—three large cockroaches scuttled away from the light. Ojisan let out a hoot of delight, and his wife a startled yelp. He took off after the little monsters with roach spray, and immobilized them and a few others that lurked out of sight. This home was extremely clean and neat. In America, roaches are associated with dirt, but they're commonplace in this tropical region—no more tolerable, though.

After my shower, I donned a pair of Ojisan's Western-style pajamas; in my haste, I'd forgotten mine. Traditionally the Japanese wear a *yukata* to sleep, but theirs were too small for me. Ojisan slept in the guest room on another futon. This surprised me because he had a bed upstairs. By sleeping near me, he was treating me as an equal and a friend.

When we had settled down in our beds, his two daughters crept in, and Ojisan started playing with them. They ran all over us and were very comic. The younger one, Chika, had been looking with fascination at a book called *Ladies English Phrase Book*, and now she lent it to me in case I needed it.

At the same time, she wasted no time in practicing her English, "Stibun wa aguri" (Steven is ugly). This caused us all to break out laughing, so she repeated herself, delighted at our reaction. She was definitely the maverick of the two.

Miyuki pounded Chika on the head, "Chika bado" (bad).

Chika, in turn, pommelled me, saying I was "bado," too, but mostly "aguri."

The girls argued over these epithets until finally Chika leaped onto my futon with the solution: "Stibu hambun (half) aguri, hambun gudo (good)." The matter resolved, she pranced off to her room.

In the space of three minutes, Miyuki fell asleep in her father's arms, and Ojisan gently laid her next to him on the tatami. Without waking her, he tucked his blanket around her. As soon as he turned off the light he began to snore, as if the light had clicked him off too.

I stayed up a long time, and by the light of the moon through the open *shōji* wall, I wrote down my thoughts. Burning punk kept the insects away. Ojisan snored pretty loudly. I just couldn't drop off to sleep the way he and Otōsan could.

At the shrine in this room there was a light, a tiny electric lantern, that was never shut off. The shrine contained a well-tended offering of beads, fruits, cakes, and real flowers as well.

The *shōji* on two sides of the room opened to the outside, so I felt as though I were sleeping outdoors. Tonight's cool night breeze disturbed me at first because I wasn't used to it. I listened to a nearby trickle of water that I followed with my mind. It fell, I remembered, from a bamboo spigot into the rock-lined stream that flowed through Ojisan's garden and into a tiny carp pond.

Casting a Net

Week 7: August
Tuesday

Today I learned to cast a net—one of the complicated, circular nets used by Japanese fishermen.

Early that morning the grandfather of the family had gone to fish at a calm place in the river that ran past the house, and I encountered him when I wandered down there for a walk after waking. He wore beige work garb that I at first took for pajamas.

I watched him for a while from the bushy trail before he saw me. He stood solidly and comfortably on a thin pier no wider than his feet that jutted 10 yards into the river. He was casting a net.

He drew gently on the rugged brown netting, countering the flow of the river. It appeared that he could feel the bottom of the river in the hundreds of strings that made up the peak of the cone-shaped net. He sighed as he leaned back to haul the net out of the water.

The bottom of the net had closed like a mouth around some fish, and he ran his fingers, without looking, around the lip of the net, grabbing them—big and little—plus a few crayfish-like creatures. He tossed his catch into a wide, shallow basket floating next to him, a bamboo frame with resin-coated paper stretched over it.

He saw me, and I approached him, walking unsteadily

onto the sliver of a pier. He didn't speak, but his smile expressed friendship, and his manner suggested equal silence on my part. He proceeded to teach me to cast the net.

The rim of the net—its large "mouth" —was made of elaborate baffles and folds that must be separated and straightened if the casting is to succeed. He deftly pulled and pushed the edges, then flipped the net over to repeat the intricate process until it was ready.

He passed the net to me, demonstrating with his empty, gnarled hands what he would do. Then he retrieved the net from me, swinging its great weight onto his left shoulder and all the way down his left arm. With a great heave of his right arm and twist of his wrist, he threw the net—with all its folds, baffles, and lead weights.

The net flew like a discus but very slowly, a perfect circle, beautiful against the morning light and the black river's calm. It seemed to hang in the air for a long time.

The circular splash looked like a cherry blossom as it rippled out and washed against the pier. The old man seemed to be taking in all this, too, as he stood there beside me on the tiny pier. I had great trouble standing still because the pier was shifting, and it was difficult to keep my balance. He had never moved his bare feet, not even his toes.

He began to drag on the net now. He seemed to feel the fish through the net in his fingers. He pulled from different angles to negotiate the awkward load along the intricate river bottom. As the main part of the net drew near, he handed the whole thing to me.

From the platform I couldn't lift the net out of the water. I nearly toppled in because I'd misjudged its weight—he'd made it look so easy. So I gingerly sat down on the pier and hauled the net into my lap. It wasn't the fish that were heavy but the net.

Contrary to popular belief, casting for fish does not bring in a haul of large, flopping fish every time. There were two big and three small fish, and a lot of tiny ones that should have escaped through the mesh but were caught in the lace-like baffles.

I started at the lip and worked my way around, gathering the net. Smack! One of the big fish kicked itself out of my fingers and back into the river.

I tossed what I didn't let slip away into the paper basket that floated at my knees, half full of flipping, sighing fish. I had the baffles pretty much straightened out now, so I stood up with the net and looked at the man. He nodded for me to proceed, and I threw the net over my left shoulder.

In doing this, I managed to hit him with part of the net that had shot loose. Too much of the net dropped over my shoulder, and I felt myself losing it down my back. I was about to tumble in so I let go, and the net sank into the water. Still off balance, I hung there for a long moment, bent over backwards, flailing my arms in the air, desperately seeking something to grab. Then I fell in after the net.

When I surfaced, I shook my head and looked up. I half expected him to be angry with me, but instead he offered his hand, grinning broadly while pulling both me and the net out of the river.

While I held the net, he straightened the folds. It's like trying to close an umbrella — just the cloth and rods but no central stick — with one hand. Then he brought it up to my shoulder in a straight line, not in a curve as I'd done for momentum. Once the net was supported by my shoulder, he pulled part of it down on my left arm and pantomimed many times how to whip it out and follow through with the whole arm and shoulder.

I yanked the net out, but it jerked my arm back, sliding

down my arm, chest, and leg, and dribbling into the water at my feet. I grabbed the edge because I didn't want to go swimming for it again.

We spent the morning like this. He must have missed most of his catch, and I can't see how there was a fish left in the water because I was so clumsy and noisy.

By the time the sun was approaching its zenith, I was getting the hang—or cast—of things. I must have seemed dense and wooden, but he treated each new time like the first, demonstrating wordlessly and with great patience.

My casts were improving. They flew out a couple of meters and landed at least in the shape of a smile, although not in the perfect chrysanthemum that his casts had formed.

With my last cast I caught a fish. I may have caught fish before but I'd lost them while recalling the net. This time the old man seemed to know I'd caught a fish, and he guided my hands as I pulled it in. After I tossed the fish into the basket, he gathered the net onto his shoulder, and we walked off the pier.

It began to dawn on me that I'd just participated in a very special experience. Although we hadn't spoken a word, we'd communicated on the most cordial and effective level, and I'd acquired a skill, aided by his guiding hands and my sheepish grins. It was as if we could understand everything important without needing language. Nonetheless I felt I should try to say something in words.

"Anata wa gyofu sugoi des" (You are a very good fisherman), I said, in my very limited Japanese.

"No," he smiled, with a modest shrug. "I am not so good."

After I returned from my stroll and unexpected fishing lesson, breakfast awaited in the form of many plates of delicacies—small, live mollusks still in their shells and all kinds of pickles, seaweed, and other Japanese specialties. We ate late because Ojisan hadn't wanted to disturb my net-casting.

Ojisan's pride—next to his fine new house—was the large wood and wire-mesh shed area, where he kept bantam hens and a rooster. One of his hens had just laid eggs. The family loved to eat these fresh, half-size eggs. He also stored his many craftsman's tools here.

At lunchtime we ate at an Italian restaurant—complete with rice and *ohashi*. Ojisan's wife joined us but finished quickly so she could go shopping nearby for a dinner of sashimi because she knew I liked it.

Ojisan announced, "Stibu, kantri rest go" (Steven, country let's go), then drove me and his daughters some distance to a large gorge cutting a dark-green gash through the flat rice paddies that filled all the space except for mountains, rivers, and roads. For hundreds of years Buddhist priests had maintained this gorge as a natural cathedral, carving an access path of narrow steps into the sheer rock sides of the gorge.

We changed into special climbing sandals, available from a rack, before descending the tiny stone staircase about 100 feet to the bottom, where the gorge was only as wide as a car. A clammy cold, stirred by the current of the river, clung to the sides of the gorge.

The bottom of the gorge was an intensely beautiful chiaroscuro, its river frothing white over gray-black rocks. Looking up I saw the lush green tropical rainforest teetering at the edge of the gorge and sometimes the sun peeking through the palmy leaves.

Along the bottom, in parts, a bamboo walkway hung from the side of the gorge. Soon we hopped off the walkway and onto a large raft made of whole bamboo trunks—green bamboo logs half-a-foot thick and wired together. We pulled our raft upstream by means of a rope secured ahead. The rafts could navigate only a short way upstream before being cut off by rapids, where we clambered from rock to rock, hauling our raft into the next node of calm.

In some places we let the raft drift back downstream and waited until a raft abandoned at the stop ahead drifted back to us. Sometimes we had to wade a short distance—or try to follow the intermittently reliable old Buddhist path along the sides of the gorge.

At one particularly tough part, Ojisan's sunglasses tumbled out of his shirt pocket and into the water. He had lunged forward to keep from being swept backward by the current, then nearly lost his balance trying unsuccessfully to grab them before they disappeared below the foam. The sunglasses we'd rescued only a few days before were gone for good.

He got a fright because his omnipresent, expensive camera would have been ruined had he been able to salvage the sunglasses.

Part of a bamboo-raft collapsed under me, as two logs broke from their wire brackets and rolled out into the river. To get off in time, I had to jump onto the rocks on the other side of the gorge and wait there until Ojisan came along with another raft that would support me. I felt like the star of "Indiana Jones and the Gorge of Gloom."

Following adeptly, Chika and Miyuki held my backpack when I took a photo or jumped, then handed it back. The bag contained my best things—my camera and diary—and couldn't be lost. The girls both wanted to carry it and fought with each other over it.

We passed the area where most people turn back, a cluster of rocks big enough to picnic on. The girls waited here for us while we stripped to our shorts and headed on to the waterfall I could hear ahead, our pot of gold at the end of the rainbow.

Ojisan waded behind me with the cameras while I

found a sure path. Often we had to throw ourselves against rocks to keep from being carried away by the current.

We rounded a corner, and there it was, a beautiful waterfall. Perfect. At first I thought this frothy crescent was rather small to have traveled so far for, but maybe small in this case was better. Though several storeys tall, the waterfall wasn't larger than life; it was a waterfall on a human scale. It was my personal waterfall, even though it had been there, carving this gorge, for thousands of years.

I felt as if I'd been let in on a secret. Clasping my hands, I meditated under the ice-cold waterfall in the deep darkness of the gorge.

Returning was easier because it was downstream and we knew the terrain. As the four of us climbed back up the stone ladder to the beginning of the trail, I felt again the weight of the muggy, sultry heat.

In the late afternoon, we returned home to pick up Ojisan's wife and drive to the ancient family home where her parents still lived, a big, old, single-storey house surrounded by a farm. Once the home of samurai, it prominently displayed the samurai's own insignia baked into the tiered tiles of its roof.

The samurai's original bath, housed in its own shed, required a fire underneath for hot water. Toilets were pits in the ground with a shed over them. The home itself was magnificent: all wood, reed, tile, and paper. A few inches lower than the rest of the house, the kitchen had a hard, earthen floor, easy access to the well, and an open fireplace outside. A grill and water tap had been installed inside for the comfort of the present occupants.

The living room, where we settled down, displayed a large shrine like the one in Ojisan's dining-room, and also a French doll among a collection of Japanese dolls. Centerstage, though, was a perfect, knee-high mock-up of a ferocious samurai archer, perfectly detailed with armor, queue, and bamboo bow and arrows.

We munched on Japanese cakes—puffy, sponge-like, dough filled with sweet beanpaste. Ojisan took a short nap, and I did too, on the room's tatami floor.

The first day of my visit to Oita, on the way home from the airport, I'd eaten tempura with the Andos and Ojisan. My legs hadn't fit under the low table, and everyone in the restaurant had stared at me. But in one respect I did fit in: I could use chopsticks. Ojisan now kept his promise to show me how to make *ohashi*. I prized the chance to learn more about traditional ways from him and his family.

Selecting one of the largest bamboo trees from a grove near the house, he began chopping it down with his *kama*. Its wood was extremely tough. We took turns at the arduous job. It had to be hacked all the way through its 5-inch diameter; it couldn't be snapped because of its continuous vertical grain. The tree finally fell and was actually light for its strength and size. I'd admired the bamboo bow and arrows on the samurai statue, and now we crafted a full-size bow and arrows as well as chopsticks from the bamboo.

Later we visited the family's Shinto cemetery behind the farmhouse. It'd been there a long time. There were many little family graves instead of the one big one in Buddhist cemeteries like the Andos'. The grandmother brought a big handful of incense, a bucket of water, and wildflowers, and she spent about half an hour decorating and washing nearly ten graves, clapping her hands and murmuring something at each.

Once the cleaning and ceremony were over, Chika and Miyuki amused themselves by placing a lit stick of incense on each grave. Ojisan added candles. He poured tea from a jar into a cup at the base of one tombstone, and some of his coffee into a cup below another.

Before dinner Ojisan picked a sour kabosu fruit from the tree by the doorway to flavor his sashimi and cut down a sunflower-head snack. Dinner was sushi, sashimi, and purple octopus prepared by Ojisan's wife and her mother while we'd been creating the bamboo bow.

As usual, Ojisan's wife didn't eat with us, and neither did her family, though her mother waited on us and smiled at me a lot. It was an especially satisfying meal because everything felt so original and genuine in the old house. Except for a silly baseball cap that Ojisan was wearing backwards, there was little I could point to that gave away the fact that we were in the twentieth century.

The family, whom I'd barely met, surprised me with gifts. There was a big box of tomatoes for the otōsan of my family. And because I'd eaten and enjoyed their sugared and pickled baby onions, they gave me a whole jar of them. "Take to America," Ojisan suggested.

As we left, the grandmother rushed out to hand me a pretty envelope. Inside was 2,000 yen (about $17), nicely wrapped as a present. I couldn't understand it. I'd eaten their dinner, chopped down one of their trees, and monopolized their living room for an evening. I didn't merit a gift, not even the onions.

"Why?" I asked, as we drove off.

"Stibu hapi nau, mahni" (Steven happy now, money), Ojisan laughed. But I still couldn't understand.

From a distance we spotted a festival in progress. We only paused to watch and didn't attend because there was no possibility of parking near it. We saw people dancing and heard the traditional monotone drum and cymbals and what sounded like a giant tambourine. The fireworks weren't big, but they were bright because we stood in a field next to and just above the launching platform.

I walked into the rice paddies to pee. People freely used paddies as toilets. Many years ago paddies were the ultimate toilet, and only recently did they stop carting night soil from the cities to the countryside for fertilizer.

While in the paddy I came across a snake. Ojisan had followed me in, but now pulled me back and pointed, "Deinjya" (danger). It was dull with a small head, and he said it was poisonous.

Ojisan's English was sparse. What time he had to study language he spent on Spanish. But like his more garrulous friend Otōsan, he loved new English words and converted them to easy Japanese pronunciation, taught them to his daughters, and used them whenever possible. He had a rough grasp of the English alphabet used for rōmaji spelling and liked to say "deinjya," "ninja," and "Boy Sukauto." Another phrase he uttered several times, seemingly to himself, on the way back to his home tonight was "Come back to Japan, Stibu. Come back to Japan."

Ojisan decided I should sleep over a second night. The Andos reported that I'd got a call from Mr. Tomita, so I called him back. He wanted me to take up the invitation he'd made earlier to visit his home. He'd pick me up at noon the next day.

To convey all this to Ojisan, I had to call Shika about four times for translation of all the arrangements. We'd gotten along so well the whole day that it was strange to realize now that our mutual vocabulary was limited to a dozen words.

Ojisan's wife did a special load of wash for me that night. She indicated that I couldn't go back to the Andos' with dirty clothes. One sock had a hole in it, and when she returned it, the hole had been carefully patched, and a matching patch sewn on the other sock to keep them symmetrical and neat.

Week 7: August
Wednesday
When I arrived from Ojisan's at about 10:30, I prepared to leave again at noon for an overnight stay with the Tomitas.

On my desk I found another gift picture of Wink from Mākun. I labelled it "YAWP" ("Yet Another Wink Picture") and tucked it in my photo album.

While I was away he'd bought their "Heart on Wave" video, as he'd planned. Where did he get the money to buy all the Wink paraphernalia? I asked Shika, who said with some distaste that he was using his traditional New Year's gift money from his parents.

Shika acted like a father and mother to the rest of the children in matters where parents weren't supposed to interfere, or in place of Otōsan because he was frequently out, or in place of Okāsan on the rare occasions when she wasn't around. Shika was protective of Dai and instructed him. She also commanded the respect of the other children, including me.

Today she had a talk with Mākun about the Wink craze. It was partly to reprimand him for spending so much money—the Japanese don't like to be considered thrifty, but they are. And partly to tell him that Wink is popular now, but soon won't be, so he shouldn't become too attached to them.

Okāsan had flown to Osaka, to a memorial service for a relative. As he did when Okāsan was not around, Otōsan ordered lunch from town. Bowls of steaming *ramen*, noodle soup, were delivered by a middle-aged man on a moped.

Both lunch and Mr. Tomita arrived on time, and at the

same time, so he came in for a chat with Otōsan while I ate. This was *de rigueur* because the two were important men and had never met. They went through an elaborate ritual of exchanging bows and volleys of salutations, a bit like a tennis match, to see who was more honored to see the other. Otōsan won, as the host usually does.

We talked for some time. Or at least they talked and became quite sociable. For politeness' sake, Teacher Tomita switched to English to ask me, "And what do you find most interesting about your Japanese family?"

I said that they were much like my family in America, very close, and they treated me as one of them. I also mentioned that I was amazed by my "uncle," who wasn't really the family's uncle but a friend so close that they'd adopted him as an uncle.

What astonished me, I said, was the strong friendship that had developed between my "father" and "uncle." I concluded, "When I grow up, I only hope I will have a friend whom I can call 'uncle'."

When Otōsan heard this, he somehow thought I was asking Mr. Tomita to let me call him "ojisan," uncle, which would have been – if taken at face value – presumptuous of me and out of order.

To smoothe over my gaucherie, Otōsan started praising Mr. Tomita in the proper way, to sweeten him up to consider my odd request. At the time, neither Mr. Tomita nor I understood why Otōsan was behaving this way. Mr. Tomita had correctly understood my meaning.

Otōsan said things like, "You cannot call Tomita-san 'ojisan' because he is very respected teacher . . ." And the whole conversation was thrown into confusion when Mr. Tomita and I tried to comprehend.

An awkward silence fell because Otōsan was grinning broadly, thinking he was helping me out of a predicament and waiting for Mr. Tomita's reply. Teacher Tomita looked numbed by it all. I was trying to blend into the garden. Otōsan wore such an eager, expectant look that we couldn't just start another conversation, so the silence dragged on.

Fortunately, Mr. Tomita liked to nod in the casual way that the Japanese do, and say "yes" all the time to fill awkward spaces. I'd seen him do this on several occasions, and fortunately he did it now. Otōsan took this for "yes," that Mr. Tomita would be my "uncle" in spite of social convention. Otōsan was overjoyed and clapped us both on the shoulders because now Mr. Tomita was part of the family, through me, in some inscrutable way. He exulted, "Good! Good, good, good. Good, good."

Mr. Tomita and I were bewildered, yet relieved, as we climbed into his car and headed for his home in the farthest corner of the prefecture. He showed me landmarks on the way, pointed out pretty sights, and told me a little about himself, too.

He'd taught English at his village high school for many years. Four years ago he was transferred to Uenogaoka, one of the best schools in the prefecture. Though the promotion was prestigious, I thought it hadn't been such a boon for him: he rose at 5 to take the train, and he didn't have the flexibility of the teachers who lived nearby.

Mr. Tomita now shook his head, his expression grave. "I'm very, very sorry, it rained early this morning here, and they have called off the fireworks." I wasn't concerned, but he seemed to feel guilty because he'd told me we would see them.

We sped along a new bypass that cut through the middle of paddies before entering a village and turning onto a tiny, raised concrete driveway no wider than the car—I'd have been afraid to drive on it without practice. His large, barracks-like beige stucco house of nondescript style had been his family's for generations.

His wife spoke no English. His older son, a village official in his mid-twenties, was quiet and obedient in the presence of his father. The younger son, a university student, was a tour guide at Mt. Fuji for the summer, so he couldn't be with us.

Mrs. Tomita served jelly-filled snacks in the elaborate Japanese room, which became their formal dining room as soon as a knee-high table was carried in. The house was a simple rectangle with a corridor down the center and rooms off both sides in a strictly geometrical way. *Shoji* vented the house beautifully, allowing the breeze to pass through from any direction.

Mr. Tomita drove me to see a small waterfall near his home. Its river had long since been tamed and ran in a channel now, instead of roaming over the fields. Downstream, this precious, highly controlled water flowed through a concrete swimming pool constructed within the riverbed for the village's recreation.

Though the waterfall was only a 15-minute walk, Mr. Tomita had never visited it as a boy. "That's because the elders of the village told us children, for generations, that a dragon lived behind the curtain of water."

Out next stop was the ruins of an 800-year-old castle. Perched on the top of a mountain, the castle was considered impregnable in its time, even after the introduction of cannon.

"Its walls derive their strength from the angle and the placement of the massive, man-sized stones," Mr. Tomita explained, using his hands to demonstrate. "When I was a boy, there was still a need for walls like that for big buildings. The masons of the village could build them just like this, without any mortar. They were proud of their work. It didn't matter that there were easier ways to make walls because this was the tradition and it worked well.

"Today we make only walls of concrete," he continued,

a touch of melancholy descending upon his nostalgia. "I think if tomorrow we tried to make a stone wall like this, we wouldn't know how. The builders don't care about the old ways and about good sturdy walls."

We walked along the walls to the castle's edge, a stark cliff dropping off a thousand feet. The sun glinted on a lush, green valley floor quilted with paddies, where a dozen wispy gray lines reached into the air.

"Tomita-*sensei*, what are those fires among the paddies?" I asked.

"The farmers are burning piles of rice stalks after harvesting the seed. I believe you call it a compost pile? We do not have space to store all the stalks to let them rot. And besides, these farmers harvest the land two or three times a year, so if they did not return the stalks as ash to the soil right away they would . . . use up the land."

"Why, then, are some of the paddies empty? Are they being left to rest?" I was still curious about how rice is grown.

"Which do you mean?" Mr. Tomita looked left to see what I was pointing to. "No, those are failed farms. The owners have left, and there is no one to take their place. The rice farmers are in a crisis, and it threatens the whole village."

"But I saw in the news that Japan protects its rice farmers," I said. "I think American rice costs only a small fraction of what Japanese rice costs because of that."

"It is a crisis of *will*," he explained, after searching for the right word. "The rice farmer is protected in Japan. He holds a special place in our hearts. Even the Emperor is a rice farmer. The rice farmer is a simple man, but he thinks he is the happiest person in the world and he doesn't want anything more. But when that farmer dies, who is there to fill his shoes today? The son has moved to the city. He never wanted to farm."

"Why's that?" I pressed, when Mr. Tomita paused in thought.

"I think that is because of television," Mr. Tomita replied, meditatively. "It makes the young people want to go to Tokyo, dress like Americans. The other young people are already there. In the parks they dance like Elvis all day. They hang out in the bars at night. The farm cannot compete with that.

"And if the son does take his father's farm, who does he marry? The countryside offers the young woman even less than the young man. Our young farmers face a 'bride famine.' The young people leave for the city—Tokyo if they can—after high school. They become part of what we elders call the *shinjinrui*, a 'new breed of person' who just wants to spend money and pursue Western pop culture. That is what we mean when we say there is a rice-farmer crisis."

A sleek, modern tourist bus with immense, dark windows pulled up to the castle, disgorging forty elderly Japanese, blinking into the bright sun. We were not alone on the ramparts anymore. The newcomers energetically scuttled about taking pictures of each other. I disrupted our serious talk with a chuckled observation, "There isn't a tourist here under 70."

Mr. Tomita sighed, "I think it is a shame for us that the young do not take an interest in the old castles either. They are only interested in foreign travel. They want to go to France, New York. They do not hold precious the same things that we do. They use Japan's new money to forget who they are. I only hope that where they go, they do not create resentment. There is a lot of goodwill that can disappear if they do.

"I fear that our young people may not behave as they should when they visit America." He looked at his feet and shook his head from side to side. "They don't respect America anymore, which makes me sad."

"But they seem to love America, from what I've seen," I said, trying to point to a brighter side.

"Yes, but liking a place is not the same as respecting a place," Tomita-sensei cautioned. "When they don't respect it, they no longer look there for progress. The older generation has deeply respected American leaders since MacArthur's days. But the young people and young politicians do not because they do not see how these leaders could have let so many problems grow up within their own country."

Blinking, Mr. Tomita gazed far off for a moment, his unaccustomed candor causing him apparent discomfort. As if to absolve me personally, he added, "I think that your movies and popular culture give young people the wrong impression about America.

"The young are so proud of Japan's new wealth, and they see nothing to copy from America anymore. I guess I should not worry, but I do. I worry about my own students. They look to America only to . . . perhaps for the wrong things. They want pop culture only."

Again he seemed to make an effort to suppress emotion, adding brightly, "I like what Mr. Ando and Youth for Understanding are trying to accomplish in bringing you and other young exchangers over here, to show us a better side of America. Our young people need to see the whole of America, not just its rock music and Terminator movies. They need to understand foreign cultures more thoroughly . . . but at the same time they shouldn't forget their own."

Before I could thank him for his praise or add my own thoughts, Mr. Tomita seemed to become overly self-conscious and wrapped up his commentary: "Anyway, we have to hurry home, or Mrs. Tomita will be angry that we are late for dinner."

Dinner was Mrs. Tomita's freshly made sashimi. Mr. Tomita told me he enjoys octopus more than anything else, so he served me a couple of varieties of it in addition to the slices of fish and eel. His two nephews had caught the eel that afternoon.

There was no shower, so I took a traditional bath while the Tomitas laid out a futon for me in the guest room. Mr. Tomita was aware that Japanese baths (scrub and rinse before entering the tub, then soak) were alien to most *gaijin*. He made several attempts to explain the custom to me, but seemed nervous. Finally he threw up his hands and said, "Anyway, you may bathe any way you like!"

Week 7: August
Thursday

I slept well, and early the next day took the train home because it would have been a long round-trip drive for Mr. Tomita, who didn't need to go to school today. He was torn over the decision about whether I should take the train and travel without companionship, so he had me choose. I said the train would be fine.

Before I left, he gave me a wonderful gift—a book of entertaining ghost stories of old Japan set down in English by Lafcadio Hearn, the first Westerner to become a Japanese citizen. Hearn married a Japanese woman, took a Japanese name, and set about preserving their traditional, oral stories in English.

Mr. Tomita's wife slipped into my hand a thank-you note for being her guest. "Dear Steven, I'm glad to see you." —the letter began before switching to Japanese to express how honored she was to be my host.

Mr. Tomita accompanied me onto the train to help me find a seat, while his wife paid for my ticket from money he'd given her. He located some Japanese college students, two boys and a girl, also bound for Oita. After a few words with them, he attached me to their group. My joining a group made him look immensely more secure, and he left me with several rounds of good-byes. I liked the idea of traveling alone, even though I was carefully guided through every step of the way, as always.

The college boys were nervous, but they asked the standard questions, "How old? Where from? What are you like, hobbies? Do you like Bon Jovi? Is Japan wonderful?" When I showed them my selection of magic tricks, the inhibitions vanished from all of us.

I don't think I could have simply linked up with a group like this in America. And maybe a Japanese boy couldn't have done it in Japan. It always amazed me how, as in the soccer game during Class Match, I could attach myself to a group and be accepted — paradoxically because of my differentness.

One of the boys asked me, with mock gravity, about the girl sitting next to me, "Do you think she is pretty?" I assumed an attitude of deep thought. She turned red with embarrassment, and the two boys laughed hard.

Cocking my head, I replied, "Pretty nai, ichiban pretty!" (Not just pretty, the prettiest!). She curled up into a ball, hiding her face, which made the boys howl again.

I worried that I'd offended her, but after more magic tricks — which she peeked at through her fingers — she passed me a note that said "Thank you very much."

To do my disappearing card trick with the greatest effect, I always asked the audience to give me one of their handy *terehon kādo*s (telephone cards), used in phone booths instead of coins. Now one of the students produced a brand new one.

The assorted people in our railroad car took great interest in my magic, straining to see what I was doing, while pretending not to be looking. The disappearing *terehon kādo* trick caused an uproar behind me because they could see where it went.

After I showed the students how the trick was done, I handed the card back to the student for him to practice. He shook his head and returned it with two hands, gift-style: "No, this is present. You have made me happy." Japan or anywhere, that's the reason I like magic.

When we reached Oita, I lost the three students in the crowded station. I'd wanted to ask them where Tokiwa was so I could pick up the hanko I'd ordered with my initials.

I wandered around for a while, but couldn't find the store. I was in the vicinity, I knew, but walking these grids of streets made me nervous about getting lost. I decided to ask the next person to point me in the right direction, "Doko Tokiwa desuka?"

The young, upright-looking man in khaki slacks and polo shirt turned out to be a disciple of an obscure religious sect. As I approached him, he asked me in loud and shaky English, "OK I pray you happy?" and proceeded to secure my happiness without waiting for my answer. His shirt proclaimed, in English letters, "Shinji Shumeikai." Later I asked him the name of the ceremony: "Jyōrei" (purification of the spirit). No one I later asked knew anything about this religious group.

In the middle of the pedestrian mall outside the train station, he motioned for me to clap my hands, then we bowed our heads and shut our eyes for nearly two minutes while he finished a prayer for my benefit. I didn't move, wondering the whole time whether he'd drop the pretense and try to mug me, but he was sincere.

Suddenly it was over. We clapped hands, I repeated something after him three times, and he began to walk me to Tokiwa.

When we reached the store, he said in English, "This is Tokiwa, but I am sorry, sorry, it is sleeping." He rested his head on his hands, adding "Oyasumi" (Good Night) before vanishing. He was kind, but he could have told me back at the train station that the store was closed.

Returning to the station, I phoned home, and Mr. Ando directed me to take a taxi. The cabbie didn't yet know where "De a i no mura" was, but we found the house without any problem.

Soon the entire family piled into Otōsan's new car—Dai, Minori, Shika, Mākun, Otōsan, and I—to pick up Okāsan at the airport, almost two hours away. It was little things like this—the whole family picking someone up after a flight—that demonstrated the love and togetherness in this family.

In the car Otōsan confessed to me that, during a conversation he'd had with my mother several days ago, he'd been nervous about his English. "I make mistake, your mother think Stibu bad English teacher for us. I don't want you lose face," he chuckled.

We arrived at the airport after a long, stomach-churning ride, but it turned out that Okāsan had taken already taken the bus to Oita. We'd missed her by less than 15 minutes. She hadn't wanted the family to go out of its way for her. I was reminded of the famous O. Henry story.

"The Farmer and the Cowman"

Week 7: August
Friday

Today Otōsan, Okāsan, Ojisan and his wife, Mākun, Minori, Chika, Miyuki, and I left on a rainy afternoon for a long ride in the van to Fukuoka, where an annual international trade fair, the Yokatopia, was taking place. This—not "the bomb at Hiroshima" —turned out to be the big, mysterious family expedition I'd heard alluded to.

We made a tourist trip of it, stopping at sights along the way and sleeping overnight in special temporary tents set up on the beach to accommodate the crowds. The next morning we saw what Coca-Cola, Bhutan, Sony, Oakland, California, and others had to offer the world.

Arriving home, I noticed two used futons in the Japanese room and asked Shika why they were there. She said that while we were gone, she and Dai had slept there, rather than alone at opposite ends of the house.

I was puzzled. After some prompting and a sheepish grin, she admitted she'd been frightened of ghosts. "On a normal night," she explained, "if I were attacked by a ghost, I could scream and there would be other people around. Last night I was a little lonely, and of course," she readily added, "I didn't want Dai to be scared."

This morning's downpour was torrential. The outer arm of a taifun had caught us and was going to pound us for nearly a week.

I still needed to get to Tokiwa to pick up my *hanko*; Ojisan was driving into that part of town to get film developed, so he took me along. There, I had to test the *hanko* in front of the craftsman, who indicated he'd do it again if I wasn't thoroughly satisfied.

At an electronics shop Ojisan bought a compact Sony video-camera, paying in cash from the tiny satchel he always carried on his wrist.

"Otōsan will take us with him to Yufuin tomorrow," Shika announced when I returned. She said she might not be able to go because of all the work she had to do. Her regular classes would begin again on the day I left for America, and she'd be late because of seeing me off at the airport. In addition, she knew she wasn't going to get all her summer assignments finished.

Nevertheless she seemed in a mood to chat. "Coming back from America has left me feeling unsettled," she remarked, contemplatively. "My friends are no longer in the school—they've graduated. I'm in a dilemma. I have seen America and its possibilities, and now I feel torn between the two worlds. I like the opportunities, especially those for women, in America, but I know I'm still part of Japan."

She made up her mind, while we were talking, to go to Yufuin with me. She knew she shouldn't, and she'd seen the sights many times before, but she'd go because it would be my last trip with the family.

Week 8: August
Monday

It rained lightly as Ojisan, Shika, Otōsan, Dai, and I headed for Yufuin. Mākun was in school. Dai happily carried his father's briefcase and umbrella.

During the hour's drive, we listened to tape-recorded Spanish lessons, courtesy of Ojisan, who's in charge of the trip to Spain that he and Otōsan plan later this year.

"You can probably get by with just English in Spain," I told Otōsan and Ojisan, "because many people who deal with tourists there speak English."

"No, Stibu," Otōsan protested. "With learning Spanish I talk to the people, donchyu, and I understand directly." He truly wanted to foster mutual understanding among peoples, and he was always willing to put in the effort.

In the car we discovered that Ojisan and Otōsan, in their excitement about their forthcoming trip to Spain, had started a "Spain Club" the day before, and as their first order of business had printed up membership cards in English. Otōsan was the President and Ojisan the Manager of the Spain Club. So far they were the only members. Shika began the laughter, which caught on, and soon we were all giggling so much that Ojisan and Otōsan laughed too.

Our first stop was Otōsan's *pension*, one of two hotels he owns with a partner. The grounds were park-like and filled with small, modern A-frame units—in a rustic, Alpine style that included tatami mats, futons, and TVs. The units were built for family or group getaways, such as office parties or high-school reunions, in a picturesque part of an old village surrounded by mountains.

We met Otōsan's partner, a polite younger man. His two children were about Dai's age, and the three of them hurried off to play, while Shika, Ojisan, Otōsan, the partner, and I ate lunch and toured the grounds. In addition to its handsome surroundings, the *pension*'s major attractions were its traditional-style gift shop, a rock garden with a semi-concealed hot bath planted in the middle of it, and some new carp swimming in a circular creek system outside the window of the dining area. The partner was especially proud of the new fish.

Yufuin was a peaceful resort, with old, preserved homes and few signs of development. The town had deliberately been kept quiet. There were plenty of tourists, though. With nature-seeking tourism increasingly popular, Otōsan said, more and more people were leaving the glitz of Beppu for the peace of Yufuin.

Otōsan dropped us off at a museum of early life in southern Japan, where craftsmen demonstrated such skills as paper-making, glass-blowing, and sword-making and sold their handiwork, while he tended to business.

We met up with him later, at another hotel. The owner might be a competitor, but friendliness was part of business here, and the two men were clearly good friends. The host made a cold drink for us, pouring freshly brewed coffee over ice.

On a skylight in the roof I saw the footprints of a raccoon that had tried to pry its way inside. I noticed the skylight because I'd just banged my head on a beam. During my stay in Japan, I'd hit my head 17 times. I'd gotten so used to it that sometimes I ducked without being conscious of any barrier overhead.

The owner asked whether Otōsan and I would like to take a bath. This hotel had more elaborate baths than Otōsan's *pension* because it was a spa. We walked along a narrow, slanting, wood corridor giving access to natural rock cavities that held baths of different temperatures, open to the sky.

I took a bath, naked, with Otōsan. He was already in the water by the time I got there.

The bath was too hot to enter quickly. I had to move slowly, adjusting to the intense heat. As we lay there, Otōsan didn't talk, and I couldn't because I was choking on the steam that rose copiously around me before hanging densely about five feet overhead. We soaked for about ten minutes.

As I crawled out, I felt the chill in the air. Fall was approaching. Stepping from the steaming tub, my thighs and chest felt weak, as if I'd finished a double round of karate class. I was tired, too, suddenly feeling enervated and very old. This was strange because many Japanese believe that a good bath makes you young.

With a slap on the back, a reinvigorated Otōsan attempted to pep me up, "Bath makes the blood flow smoothly because it soothes the blood through the skin." Seeing that this information had no visible effect on my slumping body, he added, "This bath not so hot, only medium for you. Next door my bijines friend is in *hot* bath!"

Driving home through a blinding taifun, Otōsan decided that tonight, my last night, we should have a celebratory dinner. From home he made reservations at a fancy restaurant.

Later, encountering heavy traffic only a block away from the downtown restaurant, Ojisan drove across a sidewalk to pull into the parking lot. This escapade brought squeals from everyone—"Bado!"—which made him glow.

It was a big dinner, and one of the best I've ever had, in spite of the fact that I'd eaten a lot already that day and felt uncomfortably full.

I also felt weird about what I was eating. A large red

snapper, shining brightly in its gold-red skin, was plopped in front of us on a platter. Its belly had been carved into sashimi that were left in place, for us to pick out with our chopsticks. The fish lay in a bed of rice, with decorative seaweed encircling it—so fresh it seemed alive. In fact, its tail gave an occasional flap, its mouth still opened and shut, and its eyes jerked spasmodically. Trying to disregard the watch it kept on me, I ate my slices, and it was good.

Mākun volunteered a piece of his raw horse meat for me to try. He loved this dish and wanted to see my reaction. In a culture that has for millennia eaten raw squid and other creatures, it's difficult to worry about your insignificant self trying something new, yet so very old. Immersing yourself in the atmosphere, you chew bean curd, put fish skin on your rice, and nibble tiny, dried fish instead of popcorn in front of the TV.

We sucked out live oysters and clams and picked gooey, raw parts of baby lobsters from their shells. Otōsan launched into brief, fast-moving comments about the importance of international understanding that I only partly understood, even though he was speaking English.

After a final round of *kampais*, Otōsan revealed things about himself he'd never told me before, though I'd heard some of it from others.

"I began as barber, and I did only clean-up, getting ready for other barbers. But I always try hard. Always," he emphasized. "Next, I good enough to learn cut hair."

A number of years ago Otōsan was successful enough to build his own building in town with the help of many people's money, which he was obliged to pay back in twenty years. He did so well with his venture, as Japan took off like a rocket, that he paid them all back in ten. Now he owned that building and was proud of it.

His building was worth much more now than it cost to

build, of course, a prosperous establishment in a flourishing and popular area. Next he invested with a partner in two hotels in Yufuin.

He enlarged his parents' house, while his own growing family lived in a small apartment.

Then he repeated something that he'd told me before: now that he's possessed of a large house, he plans to have exchange students visit from all over the world, forever. Otōsan wanted to do this, from what I could see, for three reasons: because he was truly interested in increasing international understanding, because he wanted himself and his family to learn to be "international," and also because he was naturally outgoing and convivial.

At home, I brought out my good-bye presents for everyone in the family. Otōsan wasn't there—we'd dropped him at his office in town—so I saved his for tomorrow.

This second round of gifts from the U.S. was a little more appropriate than the first. I gave Mākun a soccer shirt and Ojisan a red-white-and-blue striped shirt. For Okāsan I'd brought a Wedgewood pendant, and for Shika and Minori some Mickey Mouse clothes that they loved and immediately changed into. Dai got a kiwi shirt and pennant from New Zealand.

Taken by surprise, Shika struggled to find a present for me. She came up with a purple charm representing the Shinto spirit of academics. "It will get you into Harvard," she said, explaining that these *omamori* (charms) are purchased from vendors at shrines, for good luck. Some Japanese hang these teabag-sized brocade pouches from rearview mirrors, like foam dice. The pouches don't have anything in them; you simply rub them like a rabbit's foot. Not surprisingly, academic charms are especially popular around exam time.

Okāsan gave me another set of finely crafted disposable chopsticks. Dai gave me some string with a red ribbon attached at one end that I could twirl; he put a bow on it from one of his hospital presents to make it clear that it was a gift.

Week 8: August
Tuesday

On my last day Okāsan accompanied me to the school to say good-bye to my teachers and meet with my class for the last time. Only Teachers Tomita and Suzuki were in the teachers' lounge, so I gave the rest of my small presents to Mr. Tomita to deliver. I thanked them for their kindness to me.

In Japan presents are usually given earlier rather than later. Because I gave these out at the last moment, the recipients were embarrassed that they had nothing to give in return, even though they'd all given me presents earlier.

"Come back to Japan," said Mrs. Suzuki as she waved good-bye.

I received my letter of recommendation from Tomita-*sensei*, finally. Wisely he'd held it until the last day, to ensure I'd remain on my best behavior.

In the letter he listed my courses and clubs and surprised me by bestowing on me the title of Assistant Teacher. Then he added words that echoed for me his nostalgic thoughts at the castle. "We Japanese are said to be a polite people. And I myself have been sure it is true. But I am kind of surprised to find Steven more polite and considerate than almost any of the Japanese students. What is more, he is an earnest student. Each time I called him by name, he replied to me, 'Hai!' in Japanese. It is a satisfying traditional way to respond to a senior here in

Japan. I think he appreciates the proverb, 'When in Rome, do as the Romans do.'

"From his personality, abilities, and ambition, it is natural that he should have a good college education. Then I hope he will be one of the most important persons representing your country in the future."

I met the principal for the first time. Previously I'd seen him only on the platform at assemblies. He sat unsmiling in the center of the teachers' crowded room, an obvious buffer of space between him and the other teachers. He spoke to Okāsan, nodding without emotion. He seemed stiff, even a little taciturn. Head bowed, Okāsan was extremely formal and polite in his presence.

Okāsan told me later, through Shika, that he told her that the school had been honored by my exemplary conduct.

Shika said I should be pleased with myself, especially since it had taken a visit by Otōsan to convince the principal to allow me to attend Uenogaoka High School. The principal hadn't wanted any disruptions during the examination period. Otōsan had pointed out to him the equally important need for the students to be "international." I was glad the persuasive Otōsan had prevailed.

As Okāsan and I climbed the stairs to my homeroom, I noticed with chagrin that I'd been wearing my shoes during my visit with the principal. I hurried down to exchange them for the slippers in my personalized locker.

Pausing at the window in the classroom door, I heard gasps of surprise. I'd wondered if the stern old math teacher would let me talk, or resent the interruption. He clearly couldn't continue, because the students were already distracted.

In my quandary I waited respectfully outside the doorway to see what would happen. Okāsan walked in and politely asked the teacher if I could speak with him and the class. He smiled graciously, invited me in with a generous bow, and waved me to the rostrum.

"Today is my last day," I told them, speaking slowly and distinctly because I wanted to be sure they understood my words and feelings. "I've had fun, and am sad to be going home." I wrote on the board, "I am sad," just to be sure.

I looked out at the group, who'd been so good to me, accepted me as their own, shared their thoughts, lives, and lunches with me. I felt a tremor in my chest and a rush of sorrow that I managed to cover up, but only felt the more.

I walked around the room to shake everyone's hand — which caused another stir — and call them all by their English names. I slipped in personal comments. "You are cool, 3-D." "Oh, Tom Cruise!" "Hebi Metaa!" (Heavy Metal).

"Best!" Johnny shouted out what had become his usual salutation for me. Whipping a box of small, wrapped cakes from his bookbag, he plopped one into my open hand.

Mister Sumo bowed to me in a wobbly, jesting way, as though he didn't know how to do it. I faked a handshake and swept back my hair instead, something Mākun likes to do. He and I shared a laugh, then shook hands heartily.

Some of the girls started crying, which made me feel worse. I bade them all farewell with little eloquence, but with words and moist eyes that they could easily understand: "You are *good* class."

At home I gave Otōsan his presents, a picture frame with a photo of the four Wardells and a Western neckerchief that he immediately tied around his neck. It made him look even more like the cowboy he told me he wanted to be. I also presented him with a flagpole-sized American flag to fly on special occasions at "De a i no mura."

Otōsan took the occasion to remind me of his main message and why he'd said, "We will" to the possibility of another exchange student last spring. "I want to help people understand each other, all people. I mean cowboys, and I mean people who plant rice. Everyone must be friends, donchyu?"

For a split second I heard in my head a song from "Oklahoma," my high school musical: "Oh, the farmer and the cowman should be friends." People have said the like in the past, but no one more seriously and sincerely than he did then.

Ojisan delighted me with an album of the pictures he'd taken during my stay.

When things calmed down, Mākun mysteriously pulled me out of the group and down the stairs to the storeroom. "See, see. Come! More presents!" The Japanese holiday comparable to Christmas would occur soon, and he knew his parents had some presents in hiding for him. He'd searched the house for days, and like most children, he'd found them—packed in opaque plastic bags in an obscure part of the storeroom.

Secretively, he revealed to me that his big gift would be a personal computer. He was tickled to be receiving it, but even more to have discovered it.

During the morning I called at the grandparents', bringing Shika along because I had some important farewells to say. I gave the grandfather some pictures of ancient Greek comic and tragic masks, which reminded me of his Noh masks, and which I'd had my parents send. He took an interest in these masks right away, seeming to study them for ideas.

I gave the grandmother some kitchen gadgets I'd brought from the U.S., including an egg slicer and a timer—items that she might already have owned.

The grandparents performed for me as their farewell.

The grandmother donned a patterned headband and, waving a fan, danced an ancestral dance to tape-recorded *samisen* (Japanese stringed instrument) music. In his powerful voice, the grandfather sang another Buddhist chant—monotone and staccato—from an ancient scroll. I was grateful that within the three generations of this one family, I'd had a chance to experience old ways as well as new.

Back home, Ojisan took pictures of me with both his still camera and his new video-camera.

I didn't feel as though I was leaving. I just felt as though I was making another trip. One family saying farewell, another family awaiting me. Actually I felt a little lost, as if the true significance of what I was doing hadn't sunk in.

Ten of us squeezed into the van and took off for the airport: Ojisan, Chika, Miyuki, Shika, Mākun, Dai, Minori, Otōsan, Okāsan, and I. Girls and boys in school uniforms biked to school clubs or exam-prep courses. Construction workers erected more concrete-block walls around the new houses on Cherry Blossom Hill. Though these things were ending for me, the rest of the country went about its business as usual, helping me to ignore my imminent, and seemingly unreal, disappearance from the scene.

From the highway I could see the tops of rice-plants swaying heavily in the wind and smell the smoke from the already-harvested stalks.

Mākun fell asleep against my shoulder during the two-hour ride. We were all tired and now sad. Arriving at the airport an hour early, Okāsan bought green-tea ice cream for everyone, and we savored each other's company, ate, and joked.

Ojisan videotaped all this. I wouldn't have been surprised if he'd spent this last hour with the video-camera at one eye and his still camera at the other, clicking away.

At the departure gate I shook hands with Dai for a long time. He held on, shaking my hand again and again, while he smiled directly into my eyes in a heart-tugging way. Otōsan gave my hand one hard shake with both of his. With a wistful smile, Okāsan hugged me and buttoned up the collar of my travel shirt.

Ojisan gave me a quick, back-thumping embrace, "Sankyu." Chika hugged my leg, and I patted her on the head. Miyuki ran away from me. So did Minori at first, but she soon slipped back to shake my hand, and Shika hugged me. As I got in line to go through security, Ojisan whipped the videotape out of his camera and pressed it into my hand.

Mākun had disappeared but showed up again not a minute too soon with a box of cookies for me to take to my family. He'd bought it at the airport gift shop because he hadn't been able to come up with a good-bye gift for me last night.

It was an awkward moment. They all waved, and I shook hands and hugged everyone. Okāsan was crying. Suddenly the line bogged down and stopped, with me still standing within touching distance, so we said more good-byes and waved. Before I knew it the line lurched forward, and I was around the corner, boarding the plane.

They climbed to the roof terrace and waved some more. I knew I'd miss the Andos and Ojisan and his family. In just two short months and in spite of our differences of language and culture—large in some cases and insignificant in others—this had become home to me. As at my farewell to my parents at LaGuardia in June, I even felt a bit nonchalant about the parting, knowing I'd be back . . . later.

During the flight I asked myself the first question Otō-san had posed during our flight into Oita. "What is it, Japan?" To help find an answer and sum up my experience, I scanned parts of my diary. When a stewardess handed me *Time* and *Newsweek* to read, I felt far away already.

I reached into my bag to see if the photo album that Ojisan had given me held any clues to this puzzling country of old and new, strange and familiar, rice-farmers and—yes—American-style cowboys. Paradoxes, I reminded myself, can be true, without contradiction.

Instead of my album, I found I'd pulled out Mākun's gift of cookies, and a napkin fell out of the box. On it he'd hastily written me a message: "Next time come to Japan." I think, and hope, he meant "Come back to Japan."

Shika's Story

by Shika Ando

Steven was a special exchange student—you could also call him unique or strange—at our house that summer.

He was interested in our daily life, even in the smallest things, and he took notes all the time. He observed everything carefully, and he now remembers very well. He kept a detailed diary every day, every moment. I think there must have been a lot of new, fresh, interesting, funny things for him during those two months.

As I read his diary, it reminds me clearly of every moment we had together. It's interesting to me because it's the true story of what happened to a 17-year-old American boy in a strange country. It also compares the U.S. and Japan from a teenager's point of view.

I should point out that my family is not a typical Japanese family. We have six members, which is pretty big for a Japanese family nowadays. Also, we call our house "International Village" or "International House of Friendship." That's because my father is very interested in foreign countries and has many foreign friends. These friends often visit our house and have fun with us.

At first we worried about whether Steven would like this unusual family because, according to the information we received from the exchange program about him, he seemed to be interested in very old Japan and its traditions. Fortunately, my father has a very good friend – Steven, too, calls him "Ojisan," or uncle – who has an office in our house. To me he's not a classical-type Japanese man, but he learned many traditional skills as a child, such as making bamboo crafts, exploring, fishing . . . which fascinated Steven.

My parents are used to communicating with foreigners, so they never thought of Steve as a guest but rather treated him like a son, a real member of our family. On the other hand, Steve was Ojisan's first friend from overseas, so it must have been quite an experience not only for Ojisan but also for his family to make close friends with a foreigner.

We enjoyed hosting Steven. He was very popular at school, not only because he's tall and has blond hair, but also because he's very active and tried to learn a lot from Japanese teenagers.

He was a nice brother at home, even though he argued and fought with my brother Mākun, and he teased me and my sister Minori. Yes, in all these ways we're really like sisters and brothers.

He and Mākun shared a room, and they became especially close. Mākun is usually shy and not a very active person, but once he started talking about Wink (two girl singers who were very popular when Steve was in Japan), he worked hard to get Steven involved in Wink. I'm not sure whether Steven really got involved or not.

Mākun and Steve were always complaining about each other. For instance, "Mākun never lets me sleep, he keeps talking to me all night," and "Steve makes a mess, he doesn't clean the room." They never said or acted like "I like you!" but I'm sure they miss each other very much.

My mother was pleased with the fact that Steve ate everything she cooked and said "oishī."

Steve was also an English teacher for us. He corrected my English, which I was not pleased at, but which was actually very useful. He helped me and my sister with our homework. He and I came to realize that there are some things that I do better in English than he does, and there are some things that he knows better about Japan than I do.

I was impressed that he knows many historical things. I don't remember whether we had any normal conversations, such as "How are you?" or "How was your class?" But I do remember that he often spoke about the history of Japan, and I was always his student then. Even when I got a chance to be his teacher on a subject, he wasn't my student but my colleague.

It's a while since Steven went back to the U.S. His parents have sent us gifts, and everybody is happy with them. Unfortunately, I'm the only person who can write to Steve and his parents in English. My family and Ojisan's do appreciate the gifts, but they can't really thank his parents. I wish I could write for them, but I'm at college and live alone in a small student apartment in Tokyo.

My father speaks English pretty well and now has a larger vocabulary than I do, but he's sorry that he can't really write or read it.

My father is a different sort of Japanese because he makes much of his leisure and enjoyment of life. He always says, "Enjoying one's life is the most important thing." How many people are there in Japan who understand this but can't do anything about it and just work?

My father doesn't work like a typical middle-aged Japanese man, although he's made a great effort to get what he has. The most precious thing for him now is "Time for himself," doing something interesting. At this point he has great respect for American people or others who place importance on their private lives, not on money and their financial lives. He doesn't want to be the "Japanese businessman" who can work for 24 hours, like the ones in the Regain vitamin-drink song that Steve loved and learned to sing. "Can you work 24 hours, you Japanese businessman?"

My father thus makes our family unusual. But I hope that other Japanese families are becoming more like ours. I think they've been realizing the importance of family life and have noticed that money isn't everything, especially now that the Japanese economy has reached its peak and has been steady or, I'm afraid, is declining.

My mother's also been keeping busy, taking care of the rest of the family. Minori passed her entrance examinations for art school in Osaka, and everyone is happy for her. My brothers Mākun and Dai are both fine. Mākun is doing well at school. He said he'd like to be an exchange student sometime. The funny thing is that he doesn't like Wink anymore. He says they're too old for him—that is, not young enough—now.

Dai is crazy about basketball. He doesn't play with his friends in the park anymore, but practices basketball with the members of the team. His team is the No. 1 elementary-school team in Oita Prefecture, and he is the sub-captain. So my mother is busy with the extra work that his new position creates. My parents and Dai will be coming to Tokyo soon, when he plays in the national finals, which will be an exciting time for me, too.

As for me, I go to Sophia, or Jochi, University and am majoring in Business Management. The courses are hard, but interesting, and I find them very worthwhile. I love my university the way I know Steven loves Harvard.

At Sophia I belong to the club called ESAS, the English Speaking Association of Sophia, where I brush up my

English and make friends with exchange students. We meet twice a week after school.

The rest of the week I hold down two part-time jobs. One is as an assistant at an English conversation school, and the other one is as tutor at a *jūku* (private, exam-study school; cram school). I leave my apartment at 6 a.m. to work at the English school from 7 to 9, then go to college classes. After school I become a *sensei* at the *jūku*, teaching English to high-school students.

Tutoring at the *jūku* is much harder than being an assistant at the English school, though. It's easy to teach those who are eager to learn, but it's hard to teach those who are forced, urged to learn only to get into college. But as I get used to it, it's becoming less difficult.

Because we teachers at the *jūku* are young and friendly to the students, we don't teach in the formal way that Steve saw at Uenogaoka High School. Once the students know us, they are not shy about asking questions or making mistakes.

My two part-time jobs are a lot to handle, but I've learned much through these experiences. I think it's worth working because we young Japanese have been packed into the "Education Box," where we study only to get into the best schools, but we don't know much about what's actually going on around us in the world. Working is a good opportunity to learn *real* social studies.

Then I hope Steve won't have to say, "You've lived in Japan nearly 20 years and you don't *know*?" I always felt bad when I said "I don't know" to Steve. It was either because I didn't actually know or because I didn't know how to explain whatever it was in English.

Anyway, I work at the *jūku* from late afternoon until 9 p.m., and get home around 10. When do I study? At the library in between classes and late at night.

Actually, nothing has changed very much, except that

Steve has left a vacant place in the "International Village," and in Ojisan's family and mine. I hope he can come back and visit us and fill up the hole sometime.

Thank you, Steven, for the nice summer.

Afterword

The day after I returned to the U.S. I drove with my parents to Harvard for an interview, where I presented my references from the students and Mr. Tomita.

My body was running at 3 a.m. Japan time. I hadn't had a regular night's sleep for two months, and I nearly dozed off while the interviewer sorted through my file. She seemed to pay particular attention to the letters, and I hoped my Japanese friends' words, and Shika's Shinto charm in my pocket, would work their magic.

In December of that year, I was accepted. At about the same time, Shika was admitted to her first choice, Sophia.

Two summers later I stayed again with the Andos en route to Tokyo. "De a i no mura" was much quieter. Minori and Shika were away at college. The others were making preparations for an American girl who'd be this summer's exchange student.

Okāsan's life had changed little. She was avidly learning English "to prepare for future exchange students," she said. Practicing her new words, she reflected on world politics, "In the World War, Japan fought a lie because the government lied to the people." She thought that the same thing may have happened to the countries, like Iraq, that have been disturbing the peace more recently.

A serious scholar, Mākun spent his time studying, and English was still his favorite subject. During the time we spent together he was very talkative in English, and I was pleased to see he'd become quite fluent in the language and, what's more, was relaxed about any mistakes he made. The Wink poster had been replaced by the picture of a female rock singer named Jyunko. Chuckling about "old times," he presented me with two of his old Wink tapes.

Dai now slept in my old bunk. Unchanged, he was as cheerful as ever. He was captain of his basketball team, although still the smallest member. His idol was Michael Jordan.

Now specializing in re-creating traditional Japanese homes, Ojisan was building a wood and paper house for a prosperous farmer. The large house he took me to see was almost complete, with its stone and sand garden, steps made from a 200-year-old tree, tatami, and tea-ceremony room. The house replaced a 1950s-era concrete box of a house, and reminded me of Ojisan's sketches of the ancient houses we passed during our travels that summer.

In the Andos' courtyard Ojisan had built a birdhouse and labelled it with his first name, "Takumi." It gave him a presence there, he explained, even when he's away. And he was creating a tiny pond outside Mākun's window, where the wild grass bamboo used to shoot up.

Minori attended art college in Osaka. I met her later in Tokyo, where she was working at a part-time job while waiting to accompany Shika on a visit to family friends in the Philippines.

Shika loved Sophia, her business courses, and life in Tokyo, but was also eager to do an MBA in the U.S., perhaps at Georgetown, Sophia's sister school. She won a prize at Sophia that entitled her to spend a semester at the University of California at Santa Clara. Otōsan wanted her to support herself as much as possible, so she somehow managed to work at two part-time jobs.

Grandfather Ando had good news. One of his Noh masks had received high praise from a famous Noh actor. Otōsan promised me he'd ask his father to make a mask for my college graduation present. The grandparents had purchased a globe, which sat on their TV, so they could locate the homes of the exchange students who were visiting each summer from the big house down the road.

Diana was home on vacation from her two-year college in a nearby city. She called on the Andos before I arrived to deliver a tea set for me, then telephoned later, passing the phone among her friends, who—between giggles—asked whether Harvard was hard, whether I liked Japan, and whether I was in love with Diana. Bobby didn't get into the imperial university he'd hoped for, but he liked his law and government courses at Fukuoka University.

Otōsan was the most transformed. Now a man of leisure, he was searching for a new direction. If this was a mid-life crisis, it was a relaxed, pleasant one.

"What shall I do from here? What do they do in America to be happy?" he asked me in polished English. He spoke to me as his equal now, and half expected me to know the answers. His years of sacrifice were clearly over.

His employees now ran the hotels as well as cut people's hair, so he was at home much of the time, more the manager than the entrepreneur. He devoted even more time to practicing his saxophone, which had become slightly more tuneful.

Otōsan had acquired a bantam rooster, eight hens, and some chicks who lived in a large cage that Ojisan constructed in the courtyard. He woke every morning at 4:30 to quiet the fowls with food before starting his day or returning to sleep. Like Candide, he seemed content for the moment to cultivate his garden, now completed in a Western style and brightly blooming.

I told Otōsan I wanted to write about my experiences

with him and his family. He nodded serenely and without surprise, "Yes, yes."

Wanting to be sure this "yes" really meant yes— though I should have remembered that in his case it surely would—I asked what he thought about the possibility of publication and whether he'd like his family to be camouflaged with assumed names.

Quick on the draw, as always, Otōsan replied, "We are honored to be in your book! And yes, we want our own names. Of course! Such a book is needed if people and countries are to get to know each other, donchyu?"

He hinted that he, too, was writing some stories about "clash of cultures," as he called it, and his relationship—a happy one—with the West. I wonder if I'll find myself a character in them.

This is indeed a cowboy who also plants rice.

Glossary

Bon	a festival, August 13 to 15, when people make offerings of food and other items to their ancestors and pray for the happiness of their ancestors' souls in the next life
Futon	Japanese padded-quilt bedding
Gaijin	outsider, foreigner
Genki	spirited, in good spirits, healthy, cheerful
Gi	loose-fitting shirt and pants, used by workers, martial-arts practitioners, etc.
Hanko	stamp, seal, chop
Hiragana	roundish letters forming one of the Japanese alphabets; in general used to form the grammatical endings of kanji words
Kana	Japanese syllabic writing, consisting of two alphabets: hiragana and katakana
Kanji	Chinese characters adopted by the Japanese
Katakana	an alphabet of square-ish letters used to write in Japanese the foreign words that the Japanese have borrowed: for example, "teburu" for "table"
Manga	large, popular comic books

Miso soup	soup made of bean paste with pieces of chives and tofu
Obāsan	grandmother
Obentō	lunch box
Ohashi	chopsticks
Oishī	delicious
Ojisan	uncle
Okāsan	mother
Otōsan	father
Rōmaji	Latin letters used to spell Japanese words phonetically
Shōji	sliding door, traditionally of paper
Shinjinrui	today's young people; literally, "a new breed of person"; sometimes used pejoratively to censure young people for breaking with tradition
Tatami	woven reed floormat
Yukata	cotton kimono for summer casual wear and sleeping

Harvard undergraduate and prize-winning author Steven Wardell is the weekly "U.S. College Life" columnist for the *Shukan Student Times* edition of *The Japan Times*, Japan's largest English-language daily, and the author of an English-language textbook, *Model-based Writing*, published by the Asahi Press.

Wardell's interest in Japan began with karate lessons at age 12. In high school he won a Japanese-Diet/U.S.-Senate sponsored scholarship for a Youth for Understanding summer exchange to Japan, where he lived with the Ando family of four teenagers and their friends. He returned to Japan for a second summer to work at The Japan Times and revisit the Andos in Kyushu.

Wardell's vignettes of life in Japan have appeared in *The Wall Street Journal*, *The Christian Science Monitor*, JAL's *Winds* magazine, and Harvard's *Inside Japan*. Other stories have appeared in *The New York Times* and *Sports Illustrated*, and on the AP wire service.

Wardell lives in Ann Arbor, Michigan, and Cambridge, Massachusetts.